MW01625501

Religion and Development

Knut Holter
General Editor

Vol. 20

This book is a volume in a Peter Lang monograph series.
Every volume is peer reviewed and meets
the highest quality standards for content and production.

PETER LANG
New York · Washington, D.C./Baltimore · Bern
Frankfurt am Main · Berlin · Brussels · Vienna · Oxford

Religion and Development

Nordic Perspectives on Involvement in Africa

EDITED BY
Tomas Sundnes Drønen

PETER LANG
New York · Washington, D.C./Baltimore · Bern
Frankfurt am Main · Berlin · Brussels · Vienna · Oxford

Library of Congress Cataloging-in-Publication Data

Religion and development: Nordic perspectives on involvement in Africa /
edited by Tomas Sundnes Drønen.
pages cm — (Bible and Theology in Africa series; no. 20.)
Includes bibliographical references and index.
1. Economic development—Africa—Religious aspects—Christianity.
2. Economic assistance, Scandinavian—Africa. 3. Economic development projects—Africa.
4. Economic development—Africa—International cooperation.
I. Drønen, Tomas Sundnes.
HC900.R45 261.8325096—dc23 2013042298
ISBN 978-1-4331-2555-3 (hardcover)
ISBN 978-1-4539-1265-2 (e-book)
ISSN 1525-9846

Bibliographic information published by **Die Deutsche Nationalbibliothek**.
Die Deutsche Nationalbibliothek lists this publication in the "Deutsche Nationalbibliografie"; detailed bibliographic data is available on the Internet at http://dnb.d-nb.de/.

The paper in this book meets the guidelines for permanence and durability of the Committee on Production Guidelines for Book Longevity of the Council of Library Resources.

29 Broadway, 18th floor, New York, NY 10006
www.peterlang.com

Printed in Germany

Table of Contents

Acknowledgments

This volume is the fruit of the NOS-HS sponsored network conferences which took place in Stavanger (Norway) and Helsinki (Finland) in April and December 2012. The network conferences were successful in creating a place to meet other researchers and practitioners, to get to know each other, and to discuss a field of particular interest to us all. Several people made these rewarding encounters possible, and they all deserve to be thanked here. I would first of all like to thank Päivi Hasu from the University of Helsinki, Finland, and Magne Supphellen from NHH (Norwegian School of Economics and Business Administration) in Bergen for being co-applicants and co-organizers. Particular thanks to Päivi, who together with Minna Meyer made the Helsinki session a meeting to remember.

Due to the fact that Agnes Aboum from Kenya had to cancel her journey (and her keynote lecture) at the very last minute prior to the Stavanger meeting, our co-organizer Magne Supphellen stepped in to give us a thought-provoking keynote lecture on the economic aspects of micro finance development projects in Nairobi. His excellent example was followed by Gerrie ter Haar, *the* senior researcher on the theme of religion and development, who provided an exceptional overview of the research in the field from the last decades during the Helsinki conference. Both presentations have become valuable contributions to the present publication.

I would also like to thank all the authors who have contributed to this volume. It has been a pleasure to work with you, and I have learnt much from editing your contributions. Equal thanks go to the editor of the Peter Lang series, Professor Knut Holter, who impressed me with his efficiency and smooth cooperation. Our final gratitude goes to Nordisk samarbeidsnemnd for humanistisk og samfunnsvitenskapelig forskning (NOS-HS), which made these network meetings possible.

Stavanger, June 2013
Tomas Sundnes Drønen

CHAPTER ONE

Introduction

Päivi Hasu and Tomas Sundnes Drønen

Introduction

This collection of essays, analysing involvement in Africa through the lenses of Nordic researchers, represents a wide range of academic backgrounds: from theology and the study of religion to economics via peace and conflict studies, social anthropology and global studies. The outcome is an equally broad variety of themes presented in the different chapters. Rather than seeing this approach as a weakness, we consider this diversity to be a strength. It illustrates the multi-disciplinary nature of development studies and shows the strong historical relationship between religious organizations and development work. In order to gain more insights into the complex processes occurring within the field, a multi-disciplinary approach is needed. The workshops of the network have shown us how mind-enlarging these multi-disciplinary conversations and discussions can be.

Current developments in the field

It is now widely accepted that modernization has not led to secularization; rather, that religious ideas and institutions continue to play an important public role in many societies. Religious ideas are not just integral to the moral values for many people in the global South, but also shape the experience of poverty and decisions about personal and collective development. Besides being a significant source of values and views on human well-being, faith is crucial in basic service provision in many parts of Africa. It has been estimated that, at the beginning of the new millennium, faith groups and faith-based organizations (FBO) provided 50 per cent of all education and health services in Sub-Saharan Africa (Clarke 2006).

Several significant processes pertaining to religion and development have taken place in Sub-Saharan Africa during the past couple of decades: Pentecostal-charismatic Christianity has been growing exponentially in many countries—a phenomenon that has by now become global (Robbins 2004). This form of Christianity is now considered the fastest growing type of religiosity throughout the world, including in Latin America and parts of Asia. Furthermore, in Sub-Saharan Africa, churches have been increasingly involved in public life and political processes including service provision, democratization, peace building and reconciliation. Last but not least, during the past couple of decades, the international development aid system has witnessed the growth of NGOs and faith-based organizations in terms of both number and influence.

After some significant developments in American politics, NGOs and faith-based organizations have come to play an increasingly important role in the entire international aid system. Following the election of Ronald Reagan in 1980 and eventually George W Bush in 2001, the US witnessed an exponential growth of the Christian Right, consisting primarily of evangelicals and Pentecostals, who became influential in the passage of legislation guiding American foreign policy and international development.[1] Several legislative acts and policies culminated in the 2004 USAID ruling on Participation by Religious Orders in USAID Programs, which radically transformed the USAID policy on engagements with FBOs. Under this new ruling, USAID was not allowed to discriminate against organizations that combine development or humanitarian activities with 'inherently religious activities' such as worship, prayer meetings, religious instruction and proselytization (Clarke 2007: 82). This also reinforced the enormous growth of American evangelical and Pentecostal organizations working overseas (Hearn 2002; Hofer 2003).

During the 1980s, simultaneously with the American developments, major international monetary institutions such as World Bank and IMF as well as many donor countries became mistrustful of corrupt African governments. Consequently, structural adjustment policies were imposed as a precondition of loans to developing countries. This resulted in new international economic policies when major donor countries demanded political reforms such as democratization and multiparty systems, reduced government spending, privatisation and market liberalisation as a condition for development aid (Hofer 2003: 383). In this volume, Tomas Sundnes Drønen discusses how African scholars have interpreted the World Bank and IMF policies on the continent and how they in unison have condemned what they call the 'neoliberal globalization policies' of the Bretton Woods institutions. As many African governments were bankrupt and unable to provide health care and educational services for their citizens, the responsibility of providing a growing share of such services fell to the NGOs. At the same time, donors changed their aid distribution policies, which brought about a dramatic increase in NGOs that flourished as a result of economic neo-liberalism and the collapse of public services. For instance, the share of World Bank-sponsored projects involving NGOs increased from less than 10% in 1990 to more than 40% in 2001 (Hofer 2003: 384). In this service provision, faith-based organizations became ever more important actors. International donors have traditionally focused on supporting organizations associated with mainstream Christian churches. However, various types of FBOs are important in the lives of the poor in many different faith contexts. Apart from supporting FBOs through various partnership schemes, as Nikolai Hegertun discusses in this volume, donors are also engaged in some research on faith and development as well as in a dialogue with faith-based organizations concerning these issues. One such engagement was the conference *Faith in Civil Society: Religious Actors as Drivers of Change*, organized in 2012 in collaboration with Swedish International Development Cooperation Agency (Sida), University of Uppsala, Swedish University of Agricultural Sciences and Dag Hammarskjöld Foundation (Moksnes and Melin 2013).

Alongside the growing role of NGOs and FBOs in international development and the significant public and political role of the faith communities, Sub-Saharan Africa has witnessed the exponential growth of Pentecostal-charismatic Christianity. One of the interpretations offered for this phenomenal growth has been the failed promises of the nation-state concerning modernization and development that have opened up new avenues of religious imagination in the South (Corten and Marshall Fratani 2001). Pentecostal-charismatic faith communities have been proliferating simultaneously with the economic reforms since about the mid-1980s in many countries in Sub-Saharan Africa, where Pentecostalism is becoming ever more attractive to the rising urban middle class as well as the rural poor. Even if many new Pentecostal churches lack institutionalised social services, numerous volunteers are active community builders, with a particular focus on inclusion and human dignity (Drønen 2013). Several scholars have also discussed how Pentecostal-charismatic Christianity has two widespread features—namely, prosperity gospel and deliverance theology—that have implications for notions of human agency and development (Gifford 2001; Hasu 2012). Lauterbach makes a fresh contribution to these themes in her chapter.

Nordic involvement

Mika Vähäkangas suggests in his chapter that Nordic development cooperation has its roots in missionary efforts, a line of thought shared by several scholars, including Marianne Gullestad (2007), who describes the Norwegian situation. Today, Nordic governments engage in various partnership schemes with faith-based organizations. For instance, the Finnish government has supported NGOs since 1974 and, since 2003, the Ministry for Foreign Affairs has sponsored a number of Finnish partnership organizations through a Partnership Agreement Scheme. Approximately half of Finland's support for civil society organizations is channelled through this scheme, and five out of the ten organizations receiving this funding are faith-based. The ethical code of conduct, which is common in all the Nordic countries, prevents the faith-based organizations from using the funds for proselytizing; nor are they allowed any kind of discrimination based on religious worldviews.

What makes the Nordic situation somewhat special in Europe is the long history of a close relationship between the Lutheran churches and the Nordic states. For many years, this relationship was unproblematic in terms of development aid, but as the influence of the churches continued to decrease in the Nordic societies at large, several critical voices outside the churches were raised against the involvement of faith-based organizations in government-funded projects. This debate came to the forefront in Norway, when Minister of Development Erik Solheim claimed in a 2012 newspaper article that we had to "Take God Seriously" (Aftenposten, 11 August 2010). He claimed that, in order to succeed with development projects, religion had to be treated as an important aspect of what motivates human action. Coming from a minister representing the Socialist party with a long history of scepticism towards the close relationship between the church and state, this naturally stirred the public opinion about state-funded development work. Solheim's response was to ask the Oslo Center for Peace and Human Rights to appoint a committee of scholars and practitioners in the field in order to discuss the role of religion within Norwegian development policies. Nikolai Hegertun presents in his article some of the working committee's findings and compares the Norwegian process with similar processes in Great Britain and the Netherlands.

Peace building and reconciliation

In addition to being major service providers, churches and other faith communities have been significant actors in the public life and political arena, not least in the peace-building and reconciliation processes in countries like South Africa and

Rwanda (Gifford 1998, 2009). Since the end of the 1980s, with the collapse of the one-party system and nascent trends towards democratization, Christian churches played a remarkable role in promoting democratic values (Gifford 1998; Bompani and Frahm-Arp 2010). Many studies of these processes deal with the role of large mainline churches. Some recent scholarship on religion and politics in the public life in Africa has, however, called into question the rigid institutional separation between the state and the church. Political power and public authority are not exercised in only formal political institutions and processes, but also by many other kinds of institutions. Moreover, ostensibly non-political situations such as development projects might be revealed to be active sites of political negotiation over the implementation of public goals or the distribution of public authority. Development operators such as faith-based organizations and churches are in a particularly significant position to make strategic translations of ideas about not only development, but also public interest, authority and the state (Lund 2006). Furthermore, politics might also be understood to encompass the ways in which politics and the political as well as religious and gender identities are expressed at the grassroots by people from below (Bompani and Frahm-Arp 2010). In this volume, Kubai makes a new contribution by discussing the traditional communal faith and the re-invention of tradition in the process of the Rwandan reconciliation.

Religion, development and the economy

In a dialogue with the religious, economic and political events are the trajectories in academic development studies and the ways in which religion has been accounted for in such scholarly debates. A few scholars have suggested that the idea of development itself has a genealogy in Western Christian religion. Gerrie ter Haar argues in her chapter that 'development' is a secular translation of a millenarian belief whereby the kingdom of God should be created on earth. She further suggests that such a genealogical line can be traced all the way to the Millennium Development Goals. However, the early theories of development paid little or no attention to faith and religion because they seemed irrelevant while religion was seen as an obstacle to modernization (Ter Haar and Ellis 2006).

In the early days of development studies, interest in religion was primarily influenced by Weberian ideas about the Protestant ethic and its link to economic growth. Economic growth was seen to be dependent on such variables as the valuation of material goods, work, wealth creation, invention and population growth potentially affected by religious values (Lewis 1955). For instance, if work was positively valued as a way of using God's gifts, then religion would be conductive to economic growth (Deneulin and Bano 2009: 32). Echoing this concern about the relationship between religious ethos and economic activity in a new context, Supphellen discusses in his chapter the ways in which religious attitudes affect the level of self-determination among small-scale entrepreneurs in a Nairobi slum. More specifically, Weberian ideas about religious ethic and capitalism have resurfaced in the study of Pentecostal-charismatic Christianity and its economic ethos (e.g., P. L. Berger 2009; Freeman 2012).

Development and Human Rights

The 1970s witnessed growing discontent with equating development with economic growth, and dependency theory and related perspectives became influential in development studies. Among these was the 'basic needs approach', suggesting that basic needs included a sense of purpose in life and work. Nonetheless, religion as a major component of what gives meaning and a sense of purpose to many people's lives was seldom explicitly mentioned (Deneulin and Rakodi 2011). Eventually, in 1980, one of the first attempts towards a new research agenda was the special issue of *World Development*[2] that explored the relationship between religion and development. It went largely unnoticed at a time when international policy defined development largely in terms of economic growth and religion was neglected in the academic field of development studies. Changes in development thinking have nevertheless made the subject of religion no longer avoidable in development studies.

During the first decades of development studies, development thought and policy were dominated by the discipline of economics and, along with it, concerning religion, something one might call the 'Protestant ethic approach' to economic growth. Although the Human Rights Declaration was signed as early as 1948, it was not until the 1990s that a rights-based approach to development emerged and became a more widespread approach in development policy. However, religious freedom and other fundamental human rights are potentially incompatible and conflicting. The 2004 Human Development Report advocates that, in the case of a conflict, human development issues such as health and education take precedence over cultural and religious rights (Deneulin and Bano 2009: 41). Drawing from the rights-based approach, Ville Päivänsalo discusses in this volume the issue of health justice and collaboration between public authorities and faith-based organizations in Tanzania. Nonetheless, gender equality remains a crucial aspect of the rights-based approach to development. A human rights-based approach, therefore, integrates international human rights standards and principles in development activities, including women's human rights and the prohibition of discrimination based on gender.[3] Three chapters in this volume discuss the ways in which gender politics are articulated in faith-based development projects and how faith communities and institutions can potentially be transformative regarding perceptions of gender. Both Auli Vähäkangas and Kjetil Fretheim describe and discuss the term 'transformative masculinity' and its consequences for development projects in Africa. Vähäkangas' study analyses the role and motivation of male volunteers in serving the dying patients in the Selian Hospice and Palliative Care Programme in Arusha, Tanzania. The program, which uses trained volunteers who make regular home visits, is renowned for its success and its multidisciplinary approach in caring for dying patients. Fretheim's study is a presentation of recent gender initiatives by the World Council of Churches (WCC) and the Young Men's Christian Association (YMCA) movement, focusing on their shared commitment towards transformative masculinity. He also discusses how the term 'masculinity' in these projects relates to the more general terms 'religion', 'development' and 'gender'. Marianne Skjortnes, on the other hand, approaches the question of gender in a more traditional way than Vähäkangas and Fretheim, questioning the way in which churches in Sub-Saharan Africa play the role of active agents of change. She argues that the churches should always acknowledge the local roots of religious faith and practices while still paying attention to global developments in order to secure human-rights based standards towards gender equality.

Historically, it was not just the rights-based approach to development that heralded a change in development thought. The gradual understanding of poverty as a multi-dimensional phenomenon has made it explicit that religion is an important dimension in many people's lives in developing countries. The World Bank study *Voices of the Poor* (Narayan et al. 2000) noted that religion permeated people's concept of well-being. Consequently, the improved understanding of well-being has changed the concepts of development. The recognition of the shortcomings of increased per capita GDP as the primary indicator of progress has contributed to a re-orientation of development's aims from economic growth to more holistic concerns for human well-being. The human development approach based on the conceptual works of Amartya Sen and his capability approach has been particularly influential (Sen 1999; Alkire 2002). This has, at least in principle, enabled religion to be granted more space within development studies, although empirical applications of religion in the capability approach remain scarce. The widely accepted understanding is that religion is an important force that shapes people's values and what they consider worthwhile and valuable; it is integral to social, political and economic life as well as development (Deneulin and Rakodi 2011).

Concluding remarks

Academics and practitioners in the development policy community have now picked up on these new themes in social science scholarship. Emerging studies examine the growing engagement between donors and faith communities, the role of faith communities and faith-based development NGOs in supporting the poor, and the general relevance of faith in development (Clarke 2007: 78). Through its variation of themes and its particular focus on Africa through the lenses of Nordic researchers, this volume adds important perspectives to this debate. The African continent is going through profound changes due to recent developments in the global economy. These changes have consequences in terms of which values and human-rights based principles should colour the debate. They also have consequences in terms of how we, as researchers and practitioners, think and interact within the ever larger and ever more globalized development discourse.

References

Alkire, S. 2002. *Valuing Freedoms. Sen's Capability Approach and Poverty Reduction*. Oxford: Oxford University Press.

Berger, P. L. 2009. "Faith and Development." *Society* 46: 69–75.

Bompani, B. and Frahm-Arp, M. (eds). 2010. *Development and Politics from Below: Exploring Religious Spaces in the African State*, 1–19. Basingstoke: Palgrave Macmillan.

Clarke, G. 2006. "Faith Matters: Faith-based Organizations, Civil Society and International Development." *Journal of International Development* 18, no. 6: 835–848.

_. 2007. "Agents of Transformation? Donors, faith-based organisations and international development." *Third World Quarterly* 28, no. 1: 77–96.

_. 2013. Faith and Development: Challenges for Donors. In *Faith in Civil Society: Religious Actors as Drivers of Change*, eds. H. Moksnes and M. Melin, 13–30. Uppsala: Uppsala University.

Corten, A. and Marshall Fratani, R. 2001. "Introduction." In *Between Babel and Pentecost: Transnational Pentecostalism in Africa and Latin America*, eds. A. Corten and R. Marshall-Fratani, 1–21. Bloomington: Indiana University Press.

Deneulin, S. and Bano, M. 2009. *Religion in Development*: Rewriting the Secular Script. London: Zed.

Deneulin, S. and Rakodi, C. 2011. "Revisiting Religion: Development Studies Thirty Years On." World Development 39, no. 1: 45–54.

Drønen, T. S. 2013. *Pentecostalism, Globalisation, and Islam in Northern Cameroon. Megachurches in the Making?* Leiden: Brill.

Freeman, D. (ed). 2012. *Pentecostalism and Development: Churches, NGOs and Social Change in Africa*. Basingstoke: Palgrave Macmillan.

Gifford, P. 1998. *African Christianity: Its Public Role*. Bloomington: Indiana University Press.

_. 2001. "Complex Provenance of Some Elements of African Pentecostal Theology." In *Between Babel and Pentecost: Transnational Pentecostalism in Africa and Latin America*, eds. A. Corten and R. Marshall-Fratani, 62–79. Bloomington: Indiana University Press.

_. 2009. *Christianity, Politics and Public Life in Kenya*. London: Hurst.

Gullestad, M. 2007. *Picturing pity: Pitfalls and pleasures in cross-cultural communication: Image and word in a North Cameroon mission*. New York: Berghahn Books.

Hasu, P. 2012. "Prosperity Gospels and Enchanted World Views—Two Responses to Socio-economic Transformations in Tanzanian Pentecostal-charismatic Christianity." In *Pentecostalism and Development: Churches, NGOs and Social Change in Africa*, ed. D. Freeman, 67–86. Basingstoke: Palgrave Macmillan.

Hearn, J. 2002. "The Invisible NGO: US Evangelical Mission in Kenya." *Journal of Religion in Africa* 32, no. 1: 32–56.

Hofer, K. 2003. "The Role of Evangelical NGOs in International Development: A Comparative Case Study of Kenya and Uganda." *Afrika Spectrum* 38, no. 3: 375–398.

Lewis, A. 1955. *The Theory of Economic Growth*. London: George Allen and Unwin.

Lund, C. 2006. "Twilight Institutions: Public Authority and Local Politics in Africa." *Development and Change* 37, no. 4: 685–705.

Moksnes, H. and Melin, M. (eds). 2013. *Faith in Civil Society: Religious Actors as Drivers of Change*. Uppsala: Uppsala University.

Narayan, D., Chambers, R., Shah, M. K. and Petesch, P. 2000. *Voices of the poor: Crying out for change*. New York: Oxford University Press.

Robbins, J. 2004. "The Globalization of Pentecostal and Charismatic Christianity." *Annual Review of Anthropology* 33: 117–43.

Sen, A. 1999. *Development as Freedom*. New York: Knopf.

Ter Haar, G. and Ellis, S. 2006. "The Role of Religion in Development: Towards a New Relationship between the European Union and Africa." *European Journal of Development Research* 18, no. 3: 351–367.

Notes

1 For a more detailed description of the political developments, see Clarke (2007 and 2013).

2 World Development 8 (7-8), 1980.

3 http://www.ohchr.org/Documents/Publications/FAQen.pdf

CHAPTER TWO

Poverty and Prosperity in Africa

Gerrie ter Haar

Introduction

The West's relations with sub-Saharan Africa have traditionally been dominated by the idea that Africa is a continent in need of help in order to progress and that this help has to come from us. African realities, however, have changed quite markedly in recent years. The economic changes of the last decade in particular have surprised policymakers, who are used to thinking of Africa as the poorest continent. In 2010, Africa contained six out of the ten countries in the world with the fastest-growing economies, and it will probably have even more by the year 2015.[1] Africa's external debt has fallen enormously in ten years' time, and booming new consumer markets have arisen; a number of African countries now issue government bonds in foreign-denominated currencies, placing them in the mainstream of global capital markets (Ellis 2011).

While these new realities have been greeted with enthusiasm in the business world, which welcomes any new openings for investment, development practitioners, anthropologists and theologians tend to overlook, ignore or otherwise be unaware that Africa can no longer be considered simply in terms of poverty. This does not mean that there are no poor people left in Africa who need our attention, because there are too many of them even today.[2] Although there is a broad consensus among experts that economic growth reduces poverty, we are left with the important question of how to address the issue of grassroots poverty, or poverty at the micro-level, in a context of macro-economic prosperity.

In this chapter I want to explore an answer inspired by my knowledge as a scholar of religion with a focus on Africa, basing my discussion on both older and more recent work I have published.[3] I will first look into the concepts of religion and development from an African perspective, an analysis that I have made at some length elsewhere (Ter Haar 2011b: 10–19) but whose essence deserves to be highlighted, in my view, because of its fundamental importance. I will then look into the type of religious change that has taken place in Africa in recent decades, with particular reference to Christianity, which seems to reflect the economic changes on the continent. I will subsequently take a fresh look at the relation between religion and economy and will conclude with a plea to redefine the relationship between religion and development based on African rather than European models of history, including intellectual history.

Religion and development: Two concepts, one objective

One of the main obstacles to our understanding of the religious dimension in the lives of most people in the non-Western world, as I have persistently argued, is our lack of awareness of the different meanings of the concept of religion in different cultures and societies (Ter Haar 2011b: 10-15). In modern Western societies, religion is considered primarily in terms of its ability to provide human existence with some deeper meaning, a definition that can be traced to the German-American theologian Paul Tillich (Tillich 1959). At the same time, religion is often exclusively associated with its institutional form, notably churches. Yet in many other parts of the world, people's religious consciousness is defined largely by their belief in the existence of a spirit world—that is, an invisible world believed to be inhabited by spiritual beings, a definition that goes back to the British anthropologist Edward Burnett Tylor (Tylor 1958).

The latter clearly applies to Africa, where the belief in a spirit world continues to be strong and modernity has been shaped accordingly along non-secular lines (Ter Haar 2009). The traditional spirit orientation of African religious belief has been perpetuated in later religious traditions that were originally imported from outside the continent. It is visible in African Christianity, with its emphasis on the role of the Holy Spirit, but also in African Islam, with its long-standing Sufi tradition. The same spirit orientation is noticeable in more recent imports, such as oriental religions, as well as in new Christian traditions, such as Mormonism (the Church of the Latter-Day Saints) or the Unification Church (The Holy Spirit Association for the Unification of World Christianity) of the late Reverend Moon, and other trends whose main ideas resonate with traditional religious ideas in Africa.

For most people in Africa "religion" refers to the belief in the existence of an invisible world, distinct but not separate from the visible one, that is home to spiritual beings or entities deemed to have effective powers over the material world.[4] The invisible world, in other words, is an integral part of the world as people know it. An important observation in this respect is that the "real" world is not reduced to its visible or material form only. The human world is believed to be intimately connected to the spirit world, and a regular intercourse may take place between them, in a two-way mode. In such a holistic perception of the world it follows that people's social relations extend into the invisible world, in the sense that individuals and communities invest in their relationship with spiritual entities in order to enhance the quality of life in the same way that they try to maintain good relations with their relatives, neighbours and friends. They may enter into various forms of active communication with the spirit world in such a way as to derive information from it with a view to furthering their material welfare or interests. This can be observed in all religious traditions in Africa, including Christianity and Islam. Muslims and Christians also frequently call on the spirit world to enhance the quality of their lives. In passing, we may note that we find the same among the new religious communities that African immigrants have founded in Europe (Ter Haar 1998).

Enhancing the quality of life and furthering material welfare is also the aim of what is conventionally labelled "development." Here, too, we have to consider what development means in an African context that is historically defined by a religious consciousness. The modern idea of development has its genealogy in Western-Christian religion and can be seen as the secular translation of a millennarian belief, whereby the kingdom of God is no longer projected in heaven but can be created on earth. In both cases, a reign of peace and prosperity is held out to believers, as either a religious or a secular utopia. What binds both types of thought is the aspiration to eliminate evil in all its forms. One might even suggest that a genealogical line can be traced from early Christian ideas about the millennium and twenty-first-century ambitions as contained in the Millennium Development Goals.[5] The belief in progress that is so characteristic of modern development theory reflects the Christian idea of humankind as pilgrims on the road to their final destination, where life will be as originally intended by its creator. The creators are now human agents, but the underlying ideas have not really changed. The belief that humankind is bound to progress on a path to a better world remains central to the project of development. The religious notion of progress has become secularized and limited to material progress. As a logical consequence, the kingdom of God is no longer believed to be in heaven, but its perfect state is considered to be attainable on earth (Ter Haar 2011b: 16–17; Ter Haar and Ellis 2006: 354–55).

Once again, Africa's particular difference lies in the holistic worldview of Africans, in which the material and non-material—or spiritual—aspects of life are not separated. In such a worldview, development is not only a material, but also a spiritual matter: There can be no material progress without spiritual progress; the one comes with the other. From an African perspective, economic prosperity is deemed to be linked to inner growth, and the economic expansion of a person or a community, or "external expansion", is believed to accompany "expansion from within" (Ter Haar 2009: 85).[6] In fact, many religious believers, both inside and outside Africa, suppose that the spiritual dimension precedes the material one in the sense that economic prosperity cannot be achieved without creating the spiritual conditions conducive to it. This is as true today as it has been in the past, but even religious development organizations—so-called faith-based organizations—have nevertheless generally conceived of their business in a secular mode. Formal development practices have continuously been initiated without any reference to ideas that are central to Africa's own religious history. This notably concerns African ideas about the spirit world.

Religious change in Africa

Africa's original religious traditions—known in the literature as African Traditional Religions (ATRs)—have always been flexible, very adaptable, and able to incorporate new people and new ideas. This is largely due to their oral character, which allows for the *in*clusion of outsiders and their ideas much more easily than is the case with the "book" religions that many of us are so familiar with, which tend towards the *ex*clusion of outsiders and their ideas on the basis of written dogmas (Ter Haar 2000). A key element of African traditional religions is their sense of community, which cause them also to be known as "community religions." The belief in a dynamic spirit world is a salient aspect of these religions.

Africa's religious history has had a formative influence on the various forms of Christianity that have emerged on the continent, as is most visible in the African-initiated churches (AICs)—churches founded and led by Africans and in which the role of the Spirit is paramount. Today we find such churches also outside Africa, including in Europe, as a result of recent African migration. In my work on AICs in Europe, I coined the phrase African International Churches to refer to this new phenomenon (Ter Haar 1998: 24). These churches represent a new phase in the history of AICs, in which the meaning of the letter I in the acronym has changed several times. When they emerged on the African continent in the late nineteenth and early twentieth centuries, they became known as African *Independent* Churches. The 'I' reflected the viewpoint of the historical mainline churches that considered them as breakaway churches, in the manner of a child fleeing from the tutelage of its parent. Over the course of time, a new appellation emerged from within the AICs themselves: African *Indigenous* Churches—an appellation that changed the perspective from an outside to an inside one. At a later stage, following political independence in Africa, the name African *Instituted* Churches became common, indicating that in modern times all churches in Africa, including the historical mainline ones, were in fact led by Africans themselves and no longer by European missionaries. Among academics the neutral term African *Initiated* Churches became the preferred way to refer objectively to any church founded and led by Africans. The interesting point is that these various appellations show the different historical angles from which the phenomenon of AICs can be viewed, while in all cases retaining the same acronym (Ter Haar 1995: 159–70). In the global context in which these churches operate today, the meaning of the 'I' has changed once more. They are sometimes referred to as African *Immigrant* Churches, mainly reflecting an outsiders' perspective that sets these churches apart from those historically known in the country of destination. The term African *International* Churches, on the other hand, reflects an inside perspective. Most of the new-generation AICs refer to themselves explicitly as international churches, expressing their aspiration to be part of the global world in which they believe themselves to have a universal task—a task not restricted to Africa and with a message that is not intended exclusively for Africans. This new label takes account of their African origin while at the same time recognizing their continuity with the universal Christian tradition.

The new AICs stand in the tradition of the classical AICs in that they, too, have been founded by Africans and are led by them. But they distinguish themselves from these historical forerunners by their international orientation and universal aspiration. Hence, they can be found in all parts of the world and on all continents. The historical continuity with earlier AICs is notably visible in their most striking feature: the emphasis on the third person of the Trinity, the Holy Spirit, and the belief in its active and efficacious presence. The spirit-oriented nature of these new AICs builds on the indigenous religious traditions of Africa, which postulate the existence of a spirit world with which direct communication is possible.

In the academic literature, African churches of the new generation are habitually referred to as charismatic churches or, rather condescendingly, as "prosperity churches." The latter is of particular interest in the context of our topic as it contains an implicit reference to the way in which these new churches employ their religious resources to achieve "the good life," or—in the terms of some prominent African theologians—a life of abundance, both spiritually and materially (Magesa 1997).

Before elaborating on this, let me explain what I mean by religious resources. For those who believe in the existence of an invisible world, which in Africa is perceived as a spirit world, religion is a human resource, one that non-believers do not possess. Like other human resources, it can be employed for development purposes. I have suggested before that, for analytical purposes, we can divide religious resources into four major categories: religious ideas, religious practices, religious organization, and religious experience (Ter Haar 2011b: 8–9). In short, "religious ideas" refers to the content of belief: inquiry into religious ideas seeks to understand what people actually believe and why. "Religious practices" refers to the ways in which people act on the basis of their belief, which is often in the form of ritual behaviour. "Religious organization" refers to the community aspect of religion, or how people organize themselves on the basis of their beliefs. "Religious experience" refers to the psychic attitudes that religion can induce, particularly in individuals, such as the subjective experience of inner change or transformation, which believers themselves often describe in terms of a vision or vocation or both. Africa's religious history provides many examples of the transformational power of a profound religious experience. An individual, subjective religious experience often lies at the origin of a religious community and continues to give rise to new ones, as the Spirit is believed to act without restriction. The power of the Spirit can make itself felt to anyone. The effect and impact of becoming overpowered by the Spirit can be frequently witnessed in the new-generation AICs, where the resulting personal transformation is often described as a "born-again" experience.[7] The various dimensions of religion—religious ideas, practices, organization, and experience—produce knowledge that can be made beneficial to both individuals and communities, as well as to society at large. Dependent on the type of religion, they might differ in importance, but they are interconnected and form an integral whole.

The classical AICs on the African continent were—and continue to be—often materially poor but have a rich spiritual life that has been described by many academics. They are historically and sociologically a product of the time in which they emerged, the era of Western colonization and European missionary enterprise. The new generation of African-initiated churches, by contrast, is markedly different. They are products of the late twentieth century, when economic prosperity reached a peak worldwide (before the financial crises of recent years) and at a time when colonialism had become history for a younger generation of Africans. Many of the new religious leaders are well educated and have studied abroad. They are familiar with modern financial ideas and principles of management and perfectly capable of running their own organizations, independent of outside interference, especially since they are self-financing. Hence, they operate on their own terms, which are informed by an African, rather than a European, worldview that they share with the adherents and members of their churches—both rich and poor. A good example is the Redeemed Christian Church of God (RCCG), which has its origins in 1950s Nigeria, from where it has now spread to all parts of the world.[8] Interestingly, in the process, this church has transformed itself from a classical AIC into a modern one in the sense described above, reflecting the changing winds of time (Olowu 2011). Yet historical continuity has remained and is visible, among others, in the traditional principle of investing in the invisible world, in the hope for future returns in the form of material prosperity. As in other such churches, the historically known aspect of reciprocity in social relations is extended by believers to the realm of the invisible.

Typically, as they believe in the inseparable connection between the material and spiritual realms of life and the way they affect each other, both rich and poor people invest in the spirit world with a view to future material benefits. This has provoked much criticism from Western academics and policymakers, who have commented on the allegedly dubious moral nature of the new-generation AICs, especially in financial and wider economic matters, but often without much study of the religious ideas that sustain their religious practice in this regard. They fail to see the historical pedigree in Africa's original religious traditions, in which material prosperity is seen as a sign of blessing from the spirit world, often associated with the ancestors. In the same vein, the new AICs commonly speak of "blessings," whereas outside observers refer to (material) "prosperity." For the churches themselves, material prosperity is simply one of the forms that spiritual blessings are believed to take. Here too, it is important to realize that the link between the spiritual and the material in Africa is informed by the continent's own religious history.

Religion and economy: An African perspective

The significance of religious ideas in forming people's ideas about material prosperity is not unique to Africa, but expresses itself differently in different times and in different places. In Europe, for example, material prosperity used to be seen as a sign of virtue and divine blessing, and it is widely acknowledged that religious ideas played an important part in the development of capitalism in Europe. In Africa, the link between religion and material development is perceived differently due to a different religious history. The connection between the two, in the context of the twenty-first century, has been articulated, among others, by the Ghanaian theologian Kingsley Larbi, himself a representative of the new-generation AICs (Larbi 2001). He argues that the religious message must be placed within the social and economic realities of a country and understood in terms of traditional concepts of life. As such, prosperity refers to "the ability to live a happy and balanced life without the problem of having to think what to eat, where to sleep, what to wear, how to meet one's social expectations, like school fees, children's education and the ability to contribute to the need of one's community" (p. 313). These are all daily concerns for many people in Africa, despite spectacular economic growth figures in an increasing number of countries. Like many other Africans, Larbi confirms the traditional relation between the visible and invisible worlds in the sense that a person who is in good spiritual health can expect to also prosper materially or, as previously indicated, to achieve "abundant life."

According to Allan Anderson, a professor of Mission and Pentecostal Studies, the crucial message of these churches is that they promise access to "power which will cater for the necessities of life and protect it from its vicissitudes—a life that is full, prosperous, healthy, peaceful and secure" (Anderson 1991: 72). To put it in the terms of my analysis, these churches try to promote the good life by mobilizing their religious resources, the most important of which is the belief in the power of the Holy Spirit, with whom believers may engage actively and without intermediaries, in the same way as Africans used to do—and continue to do—in their original religious traditions. The model of active engagement with a spirit world is the opposite image of the idea of ultimate dependence on an all-powerful God who decides unilaterally to whom he will send his blessings and from whom to withhold them. The new-generation AICs thus perpetuate African religious ideas by engaging directly with the invisible powers to influence their destiny for their own benefit. It is this last point—the perceived possibility to engage with the invisible world in order to shape one's own fate—that makes it especially urgent for development practitioners to encourage the deployment of religious or spiritual resources in Africa.

However, in the face of a global financial crisis, all of us need to rethink some of our fundamental assumptions about the world and the way it is governed (Ter Haar 2012)—more precisely, the forces that are *believed* to govern it. While religious believers such as those in Africa generally ascribe significant power in this regard to spiritual entities, secular believers also tend to ascribe power to invisible forces, such as those often referred to as market forces or the invisible entity known as capital (not to be confused with money, which is simply the commonest form in which capital becomes visible). In both cases—religious and secular—invisible forces are believed to affect our material world. Both are derived from an underlying assumption that the material world is regulated by invisible forces that people can manipulate for their own benefit and that of their communities. In both cases these invisible forces—spirit as well as capital—are ascribed transcendental qualities.

If we are prepared to adopt this different—and perhaps unusual—perspective, we can see that religion and economy are less far apart in their mode of thinking than is generally admitted. In both cases we are dealing with transcendental agencies that manifest themselves in ways that vary according to the history and culture of a given society. Both emanate from particular ways of viewing the world: in the one case expressed in religious terms (spirit), in the other, in economic terms (capital). In the case of the latter, modern government and business are based on the assumption that the invisible entity called capital can (in principle) be accessed by anybody, although at the highest level access to it is mediated through a range of techniques operated by specialists such as bankers and economists, in the same way as for religious believers access to the transcendental is mediated by religious experts such as priests and theologians, who have their own techniques. In modern societies, we can say that economists have replaced theologians as the people who predict and calculate the future—or claim they can do so.

I am making these points in order to introduce some thought-provoking ideas about matters not normally considered in the same light. I am not claiming that the invisible forces that are supposedly governing our world—whether conceived of as economic or spiritual in nature—are similar in every respect. Considering how the concept of capital emerged in Europe's history enables us to see that the belief in spirits, so widespread in Africa, is not such an unusual way of thinking about the world as is commonly thought. It helps us to see that social interactions with different invisible worlds have distinctive histories that can be traced in specific locations. These social interactions have both shaped societies and been determined by them, such as in the case of Africa and Europe, respectively.

Poverty and prosperity: A moral question?

In the context of our discussion it is relevant to note that in many parts of the world the current economic crisis is perceived primarily as a moral crisis. A global opinion poll on values and ethics carried out by the World Economic Forum following the crisis of 2008 showed that a majority of respondents—more than two-thirds—considered the economic crisis to also be a crisis of ethics and values. In general, respondents believed that business of any sort should be more values-driven. The results further showed that in economies in different parts of the world, such as those of the United States, Saudi Arabia and South Africa, religion and faith are the prime drivers of values.[9] Although religion does not have a monopoly in this field, the mere fact that many people in the world derive their values primarily from their religion constitutes a reality and is, therefore, something that we should consider. Even the government of China, despite its official atheism, has now taken note of this fact and tries to respond to the reality of religion, if only to be able to control it better.[10]

Many studies have looked into the question of the relationship between religious values and economic behaviour. Does religion, for example, contribute to economic growth or to poverty alleviation? The results of these investigations are mixed, as appears from a recent assessment (De Jong 2011). Empirical research shows no grounds for believing that specific religions are either pro- or anti-growth. Rather, it appears that the values adhered to by members of the major religions change as a result of economic circumstances and political pressure (De Jong 2011: 138–40). However, this does not alter the fact that popular opinion believes there to be a connection between the breakdown of values and the breakdown of the economy.

One of the ways in which religion, morality and economic growth are considered to be connected has become apparent through an increasing interest in Islamic banking. Islamic banking—or, more precisely, Islamic financing—is a well-known phenomenon in Muslim-majority countries, where religion is not considered a purely private affair but seen as of consequence for the public sector in every area of life. Given the importance of Islam in Africa, there is a growing interest in this form of banking there too and therefore sufficient reason for Western organizations to consider this option more closely. Islamic financing is based on Qur'anic principles, which implies that financial products must be Sharia'h-compliant, although there are no global standards in this regard. The core belief in Islamic finance is that money is not an earning asset in and of itself; hence, the charging of interest or *riba* is prohibited (which is historically also known in Christianity). Financial transactions must be linked, whether directly or indirectly, to tangible economic activity. There are rules to avoid financial speculation and rules concerning the sharing of both risks and profits of financial transactions, to mention only some of the most important regulations (Khan and Thaut 2011: 187–88). The sharing of profit as well as loss is a key principle underlying the great variety of financial techniques that have been developed in Islamic banking systems.

Islamic financing is a complex matter for outsiders but the point of interest here is the way in which religious ideas are applied to material realities in the twenty-first century. It has been suggested that currently more than 300 Islamic financial institutions operate worldwide, spread over more than 50 countries, including both Muslim and non-Muslim countries, even in the so-called developing world, and including Africa[11] (Ozsoy 2011: 178). China recently awarded its first Islamic banking licence to accommodate its more than 80 million Muslim citizens, and reportedly a number of big conventional banks are currently considering how they can create Sharia'h-compliant products for their clients. In Nigeria, the governor of the Central Bank of Nigeria, the internationally respected Lamido Sanusi, recently suggested introducing Islamic banking nationwide for the benefit of the country.[12]

Irrespective of personal opinions in this matter, in view of the present discussion, a crucial point is that Islamic ways of financing are inspired by particular religious ideas, which lead to particular practices that have relevance for development.

Muslim intellectuals believe that the attachment of Islam to an equitable distribution of income by prohibiting interest can help alleviate the problem of poverty. They also believe that a potential advantage of Islamic finance is that funds must be allocated only to productive activity that is not exploitative or socially or morally harmful. Thus, Islamic finance should not promote antisocial, unethical and often destructive businesses such as gambling, prostitution, alcoholic liquor, nightclubs and narcotics, which are all considered *haram* activities and, thus, forbidden. Borrowers are obliged to invest only in *halal* or permissible activities. In this respect, Islamic finance shares many of the features of the socially responsible financing that has emerged in some secular institutions. It possesses the potential to promote more ethical investment and business practices.

Conclusion: mobilizing religious resources

One of the most important consequences of a religious worldview is that people's ideas of development are not formulated in exclusively material terms, nor is progress seen only in economic terms. For religious believers, spiritual growth is an intrinsic part of human progress, and spiritual wealth goes hand in hand with material prosperity.

In Africa, too, poverty and prosperity are not simply economic concepts to be translated into material terms alone, as is most obvious today in the new-generation AICs discussed earlier. It is of crucial importance to study the religious ideas sustaining religious communities in Africa today, both Christian and Muslim, and to do so in such a way as to situate them in the context of Africa's—not Europe's—history. While the contribution to development of religious institutions and their leaders has been recorded in many places and situations, far less has been written about the religious ideas that underlie their material behaviour and that can be considered part of the religious resources of believers. As I have emphasized in the past, there is no reason (other than ignorance or prejudice) for anybody working to improve living standards around the world to ignore one important human resource if and when it is available. It is at the point where people's individual and social interests meet that religion may become a powerful resource that can be channelled for constructive purposes by development agents.

The question is how to unlock this religious potential. Here, too, a comparison between the invisible forces of religion and those of economy may illustrate the point. In the same way as the invisible force called capital constitutes a potentiality rather than a visible reality in human society and can be realized only through a set of interrelated ideas, practices and institutions, so too do the invisible forces inherent in religion constitute a human potentiality that can only be realized through a coherent set of ideas, practices and institutions, albeit of a different nature. In both cases the question is how to turn potentiality into reality, or how to make the invisible visible in such a way as to further what we conventionally label "development." I have referred in this regard to the need for spiritual empowerment of individuals and communities in Africa (Ter Haar 2011b: 14–15).

There are recorded cases illustrating how African religious ideas can be realized successfully for development purposes. A telling example is the ecological liberation struggle in Zimbabwe that became known as the "war of the trees." In this case, traditional religious beliefs were mobilized to restore the ecological balance in the southern part of the country that had been lost as a result of rapid deforestation. The disastrous ecological situation in the late 1980s led to a unique initiative to reverse the process, in collaboration with the communities living there. The liberation of the "lost lands" took the form of the massive mobilization of peasant communities to join in tree-planting, wildlife conservation and the protection of water resources. For that purpose, they once again got the help of the spirit mediums that had previously been instrumental in winning the political liberation war (Daneel 2001).

I will be the first to admit that the mobilization of religious resources is easier said than done. At the same time, it is fair to say that as the result of a secular bias hardly any academic research has been devoted to exploring people's religious potential for development, certainly not in any systematic manner. Similarly, development policymakers, who might have little problem in engaging with religious institutions for the sake of service delivery, are not easily prepared to engage with the ideas and motivations of those who gave life to these institutions in the first place. Yet, as shown in an earlier publication, it is entirely feasible to explore in a concrete manner the relevance of religious ideas for development, including in Africa (Ter Haar and Ellis 2006).

Western ideas of development, I have suggested, come from a secularized reading of Europe's religious (Christian) history. Africa's history is different. Religious ideas have been part and parcel of its intellectual history and are central to its people's understanding of the world. Any analysis of Africa's development should be based on this fact, as well as any resulting policies. For too long, development experts have acted like modern missionaries by attempting to change people's outlook of the world rather than build on it.

References

Anderson, Allan H. 2001. "Pentecostal pneumatology and African power concepts: continuity or change?" *Missionalia* 1: 65–74.

Daneel, Marthinus L. 2001. *African Earthkeepers: Wholistic Interfaith Mission.* Maryknoll, NY: Orbis.

De Jong, Eelke. 2011. "Religious values and economic growth: A review and assessment of recent studies." In *Religion and Development: Ways of Transforming the World,* ed. Gerrie ter Haar, 111–40. London: Hurst & Co. / New York: Columbia University Press.

Ellis, Stephen. 2011. *Season of Rains: Africa in the World.* London: Hurst & Co.

Khan, Ajaz Ahmed and Thaut, Laura. 2011. "The opportunities and challenges of Islamic microfinance." In *Religion and Development: Ways of Transforming the World,* ed. Gerrie ter Haar, 183–204. London: Hurst & Co. / New York: Columbia University Press.

Larbi, E. Kingsley. 2001. *Pentecostalism: The Eddies of Ghanaian Christianity.* Accra: Centre for Pentecostal and Charismatic Studies.

Magesa, Laurenti. 1997. *African Religion: The Moral Traditions of an Abundant Life.* Maryknoll, NY: Orbis.

Milingo, Emmanuel. 1994. *Development: An African View.* Broadford, Victoria: Scripture Keys Ministry Australia. [original mimeograph 1976].

Olowu, Dele. 2011. "Faith-based organizations and development: An African indigenous organization in perspective." In *Religion and Development: Ways of Transforming the World,* ed. Gerrie ter Haar, 55–80. London: Hurst & Co. / New York: Columbia University Press.

Ozsoy, Ismail. 2011. "Islamic banking: Background, theory and practice." In *Religion and Development: Ways of Transforming the World,* ed. Gerrie ter Haar, 159–82. London: Hurst & Co. / New York: Columbia University Press.

Platvoet, Jan G. 1999a. "To define or not to define: The problem of the definition of religion". In *The Pragmatics of Defining Religion: Contexts, Concepts and Contests,* ed. Jan G. Platvoet and Arie L. Molendijk, 245–65. Leiden: Brill.

Platvoet, Jan G. 1999b. "Contexts, concepts & contests: Towards a pragmatics of defining religion". In *The Pragmatics of Defining Religion: Contexts, Concepts and Contests,* ed. Jan G. Platvoet and Arie L. Molendijk, 463–516. Leiden: Brill.

Platvoet, Jan G. and Molendijk, Arie L. (ed.). 1999. *The Pragmatics of Defining Religion: Contexts, Concepts and Contests.* Leiden: Brill.

Ter Haar, Gerrie. 1995. "African independent churches: The ideological implications of continuity and change." In *The Living Tradition: Towards an Ecumenical Hermeneutics of the Christian Tradition,* ed. A.W.J. Houtepen, 159–70. Zoetermeer: Boekencentrum.

Ter Haar, Gerrie. 1998. *Halfway to Paradise: African Christians in Europe.* Cardiff: Cardiff Academic Press.

Ter Haar, Gerrie. 2000. *World Religions and Community Religions: Where Does Africa Fit In?* Occasional Paper, Centre of African Studies, University of Copenhagen.

Ter Haar, Gerrie. 2009. *How God Became African: African Spirituality and Western Secular Thought.* Philadelphia: University of Pennsylvania Press.

Ter Haar, Gerrie. 2010. "The *mbuliuli* principle: What is in a name?" In *Development and Politics from Below: Exploring Religious Spaces in the African State*, ed. Barbara Bompani and Maria Frahm, 40–55. Basingstoke: Palgrave Macmillan.

Ter Haar, Gerrie (ed.). 2011a. *Religion and Development: Ways of Transforming the World*. London: Hurst & Co. / New York: Columbia University Press.

Ter Haar, Gerrie. 2011b. "Religion and development: Introducing a new debate." In *Religion and Development: Ways of Transforming the World*, ed. Gerrie ter Haar, 3–25. London: Hurst & Co. / New York: Columbia University Press.

Ter Haar, Gerrie. 2012. "The invisible worlds of religion and economy." Farewell speech delivered at the International Institute of Social Studies of Erasmus University Rotterdam on 9 February 2012. [Available from www.iss.nl].

Ter Haar, Gerrie and Ellis, Stephen. 2006. "The role of religion in development: Towards a new relationship between the European Union and Africa." *The European Journal of Development Research* 18, no. 3: 351–67.

Tillich, Paul. 1959. *Theology of Culture*. New York: Oxford University Press.

Tylor, Edward B. 1958. *Religion in Primitive Culture*. New York: Harper. [Originally published in 1871 under the title Primitive Culture].

Notes

1 These six countries were Angola, Nigeria, Ethiopia, Chad, Mozambique, and Rwanda. In 2015, Ethiopia, Mozambique, Tanzania, Congo, Ghana, Zambia, and Nigeria are expected to be among the world's fastest growing economies (source The Economist).

2 According to the 2012 World Hunger and Poverty Statistics, in 2010 there were 239 million people in Africa going hungry, out of a world total of 925 million. Hunger is defined here as "the want or scarcity of food in a country."

3 Certain passages have been taken directly from my publications and incorporated into the present chapter. Ter Haar 2011a provides a discussion of the relationship between religion and development from various perspectives.

4 This is a neo-Tylorian definition, which I have consistently used in my work on religion in Africa as an operational definition. An operational definition is a heuristic instrument that emerges from the context under study-in this case, an African context (Platvoet 1999a: 262, 1999b: 510-12).

5 The Millennium Development Goals (MDGs) were agreed upon in 2000 by the United Nations, to be achieved by the year 2015. The eight goals are: eradicating extreme poverty and hunger, achieving universal primary education, promoting gender equality and empowerment of women, reducing child mortality, improving maternal health, combating HIV/AIDS, ensuring environmental sustainability, and developing a global partnership for development.

6 The expression comes from former Zambian archbishop Emmanuel Milingo, who wrote a number of pamphlets on development in Africa in 2004-2005, which remain unpublished.

Another pamphlet by Milingo on the same subject was written in 1976 but only published in 1994 (see bibliography). See also Ter Haar 2010.

7 This is a description, we may note in passing, that conforms to experiences historically known from initiation rites in Africa.

8 In 2010, the church was operating in 114 countries in all continents (Olowu 2011: 66), more than forty of them in Europe.

9 "Faith and the Global Agenda: Values for the Post-Crisis Economy." A report published by the World Economic Forum in Geneva, 2010.

10 In December 2012 the Chinese Academy of Social Sciences, in collaboration with the Chinese government, hosted a conference called Religious Charities and Social Development to consider the various ways in which religion might benefit Chinese society.

11 Examples include Djibouti, Gambia, Mauritania, Niger, Nigeria, Senegal, and Sudan.

12 In July 2012, this led to a heated debate in the Nigerian press-not for the first time-with some eminent Christian leaders considering such a proposal as a Muslim conspiracy to Islamize Nigerian society at the expense of its Christian population.

CHAPTER THREE

Globalization, Religion and Development

Perspectives from Africa

Tomas Sundnes Drønen

Introduction

Globalization, religion and development are three analytical terms which on their own could fill several bookshelves. In this chapter, the three concepts are brought together in an attempt to show how they might shed light on one another when the particular case discussed is development in an African context. The first part of the chapter will present some personal experiences from northern Cameroon which will serve as an example of how a small religious community can act as the facilitator for a multilateral development project in a globalized world. The case reveals that the relationship among development, religion and globalization is complicated. The rest of the chapter will serve as an effort to highlight the need for in-depth studies of the involved terms from a contextual perspective in order for an academic discussion to be relevant in an African setting. This will be done through a general presentation of the need to rethink the role of religion in a globalized world, followed by a close reading of how some of the most prominent African social scientists interpret the term *globalization* from their own social and economic context. Finally, a few words will be added about the relevance of the discussion.

Social reconstruction: A snapshot from northern Cameroon

The development discourse in Africa in the last decades has had AIDS and HIV infections high on the agenda. For many years, the fight against the pandemic appeared to be a lost case, and the lack of constructive dialogue between the Western development agencies and the population they sought to address was discouraging to watch. Having lived for many years in northern Cameroon, this was for me personally much more than an academic or theoretical issue. It was a question of everyday life, everyday practices, and everyday grief. When I look back at the friends I made in the area between 1998 and 2008, I would estimate that nearly one third of the people I met on a regular basis are today dead from AIDS. Still, every evening when I turned on the TV to watch the state-owned CRTV channel (the only channel to which I had access), there were long info-commercials about the use of condoms and information about how the HIV virus spread. When I drove down to the town centre, I could see anti-AIDS billboards wherever I turned my head, all funded by UNICEF and the Gates Foundation . Yet on no occasion prior to 2003 did I have a sound and balanced conversation with any of my friends about this burning issue—not even with a man employed in my house who was HIV-positive. I knew about his status, and he knew that I knew, yet the topic was taboo. The global flow of images and information, through infotainment on TV, images and slogans on large billboards, and instruction at schools and in hospitals, did not seem to affect people around me at all. A somewhat peculiar discourse of neo-colonial oppression mixed with conspiracy theories of various sorts was the closest I came to reasonable discussions about the lethal disease.

Then one day something strange happened: The church I attended was visited by the national church president of the Lutheran church (EELC), who on this occasion entered the pulpit with a red ribbon attached to his cassock. For the first time I heard a pastor in northern Cameroon speak openly about AIDS, including how the disease was transmitted, contraception, consequences and morality. The rest of the church was as surprised as I was. We had all been part of an historic event. What had happened? After countless public and private projects in education and health sectors all over northern Cameroon, a Norwegian NGO had launched a new project, *All against AIDS*, in the Lutheran church. The NGO had good contacts among the church leadership, so they initiated the project by gathering all the pastors in the church for a two-day seminar, engaging the church president to lead the meeting. During the next several months, I witnessed a silent revolution. A theme that until recently had been taboo was suddenly spoken about from pulpits all over northern Cameroon.

The role of religion in a globalized world

Defining globalization

What is the role of religion in a globalized world? In order to answer this question, a few words have to be said about the two terms themselves: globalization and religion. The first term has been described in detail by numerous studies during the last decades, yet it can hardly be argued that an overall consensus has been reached in order to describe a word so slippery that it can be used to promote and/or contest almost any recent social action. However, some elements have been agreed upon by the majority of social scientists for describing processes which influence our current global condition, and an equal majority agree upon the fact that the term is so embedded that it has to be narrowed down and defined according to the academic field in which we wish to employ it. Within social sciences and cultural analysis, Anthony Giddens' reflections upon the changes in the perception of *space* and *time* (Giddens 1990) have been of importance in the search for common analytical ground. The technological development has increased our ability to be present in and influence social relations "across indefinite spans of time-space" (1990: 21), and both time and space have according to Giddens been "stretched," allowing social systems to be "embedded" and lifted out from their geographical location. Jan Art Scholte used the terms "transplanetary connections" and "supraterritoriality" (Scholte 2005) to underscore Giddens' point. Scholte further argued, with much right, that this new perspective within social sciences has serious methodological implications. We might like, or dislike, new and fancy academic buzzwords, among which globalization most certainly has its place, but the rapid technological changes that the last decades have brought about force us to look at social relations from a radically different angle.

There are two aspects of the globalization debate that I would like to place at the forefront when globalization is discussed together with the terms development and religion from an African perspective, and both derive from the unfinished thinking of Roland Robertson. The first aspect has to do with what Robertson somewhat loosely called global consciousness (Robertson 1992) in an attempt to define the fact that more and more people across the planet actually engage in mental and social processes which have important elements in common. The most obvious historical example of this development would be the spread of the world religions. From the Jewish people emerged the idea of the one God in opposition to the many gods which were present in most indigenous practices, from the traditional Nordic religions to the richly populated African cosmology. Christianity slowly transformed large regions of the world by introducing new rites and practices which made people reorient their minds and their bodies from earlier practices inherited from their forefathers. New concepts of time were introduced, along with the tools to rest on the seventh day of the week, and new religious festivals saw the light of day. When Islam penetrated the Saharan desert, a written language which made communication across yet undefined distances possible enlarged the intellectual horizon. Space acquired new meaning as everyone had to turn towards a particular geographical direction when praying; and the dream of crossing deserts and seas in order to join other Muslims on pilgrimage to Mecca transformed and inspired the religious imagination.

This way of analysing a global movement towards common consciousness is also shared by Jeffrey Haynes, who focused on the increased "common activity" that globalization engages individuals (2007: 31). He mentioned wars, crime, trade and culture as activities transcending national and cultural borders and influencing humans across the globe. Peter Geschiere and Birgit Meyer added their perspectives to this line of thought, even if they were more occupied with the cognitive aspects of these activities. They initiated an interesting debate about globalization and identity through their book about *Dialects of Flow and Closure* (Geschiere and Meyer 1998), and several authors have since picked up that gauntlet. André Corten and Ruth Marshall-Fratani described the global processes which the new Pentecostal churches in Africa go through as

> the development of an increasingly complex web of transnational Pentecostal networks, where flows of people, money, ideas, and images circulate with growing speed and intensity, defying all attempts to pin them down to any particular source or destination. (Corten and Marshall-Fratani 2001: 1)

This flow of people, money, ideas, images and discourses is not limited to the growth of Pentecostalism, but shows how globalization is a fruitful analytical concept which can be applied to changes in social behaviour in many different fields. It is but obvious that, as the academic field *per se* is preoccupied with global relations and global change, development studies have to become engaged in the globalization debate as well as have the necessary credibility and competence to do so. The development discourse is strong because it is as full of ideology as it is of money; therefore, it is likely that it will influence practices and consciousness among all its participants.

The second aspect of Robertson's contributions to the globalization debate that I would like to mention briefly is the much used, but not so much discussed, term *glocalization*. Robertson's (1992; 1995) suggestion to replace the term globalization with the somewhat more obscure word glocalization did not attract many followers, but the latter term survived and flourished. It was actually first applied by

Japanese farmers who introduced foreign technology to their local way of farming, thus merging the "global" with the "local." The reason why the term has survived is because it is one of those terms which actually describes very wide processes and is applicable to a large variety of analytical contexts. We could with other words ask how local communities are influenced by global trends and then use the glocalization label to describe both the acceptance and the resistance which the external influence has as its result. In order to give the term more exact meaning, several scholars (Eriksen 2007; Holter 2013) have used it in order to show how the global influence has been applied on local practices in a new and creative way, thereby inventing qualitatively new ways of answering old questions. Later in this chapter, we shall see how an African church has glocalized the development discourse as well as how resistance against the very term globalization, due to an ideological interpretation of it, has made African intellectuals reinvent the term according to their analysis from a particular geographical and socio-political viewpoint.

Religion and development: Flow and closure

> When I arrived at the World Bank in 1995, one of my main goals was to broaden the approach to development work. I believed that, however important its place and role, it was never wise to have economic growth as our primary lens . . . it struck me forcibly that religion was a pervasive force in many of the World Bank's client countries. Religion is an omnipresent and seamless part of daily life, taking an infinite variety of forms that are part of the distinctive quality of each community. (Wolfensohn 2011: xvii)

James D. Wolfensohn, looking back at his ten years as president of the World Bank, makes himself a natural spokesman for the changes which have occurred within more and more political offices the last decades. Development, understood as social transformation, can never be about economy alone, and donors and policymakers have thus turned in other directions in order to expand their horizon for what development is—or should be. Until recently, even sociologists of religion, who were among the first academics to be engaged in serious discussions about the new global condition (Robertson 2007), showed little interest in the growth of religious activity worldwide and the important social implications of this activity. Most were rather preoccupied with describing what they interpreted to be the secularization of the Western world. Robertson, in one of his recent articles entitled "Global Millennialism: A Postmortem on Secularization" (2007), described what he claims to be the misunderstood relationship between modernization and secularization among his sociologist colleagues in Europe. He called the inability to recognize the importance of religion an "ethnocentric assumption," claiming that this failure in academic circles is "indeed, one of the great shibboleths (at least, category errors) in the history of the social sciences" (2007: 18). José Casanova, probably today's most cited and influential sociologist of religion from North America, supports Robertson's claim, calling the focus on secularization "a European myth" (Casanova 2007). Robertson claimed that we have to understand that the contemporary phase of globalization has very distinct "religious overtones" (2007: 9); thus, we have to shift our focus from the close (European) surroundings to look at what is happening on the global scene. Once we start studying that scene, Robertson explained, we will detect that religion is not necessarily about rites, dogmas, and religious bureaucracy, but about spirituality. As a result of this insight, secularization should not be regarded as an inevitable process which finally wipes religion from the surface of the world. It should be regarded as an example of religious change, confined to a specific historical and cultural context. Secularization theory has to be detached from the grand narrative of modernization, and we should follow David Martin's advice and redefine our discussion to include the idea of multiple modernities (Martin 2005). This way we can come to terms with the fact that in large parts of the world an increased interest in religion has gone hand in hand with the embracement of the material and technological development we like to call "modernity."

Earlier we saw that one important aspect of globalization was the increased possibility of communication across large distances—what Geschiere and Meyer called "global flows." Both Michael Wilkinson and Peter Beyer have argued that religion is an important element within this flow (Beyer 1994; Geschiere and Meyer 1998; Wilkinson 2007). Increased communication forces the religious communities to reorient their tradition away from the cultural tradition of its origins towards the global whole, a process which has serious implications when the theme under study is religion and development. Beyer focuses on two such alternatives. The first is the fundamentalist assumption which insists that little change is necessary or desirable. The alternative response would be an openness which sees change as a "prime warrant for the continued authenticity of the tradition" (Beyer 1994: 10). Both these responses have implications for foreign actors seeking partners for development projects. The former attempts to fight the forces of change (even with means and resources provided by the new enemy); the latter engages in new projects even if it means reformulating the old content to new material situations. Both these reactions to the development discourse (understood as both arguments and actions) rest upon and depend upon communication. Regardless of whether the two different attitudes are involved in, or refuse contact with, the foreign bodies looking for partners in the global south, the communicating bodies are whirled into a global paradox of acceptance and rejection.

But how do these theoretical considerations actually materialize? What are the signs of global religious communication? How has our age become "the most religious of worlds" (Thomas 2007: 35)? Africa itself might be the most obvious example of how religion has played an integral role in the gradual movement towards global integration. Religious ideas' role—sometimes as hostage and sometimes as colonizer—might also serve as a good example of the complexity of this historic development. Through the transatlantic slave trade, religious ideas once connected to geographical sites and ethnic relations were introduced to new contexts on new continents. There are several examples of how the religious traditions of the slaves have had a lasting impact on the cultures they encountered in Brazil, Cuba, Haiti, and the Americas (Adogame 2007). From a more recent example we can state that African impulses have been important in what has become the worldwide Pentecostal revival (Wagner 2004). This complexity of global religious encounters can also be exemplified through examples from the modern mission movement. Several pioneering missionaries were actually freed slaves who returned to their old continent with a new religious tradition to share. Leading figures like Samuel Ajayi Crowther in Nigeria and Joseph Merrick in Cameroon were the result of Christian involvement in the fight against slavery; they returned to Africa in order to create new Christian congregations together with former slaves who wanted to re-settle on the continent of their ancestors. The irony of the story was that these glimpses of humanity and liberation not only paved the way for religious activities among the local population, but also unfortunately prepared the ground for the colonial "scramble for Africa" (Adogame 2007: 537).

Far from all religious traditions join the rejoicing choir in favour of the globalization-hymn. Frank J. Lechner's (2005) study of the anti-globalization movement revealed that a strong engagement exists against some of the consequences of the neoliberal market economy also among the established churches in the West. During his visit to Cuba in 1998, Pope John Paul II delivered a sermon in which he strongly condemned "the resurgence of a certain *capitalist neoliberalism* which subordinates the human person to *blind market forces* and conditions the development of people on these forces" (Lechner 2005: 122). Many church leaders also claimed to be part of the winning team when President Bill Clinton announced a foreign aid bill in 2000 which ultimately led to full debt relief for several poor countries (Lechner 2005: 118). This is not to say that the church's leading role in the anti-globalization movement is to claim that another world is possible; rather, attention should be paid to the fact that the churches not only promote or profit from global changes, but also take part in the fight against certain consequences of these changes.

This reluctant attitude towards globalization is even more visible within Islam, a religion which clearly profited from expanding trade routes and increased contact between the continents through both the trans-Saharan trade routes to West Africa and the naval connection between East Africa and the Arabian Peninsula as well as the Indian sub-continent. Even if the Sufi brotherhoods are known to have spread Islam through peaceful means across large distances, several recent dramatic events bear evidence of the deep negative feelings in some Muslim milieus against Western liberal cultural dominance. According to Mark Jurgensmeyer, the World Trade Center was not only a symbol of American capitalism, but was also a *world* trade centre, where citizens from 86 different nations were reported killed after the buildings' collapse (Jurgensmeyer 2005), showing that the 9/11 attacks were not only directed against Americans, but against the global economy. The Islamist terrorists' goal was to broadcast the message that there are strong powers which oppose the idea of one world—at least one world dictated culturally and economically from Manhattan. This strong religious anti-globalism can take many different forms, and the al Qaeda network seems to have found new ways as branches of the organization were recently established in the Saharan desert and started to attack oil installations owned by multinational companies. Even if these networks seem scattered and small, they are united in a fight for a different global content, a morally based opposition to the capitalist cultural liberalism of the West. Their idea of development and self-governance stands in radical opposition to the charters of the government-financed NGOs which operate in the same areas and are trying to "liberate" the same population.

Globalization from an African perspective

What happens when a Western academic term, describing global processes from a Western perspective, is adopted by African researchers? The term becomes glocalized: It is introduced as part of the flow of concepts and theories that make up the academic discourse to which universities worldwide have to relate in order to communicate with their Western counterparts. However, the outcome of this glocalization process has surprised many of the Western scholars who actually have taken the time to read what their African colleagues write. I have chosen to present the "African" response[1] to the globalization debate along two lines: The first line concerns the theoretical discussion which has emerged through, and is coloured by, a strong ideological interpretation of the term itself. In several publications from the continent, Africa is portrayed as marginalized in the global game in terms of economy, politics, and cultural influence on the rest of the world.[2] Numerous scholars have launched critiques against Western writers' tendencies to "post"-explain and theorize Africa out of the factual discussion about the "new world order" (Aina 2004; Ake 1995; Amin 1997). In an attempt to re-orient his Western readers, Paul Tiyambe Zeleza begins his two-volume *Rethinking Africa's 'Globalization'*[3] with the subtitle "Remapping Africa," stating:

> Africa in short, is a geography, a history, a reality and an imaginary of places, peoples and positions, both an invented intellectual construct and an object of intellectual inquiry. What is Africa in the brave new world of contemporary globalization? What are its new cartographic and cognitive boundaries, its internal and external networks? What is the intellectuals' role in clarifying and mapping Africa's place in this reconfigured world? (Zeleza 2003: 3)

Zeleza is quite critical of those scholars who claim that globalization represents a new way of conducting social research or a new way of mapping the world. His criticism is based on the notion that such claims further marginalize Africa from the academic discussion. From his historical point of view, Zeleza claims that Africa is not—and never has been—marginalized from the global community. To the contrary, he underscores that Africa has always mattered and that it still matters today for the 900 million people inhabiting the continent. It also matters for the millions who were forced into a historic slave-trade diaspora and a more or less voluntary diaspora caused by colonial and post-colonial misrule. But instead of starting his "remapping" of Africa by deploring the actual state of most African economies, Zeleza claims that Africa today plays an important role in the world's global economy. Africa's ratio of extra regional trade to GDP is actually the highest in the world, making it more "globalized" than all the other continents.[4] Zeleza then rightly asks if this globalized economy is actually Africa's main problem. How come, after five hundred years of global integration, Africa has not been able to lift its population out of poverty? (Zeleza 2003: 4–5). The question is obviously a rhetorical one and needs not be answered, but it serves as a good example of an African scholar's approach towards a debate thus far being conducted by Western economists. When Joseph Stiglitz, the 2001 Nobel Prize winner and former chief economist of the World Bank as well as the driving force behind the World Bank's globalization policy, introduces his book *Globalization and Its Discontent* with a slightly ironic question: "Why has globalization—a force that has brought so much good—become so controversial?" (Stiglitz 2002: 4), it is understandable that Zeleza and his African colleagues feel the need to engage ideologically in the academic debate.

The second line of thought evident in the African scholarly contribution to the discussions about globalization is that the word is very much tangled up in what we in the West would call the development discourse. The African social scientists, contrary to their northern colleagues, see their research first as a contribution to finding solutions to the immense problems of poverty and lack of development in large parts of sub-Saharan Africa.[5] These problems cannot be discussed in a temporal or spatial vacuum; consequently, the discussion concerning social organization is strongly historicized and thus also ideologized. The academic association which publishes most literature related to this topic on the continent is the Council for the

Development of Social Sciences in Africa (CODERSIA), one of the most vibrant and influential academic associations in this part of the world. In the CODERSIA publications which I have consulted, and which directly or indirectly deal with globalization, the term is interpreted as much as an historical period as an analytical term. In his introductory chapter to the collection of articles entitled *Globalization and Social Policy in Africa*, Tade Akin Aina wrote:

> However, any meaningful and relevant analysis of globalization and social policy in Africa must start with an understanding of the twin processes of poverty and development. It must investigate both process and context as they relate to the recent history and experience of the different countries. Such an analysis must revisit the "development process," its promises and failures, and, in particular, the recent epoch of persistent crisis and adjustment. (Aina 2004: 2–3)

According to Aina, the starting point of any discussion about globalization is a discussion about development and poverty. Globalization does not make sense as an analytical term separated from the social reality in which the researcher is situated and, when summing up the findings from the 17 authors in the volume, Aina focused attention on the main conclusion of the study, which confirms that "globalization has not been necessarily benign, as far as Africa and Africans are concerned" (Aina 2004: 5). This is a rather modest rephrasing of the way several authors through quite harsh descriptions see globalization primarily as a neo-colonial practice, a political strategy used by the rich countries in the north to continue their economic domination of the formerly colonized south. When Western involvement in Africa is discussed, including the bilateral development aid, few authors find any positive results which give hope for the future. Globalization is not interpreted as a joint venture, a process which brings opportunity for future collaboration and development; it is rather presented as a prolonged arm of historical dominance.

> [G]lobalization in one way or another has been responsible for the erosion of people's welfare, job destruction and mass unemployment. It has thrown people into deeper immiseration and resulted in tensions. . . . In sum, what marks this period, unlike the previous stages of capitalism, is the fact that what exists is what has been characterized as "disorganized capitalism." . . . The period is marked by the dominance of the "supermarket ideology" disseminated by the media, which goes as far as defining "love" in terms of the relationship between a person and his/her car, or "revolution" as a new brand of soap, a microwave or a washing machine. (Chachage and Annan-Yao 2004: 332–333)

Aina divided Africa's recent history into three phases: the colonial period, the early post-independent phase, and the crisis and adjustment era. Describing social policy during the first period, Aina underscored that the period was very complex due to influences from many different nations with a wide variety of agendas, but that the policy was selective and exclusionary and only benefited the local population if it played its defined subordinated role in the colonial structure (Aina 2004). In terms of economy the colonies played no independent role, and their integration into the world economy occurred as commodity only. This changed radically during the second period, from the late 1950s to the mid-1970s—a period marked by nationalism and optimism fuelled by independence euphoria, where nations were constructed and the economies flourished. Social subsidies played an important economic role during this period, and the national leaders, who sought legitimization through education and healthcare, provided the necessary funds (Aina 2004). However, the good times did not last very long as the global financial crises of the 1970s hit the new states with strength and led them into the last period, the crisis and adjustment era. The lack of democratic reforms within the political systems added to the economic crises and made the new African states unable to adjust to the global economic changes. Aina described the era as follows:

> This is the era that we recognise as containing that constellation of forces in the contemporary spread of global capitalism now known as globalization. It expressed the social and economic forces and dynamics now at play in the context of globalization and that have produced changes in political and economic regimes in addition to redefining patterns of social relations between economic and social groups and ethnic and gender relations. (Aina 2004: 13)

The rise and fall of the structural adjustment programs

In 1999 Thandika Mkandawire and Charles C. Soludo published the study *Our Continent Our Future. African Perspectives on Structural Adjustments*—an analysis of 30 research projects which evaluated the result of the imposed structural adjustment programs (SAP) on most sub-Saharan national economies. The SAP were introduced by the International Monetary Fund (IMF) and the World Bank in an attempt to save the sinking African economies through harsh cuts in public spending and privatization of public services. Mkandawire and Soludo's findings are discouraging reading for all those looking for positive consequences of the IMF policies' in Africa. The conclusion of the study is, in short, that the programs did not pay enough attention to the individual differences and needs of the concerned countries. The authors concluded that, if such programs were to have any effect in the future, the involved governments have to be included to a larger extent in the process of finding local solutions to local problems (Mkandawire and Soludo 1999). The programs were, in other words, interpreted as yet another version of colonial domination from the Western powers in charge of the IMF and the World Bank.[6]

Why does such total discouragement and negative attitude towards he IMF and the World Bank exist in the literature? In order to understand why so many social scientists across sub-Saharan Africa are critical of the Western development discourse (including the term *globalization*), one has to understand the prominent and influential role of the Egyptian scholar Samir Amin. His analysis of the economic historical development in the region has made a lasting impact on most social scientific scholars on the continent, and both Zeleza (2003: 4–5) and Aina (2004: 5) have drawn attention to Amin's influence on the field. Amin often "translates" the term globalization into meaning the global disorder which led to the implementation of SAP during the 1980s and 1990s. Globalization and SAP are actually viewed as identical terms; globalization has been reduced to mean a short historical period and a specific economic adjustment program introduced by the Bretton Woods institutions. The chaos that followed the IMF-initiated programs led Amin to search for an alternative humanist project of globalization focused on the renegotiation of the global/national dialectic while aiming for a more balanced relationship among the world's major regions. The ultimate goal is an open and flexible discussion of the economic relationship between countries in all parts of the world (Amin 1997).

> The predominance of this chaos should not keep us from thinking about alternative scenarios for a new "world order" even if there are many different possible future "world orders." What I am trying to do here is to call attention to questions which have been glossed over by the triumphalism of inevitable globalization at the same time as its precariousness is revealed. (Amin 1997: 2–3)

Globalization, religion and development: Concluding remarks

So what, you may ask, is the relevance of my personal experiences from northern Cameroon in a highly theoretical discussion about the relationship among globalization, development and religion in Africa? My point is that global discourses are not automatically adopted locally. Global discourses are caught in the tension between flow and closure. Global messages are always in danger of being taken hostage by either *jihad* or *McWorld* (Barber 1995). Globalization as a term is met with resistance in African academic milieus, much the same way that many Western development projects are met with resistance and neglect among the population they seek to help. Both globalization and development are often interpreted as *neo-colonial*, both as discourse and practice, and thereby met with a negative attitude from the concerned population. The two terms are met with reluctance because they are imposed from the outside and lack local groundedness. Globalization as an analytical term was interpreted by the CODERSIA authors to mean a concrete economic program imposed by the World Bank and IMF, and many of the AIDS-related advertisements were interpreted as Western countries' attempts to limit the sexual freedom of Africans. In both cases the intentions behind the involvement from the outside world was questioned.

The strength of the previously mentioned *All against AIDS* project was that, even if it was initiated from the outside world, the project had a local leadership who was well aware of the challenges and prejudices present among the people it addressed. In addition it was transmitted through a channel which was accepted by the people: a church headed by spiritual leaders with credibility among its listeners. This very brief presentation of a successful development project might serve as a good example of the role of religion and religious leaders in a globalized development discussion. Religious communities interact with believers on many different levels, and religious leaders share worldviews, beliefs and everyday challenges with the same population for which the development projects are intended. The very same leaders often act as links between the local population and the global ideas and discourses provided by NGOs and bilateral development agreements through their travels and access to information technology. In this way, the development discourse can be glocalized through religious communities who have the authority needed to convince people that change is necessary and that change can be for the better. Thus, globalization, religion and development can be transformed from contested and theoretical terms into local practices which can transform and empower the local population.

References

Adogame, Afe. 2007. "Sub-saharan Africa". In *Religion, Globalization, and Culture*, ed. Peter Beyer and Lori Beaman, 527–548. Leiden: Brill.

Aina, Tade Akin. 2004. "Introduction: How do we understand globalization and social policy in Africa?" In *Globalization and Social Policy in Africa*, ed. Tade Akin Aina, Chachage Seithy L. Chachage and Elisabeth Annan-Yao, 1–20. Dakar/Oxford: CODESRIA.

Ake, Claude. 1995. "The new world order: A view from Africa.". In *Whose world order?: Uneven globalization and the end of the cold war*, ed. Hans-Henrik Holm and Georg Sørensen, 19–42. Boulder, CO: Westview.

Amin, Samir. 1997. *Capitalism in the Age of Globalization: The Management of Contemporary Society*. London: Zed Books.

Barber, Benjamin. 1995. *Jihad vs. McWorld. Terrorism's Challenge to Democracy*. New York, NY: Ballantine Books.

Beyer, Peter. 1994. *Religion and globalization*. London: Sage.

Casanova, José. 2007. "Rethinking secularization: A global comparative perspective." In *Religion, Globalization, and Culture*, ed. Peter Beyer and Lori Beaman, 101–120. Leiden: Brill.

Chachage, Chachage Seithy L. and Annan-Yao, Elisabeth. 2004. "Conclusion—future agenda: Beyond globalization." In *Globalization and Social Policy in Africa*, ed. Tade Akin Aina, Chachage Seithy L. Chachage and Elisabeth Annan-Yao, 327–339. Dakar/Oxford: CODESRIA.

Corten, André and Marshall-Fratani, Ruth. 2001. "Introduction." In *Between Babel and Pentecost. Transnational Pentecostalism in Africa and Latin America*, ed. André Corten and Ruth Marshall-Fratani, 1–21. Bloomington, IN: Indiana University Press.

Drønen, Tomas Sundnes. 2013. *Pentecostalism, Globalisation, and Islam in Northern Cameroon. Megachurches in the Making?* Leiden: Brill.

Eriksen, Thomas Hylland. 2007. *Globalization. The Key Concepts*. London: Berg

Geschiere, Peter and Meyer, Birgit. 1998. "Globalization and identity: Dialects of flow and closure." *Development and Change* 29, no. 4: 601–615.

Giddens, Anthony. 1990. *The Consequences of Modernity*. Stanford, CA: Stanford University Press.

Haynes, Jeffrey. 2007. *Religion and Development. Conflict or Cooperation?* Hampshire: Palgrave Macmillan.

Holter, Knut. 2013. "Global tekst i lokal tapning: En nigeriansk bydelsprofets bruk av vann, olivenolje og bibeltekster til helbredelse–som eksempel på religiøs glokalisering?" *Kirke og kultur* 118, no. 2. Forthcoming.

Jurgensmeyer, Mark. 2005. "Religious antiglobalism." In *Religion in Global Civil Society*, ed. Mark Jurgensmeyer,135–148. Oxford: Oxford University Press.

Lechner, Frank J. 2005. "Religious rejections of globalization." In *Religion in Global Civil Society*, ed. Mark Jurgensmeyer, 115–133. Oxford: Oxford University Press.

Martin, David. 2005. *On Secularization: Towards a Revised General Theory*. Aldershot: Ashgate.

Mkandawire, Thandika and Soludo, Charles Chukwuma. 1999. *Our Continent, Our Future: African Perspectives on Structural Adjustment*. Trenton, NJ: Africa World Press.

Robertson, Roland. 1992. *Globalization. Social Theory and Global Culture*. London: SAGE.

Robertson, Roland. 1995. "Glocalization: Time-Space and Homogeneity-Heterogenity." In *Global Modernities*, ed. Mike Featherstone, Scott Lash and Roland Robertson, 25–44. London: Sage.

Robertson, Roland. 2007. "Global millennialism: A postmortem on secularization." In *Religion, Globalization, and Culture*, eds. Peter Beyer and Lori Beaman, 9–34. Leiden: Brill.

Scholte, Jan Art. 2005. *Globalization: A Critical Introduction*. 2nd ed. Hampshire: Palgrave Macmillan.

Stiglitz, Joseph. 2002. *Globalization and its Discontent*. London: Penguin Books.

Thomas, George M. 2007. "The Cultural and Religious Character of World Society." In *Religion, Globalization, and Culture*, ed. Peter Beyer and Lori Beaman, 35–56. Leiden: Brill.

van Binsbergen, Wim M. J. and van Dijk, Rijk. 2004. *Situating Globality: African Agency in the Appropriation of Global Culture*. Leiden: Brill.

Wagner, Peter. 2004. "Introduction." In *Out of Africa: How the Spiritual Explosion among Nigerians is Impacting the World*, 7–18. Ventura, CA: Regal Books.

Wilkinson, Michael. 2007. "Religion and global flows." In *Religion, Globalization, and Culture*, ed. Peter Beyer and Lori Beaman, 375–389. Leiden: Brill.

Wolfensohn, James D. 2011. "Foreword." In *Religion and Development. Ways of Transforming the World*, ed. Gerrie ter Haar, xvii-xviii. London: Hurst and Company.

Zeleza, Paul Tiyambe. 2003. *Rethinking Africa's Globalization: The Intellectual Challenges*. Asmara: Africa World Press, Inc.

Notes

1 This is, of course, a reduction deliberately made by me, meaning the African scholars that I have read and cite in the following.

2 For a more elaborated version of these arguments, see Drønen 2013, pp. 25-30.

3 The term globalization is even placed in quotation marks as if the intention were to question the term from the very start.

4 Whereas Europe's external trade accounts for 12.8 per cent, North America's is 13.2, Asia's is 15.2, and Latin America's is 23.7, Africa's ratio of extra regional trade in 1990 was 45.6 per cent (Zeleza 2003: 4-5).

5 Wim van Binsberger and Rijk van Dijk have edited an informative introduction to Africa's role within an emerging global culture in their book *Situating globality: African agency in the appropriation of global culture*, published in 2004.

6 IMF and the World Bank are parts of the UN system, but unlike the the UN General Assembly, representation in the IMF and World Bank direction is dependent on the economic contribution to the organization. The "gentleman's agreement" is that the chief of the World Bank always is from the US, whereas the head of the IMF is always a European.

CHAPTER FOUR

Small-Scale Entrepreneurs in the Slum Areas of Nairobi

Magne Supphellen

Introduction

Whereas classic theories of development considered religion to be irrelevant or an obstacle to economic development (e.g., Leys 1996), current researchers, governments and development organizations increasingly construe religion as an important factor with significant potential impact on the success of development efforts. In Africa, religion is undoubtedly very central to people's worldviews. Neglecting to consider the metaphysical aspects of human life has probably resulted in flawed development projects on this continent (Tyndale 2001). However, the knowledge of how religion influences development efforts is rather limited, and more empirical research has been called for (Mersland, D'Espallier and Supphellen 2012; Ter Haar and Ellis 2006). Mersland et al. (2012) suggested that researchers explore the nature and impact of religion on three arenas of development programs: recipients, providers, and the interactions between them. In this study, we focus on the recipients. Specifically, we explore how religious attitudes towards business activity among small-scale entrepreneurs in the slum areas of Nairobi influence their level of self-determination.

Self-determination is a motivational construct. When individuals are self-determined, they feel empowered or psychologically energized to act. A basic premise of self-determination theory (SDT; Deci and Ryan 1985: 1991) is that the level of self-determination is higher when the motivation to act is intrinsic—that is, rooted in a sense of personal importance, interest or enjoyment. A number of empirical studies have confirmed that intrinsic motivation increases effort, persistence and behavioural performance (see Ryan and Deci 2000). Conversely, extrinsic motivation, characterized by compliance to some kind of external demand or reward contingency, lowers self-determination and behavioural performance. Because religion provides premises for the goals, values, motivations and behaviour of people, we expect entrepreneurs' self-determination to be influenced by their worldviews or religious beliefs. We expect that the nature of this influence depends on the specific type of religious attitude in question: Some attitudes might strengthen entrepreneurial self-determination whereas others might weaken it. In this study, we briefly discuss SDT and define and develop empirical measures for three types of religious attitudes towards business activity. Hypotheses on the effects of religious attitudes on self-determination are tested on a sample of 321 small-scale entrepreneurs in the slum areas of Nairobi, Kenya. The findings support the proposition that specific religious attitudes stimulate self-determination and, thus, represent a resource for economic development (Ter Haar 2005).

Self-determination and entrepreneurs in subsistence markets

According to SDT, humans have three core psychological needs: competence, relatedness and autonomy (Ryan and Deci 2000; Deci and Ryan 2000). Competence is the perceived ability to influence important outcomes. Relatedness is the experience of having satisfying social relationships, and autonomy concerns the experience of acting with a sense of volition and choice. Nurturing feelings of autonomy, competence and relatedness facilitates self-determination, which in turn increases persistence and behavioural performance.

Self-determination is described as a continuum of motivational types distinguished by the degree to which the motivations emanate from the self (Ryan and Deci 2000). At the low end of the continuum is amotivation, the state of lacking the intention to act. When in this state, people do not value the activity; they might feel incompetent or expect an undesirable outcome. If they act, they do so without intention, based solely on some kind of external pressure. The middle and higher parts of the continuum include five kinds of motivations, with increasing levels of self-determination. In this research we are concerned with the two types of motivations with the highest level of self-determination: intrinsic motivation and integrated extrinsic motivation.

Intrinsic motivation (IM) is deeply rooted in the personal interests and personality of the individual. Intrinsically motivated actions are carried out for their inherent enjoyment, not in order to obtain some kind of external reward. IM is the highest level of self-determination with the strongest positive effects on performance.

Integrated external motivation (IEM) is described as the most autonomous form of extrinsic (externally oriented) motivation (Ryan and Deci 2000). It shares many qualities with intrinsic motivation, but is focused on separable outcomes rather than the inherent enjoyment of the action. When a behaviour or action (e.g., conducting business) has high IEM, it has been evaluated, brought into congruence with one's values and needs and assimilated to the self. Actions driven by IEM are done to confirm one's values and self-concept.

A series of studies have shown that IM and IEM facilitate more engagement, persistence and better performance than more extrinsic types of motivation (Ryan and Deci 2000). Hence, entrepreneurs with higher levels of IM and IEM probably work harder, cope better with difficulties and gain better profits than those with lower levels of these motivations. However, entrepreneurs in subsistence markets are probably driven by a mix of motivations. Certainly, there are external pressures to provide food and basic goods for the household, but people in such areas might choose from among different strategies to obtain this. Entrepreneurship is but one of several options: Some work for other people, others engage in theft and/or begging. Because the benefits of theft and begging are more certain and immediate, such activities are often chosen over other options. Thus, people who engage in entrepreneurial activity are probably not motivated by expectancies of extrinsic rewards only; they also experience some level of self-determination in terms of IM and/or IEM. We suggest that the religious attitudes of entrepreneurs towards business activity influence their level of IM and IEM.

Three religious attitudes towards business activity and their effects on self-determination

In Africa, most people are profoundly religious. According to Haynes (1995), "spiritual and material concerns interact within highly fluid boundaries in a context where many Africans relate to religion as a means of solving a number of personal problems, some of which will be material issues". In such a context, it is likely that religious beliefs and attitudes influence the way entrepreneurs think about their businesses. Thus, we used three types of sources to explore religious perspectives on business among Christian owners of micro-financed businesses (MFB). First, we reviewed the classic literature on Christian business ethics (e.g., Wingren 2004;

Curran 2002) because Kenya, as well as many other African countries, has been heavily influenced by Western missionaries. Second, we examined current analyses of Christianity in Kenya (e.g., Gifford 2009). Finally, we interviewed five local pastors (all were fluent in English) and twenty-nine local MFB owners (interviewed by three local bilingual interviewers fluent in Swahili and English).

Three different religious attitudes or orientations towards business activity emerged from the literature reviews and the interviews. First, calling orientation refers to the attitude that business is a holy calling from God. Similar to all other human capabilities, the talent for conducting business is considered to be a gift from God. Business people are called to be good stewards and gain on their talents to the benefit of people and the honour of God. Importantly, within this perspective, God is not a distant grantor of talents who withdraws to let people work on their own. Rather, God is construed as an active supporter of his people and a personal resource for advice, comfort and power. This perspective on work and business seems to draw on the classic Protestant work ethic (see, e.g., Wingren 2004), but is also consistent with current Catholic doctrines, such as the teachings of Pope John Paul II in his encyclical letters on human work from 1981 (see Curran 2002). There are good reasons to expect a positive effect of calling orientation on the self-determination of entrepreneurs. As previously noted, self-determination is rooted in three basic types of psychological needs: competence, autonomy and relatedness. The calling orientation might nurture all three of them. The notion of God-given talents might strengthen the sense of worth and competence: "Because God has invested in me, I have good chances of succeeding." The expectation of God watching over and being available to help the entrepreneur can create a context of security and relatedness, which is conducive for self-determination flourishing (Ryan and Deci 2000). What about autonomy? At first glance, we might expect that dependence on supernatural forces would reduce perceived autonomy. This is not necessarily the case. In fact, I would argue that the calling orientation has a positive effect on the sense of autonomy of entrepreneurs. Their level of choice and volition is decided by the extent to which they have an internal perceived locus of causality, which is a sense of being able to actively influence (cause) important outcomes (Ryan and Deci 2000). To our entrepreneurs, autonomy is about the perceived control of factors influencing the economic performance of their businesses. According to Ryan and Deci (2000: 74), "autonomy refers not to being independent, detached, or selfish but rather to the feeling of volition that can accompany any act, whether dependent or independent, collectivist or individualist." Because the calling orientation informs entrepreneurs that God is interested in their business, grants them talents and is available for advice and inspiration, this religious perspective on entrepreneurship probably increases the sense of control and the perceived potential for influencing outcomes.

Both historical and current empirical evidence lend credence to the idea that the calling orientation has a positive effect on the self-determination of entrepreneurs. For example, an analysis of the Norwegian lay preacher and entrepreneur Hans Nielsen Hauge (1771–1824) suggests that his remarkable success was inspired by a sense of calling which "stimulated important performance factors, such as motivation, personal agency, and alertness to market disequilibrium" (Dalgaard and Supphellen 2011). In line with this reasoning, psychological studies suggest that the sanctification of work (i.e., seeing work as a calling) is correlated with a number of positive attitudes and behaviours, such as finding work tasks more meaningful, persistence and fewer days of work missed on account of illness (Wrzesniewski et al. 1997). It seems likely that these effects are, at least partly, caused by higher levels of self-determination. Specifically, we expect that the calling orientation has a positive effect on both IM and IEM, the two motivational types with the highest level of self-determination.

H1 Calling orientation has a positive effect on (a) intrinsic motivation and (b) integrated extrinsic motivation of entrepreneurs.

The second perspective, reward orientation, stems from a major stream of African Christianity termed Winning Christianity or Prosperity Gospel (Gifford 2009). The fundamental element here is the idea that active engagement in the spiritual arena and monetary donations to the church will be rewarded in terms of financial prosperity (e.g., success in business). Hence, we termed this perspective reward orientation. This logic is fundamentally different from the calling orientation as it does not focus on talents or even on work as such. The logic of reward orientation is that the outcome of entrepreneurial activity is decided not by the talents or efforts of the entrepreneur, but by the level of effort and sacrifice on the spiritual arena. Inspired by charismatic American leaders such as Hagin (1995), adherents to this orientation perceive a direct relationship between monetary church donations and personal financial blessings (Gifford 2009). A key biblical source here is a statement of Jesus, cited in Mark 10:29–20: "no one who has left home or brothers or sisters or mother or father or children or fields for me and the gospel will fail to receive a hundred times as much in this present age"(New International Version). This passage is used to promote a general principle of material reward for sacrifice to the church: One Shilling donated to the church, will give a return of one hundred Shillings.

We expect the reward orientation to have some (temporary) effect on IEM. Entrepreneurship might serve as an arena for harvesting the rewards of sacrifices at church. The outlook for rewards can add an element of higher purpose and meaning to the business activity, which might increase the level of IEM—at least in the short run. This reasoning is consistent with Gifford's (2009) observation of people after services at Prosperity Gospel churches: "Nevertheless, talking to members after services and functions, one cannot miss the sense of determination and confidence many have derived from the church. Members will freely talk of the 'vision' they have caught which has given purpose to their lives" (p. 125). However, we do not expect the reward orientation to stimulate the level of enjoyment or satisfaction of doing business (i.e., no expected effect on IM) because the reward orientation is not concerned with the talents of the entrepreneur, the stewardship of talents or the ongoing support of God in day-to-day business operations. Consequently, the reward orientation has less potential for stimulating the entrepreneur's sense of competence and autonomy, which are the two major antecedents of IM, the strongest type of self-determination (Ryan and Deci 2000).

H2 Reward orientation has a positive effect on integrated extrinsic motivation, but no effect on intrinsic motivation of entrepreneurs.

Finally, we identified a fatalistic orientation. The interviews with local pastors informed us that some MFB owners were influenced by fatalistic beliefs even though they define themselves as Christians. These people believed that their future, including the results of their business activity, was entirely in the hands of a supernatural force. Hence, this orientation is characterized by an external locus of control: Outcomes of all events and activities of life, including entrepreneurship, are not controlled or caused by the individual, but by fate or some cosmological power.

Entrepreneurs with a fatalistic orientation probably have rather low levels of self-determination. Those who succeed quickly in their carriers without any drawbacks might conclude that they are destined for success, which can increase their sense of competence and autonomy to some extent and thus increase self-determination in the short run. However, when they experience drawbacks, there will be a serious negative change in motivation. Problems lead the fatalistic entrepreneur to conclude that "it wasn't meant to be, and there is nothing I can do about it" because it is out of their control.

Importantly, most entrepreneurs experience problems and drawbacks before they succeed (e.g., Burns 2011). This is why the net effect of a fatalistic orientation is expected to be negative on the self-determination of entrepreneurs. Also, this orientation contributes less to a sense of relatedness because people with a fatalistic orientation typically perceive God or the supernatural force as more distant than people with a calling or reward orientation.

H3 The fatalistic orientation has negative effects on (a) intrinsic motivation and (b) integrated extrinsic motivation.

Method

Sample and procedure

The hypotheses were tested on a sample of three hundred twenty-one MFB owners in the Nairobi slum areas (n=321). Approximately five hundred credit customers were drawn randomly from client lists of the Jami Bora Trust, a local micro-credit institution. Of these, one hundred seventy-nine declined, mainly for practical reasons or due to illness (response rate: 64.2 per cent). Clients were contacted via mobile phones by officials from the trust and asked to participate in exchange for a dinner meal. Approximately 97 per cent of participants were Christians and 3 per cent were Muslims; 61 per cent were females. The average number of workers, including the owner, was 2.1. Approximately 75 per cent were retailers of fast-moving consumer goods. The remaining 25 per cent provided various kinds of services, such as housekeeping services, barber shops, carpenter services, transport, repair of electronic items and tailoring services.

Participants were instructed to meet at official places close to their homes, such as community buildings, cafés and churches inside the slums. A questionnaire was first developed in English by the author and then translated into Swahili by local bilinguals at a local university. A group of six bilingual graduate students from the same university collected the data. Participants were first briefed on the purpose of the study and how to use the scales (five-point scales). They were given a sheet of paper with the scale to have in front of them while responding to the questions. The interviewers asked questions in Swahili and registered responses on the English questionnaires. The personal interview mode allowed for respondents to ask questions when they felt uncertain and for interviewers to address ambiguities or inconsistencies in the responses.

Measures

Calling orientation was measured on a five-point scale (1=completely disagree; 5=completely agree) using three items: "I believe that God has called me to use my talents in business"; "Because of God's grace, I feel obligated to exploit my talents and work hard"; and "Because God has saved me, I want to bless people through my business activity." Three items were used for the reward orientation: "God rewards a humble businessman with financial success"; "If I believe strongly enough, God will give me success in business"; and "If I submit my life completely to God, He will reward me." The fatalistic orientation also consisted of three items: "When somebody succeeds with his or her business, it is not because of the person's talents, but only because of grace"; "My effort in business is not crucial; I must wait for God to make my way"; and "Business success has little to do with my own abilities." The nine items for the three attitude orientations were submitted to an exploratory factor analysis using principal component extraction and oblique rotation. This analysis gave three factors with eigenvalues > 1 (explained variance = 63.2 per cent). Importantly, the pattern of loadings was clean and consistent with the theory. The three items for the calling orientation loaded on the same factor (loadings: .697 to .877; highest cross-loading: .074). Similar results were observed for the reward orientation (loadings: .761- to .826; highest cross-loading: .121) and the fatalistic orientation (loadings: .723 to .834; highest cross-loading: .084). Thus, we computed indexes by averaging the scores of items on each orientation.

The measures of the two motivations were based on Ryan and Deci's (2000) framework of motivational types . IEM was measured by three items (same five-point scale): "(Doing business) is personally meaningful to me"; "I feel it is the right thing for me to do"; and "I feel that I was meant to be a businessman/woman." The following items represented IM: "It is fun to do business"; "It is exciting"; and "I really enjoy it." Again we submitted all items to exploratory factor analysis using the same methods of extraction and rotation as for the religious orientations. This analysis showed two components with eigenvalues greater than 1 (explained variance=63.7 per cent). The pattern of loadings was consistent with theory: The three items describing IM loaded on the same factor (loadings: .917 to .771; highest cross-loading: .134). Likewise, items for IEM also loaded on a separate factor (loadings: .828 to .573; highest cross-loading: .131). Average scores on each motivational type were used in the subsequent analyses.

Control variables

The following control variables were included in the analyses: gender, age, business training (Yes/No) and overclaiming. Overclaiming is the tendency to respond in a socially desirable manner. Specifically, measures of overclaiming reveal the extent to which respondents overrate their knowledge in a topic area (Paulhus et al. 2003). We asked respondents about their knowledge of specific business terms: income, positioning, profit, *shadow product, money line,* and *blind market* (1= don't know at all, 5=know very well). The three latter terms (in italics) are phony, non-existent terms. Scores on these three terms were indexed and used as a measure of overclaiming. All multi-item measures in the study had satisfactory levels of reliability (Cronbach's alphas ranged from .83 to .94).

Descriptive statistics for the scaled variables are reported in Table 1. Mean scores for both motivational types are quite high. Mean scores on the calling and reward orientations are also high and above 4.5, whereas the mean score on the fatalistic orientation is rather low: 2.656. Because previous research has shown important differences between male and female entrepreneurs (Verheul, Van Stel and Thurik 2006), we also report means for the genders separately. Table 1 reveals two gender differences in our sample. The mean score on calling orientation is significantly higher for males than females ($p < .05$). Males also score marginally higher on the overclaiming index ($p < .1$).

Table 1: Descriptive statistics for scaled variables (N= 321)

Variable	Mean (st.dev)			Max	Min
	Full sample	Females	Males		
Intrinsic motivation	4.706 (.732)	4.698	4.714	1	5
Integrated extrinsic motivation	4.651 (.696)	4.667	4.624	1	5
Calling orientation	4.676 (.663)	4.580	4.772**	1	5
Reward orientation	4.750 (.628)	4.764	4.737	1	5
Fatalistic orientation	2.697 (1.406)	2.656	2.738	1	5
Overclaiming	1.332 (.892)	1.268	1.396*	1	4

Table 2: Regression analysis. Standardized coefficients (N=321)[a].

	Integrated extrinsic motivation			Intrinsic motivation		
		Females	Males		Females	Males
Calling orientation	.267**	.412***	.048	.251***	.396***	-.036
Reward orientation	.043	.166**	-.007	.004	.085	-.034
Fatalistic orientation	-.016	-.043	.003	.023	-.064	.111
Overclaiming	-.003	.048	-.058	.047	.092	-.027
Business training	.001	-.053	.051	-.061	.120*	.001
Age	.085	.104	.049	-.092	-.097	-.121
Gender	.047			.007		
R^2	.087***	.245***	$.013^{ns}$	.075***	.196***	$.025^{ns}$

[a] all scaled variables are log-transformed.

*= p > .1

**=p > .05

***=p > .01

Test of hypotheses

OLS regression was used to test H1 through H3. As shown in Table 1, several of the scaled variables were skewed, either towards the low end (overclaiming and fatalistic orientation) or the high end of the scale (calling orientation, reward orientation, IM and IEM). These variables were log transformed before we ran the regressions in order to normalize distributions. The results of regressions with intrinsic motivation and integrated extrinsic motivation as the dependent variables are shown in Table 2, including separate regressions for each gender. Calling orientation has a positive effect on both IM (ß= .251, $p < .01$) and IEM (ß = .267, $p < .05$). Hence, H1a and H1b are supported. However, the gender-specific analyses revealed that these effects are due to the female entrepreneurs in our sample; we find no significant effects of calling orientation in the male subsample. Hypothesis 2 on the effect of reward orientation is also supported, but only for females. For this subsample, there is a positive effect of reward orientation on IEM (ß = .166, $p < .05$), but not on IM (ß = .085, $p > .1$), as we expected. According to H3, there would be negative effects of the fatalistic orientation on both types of motivation. This hypothesis is not supported. No coefficients reach significance ($p > .1$). Separate analyses for each gender show the same result. Interestingly, we observed a positive effect of business training on IM for females, although this effect is only marginally significant (ß = .120, $p < .1$).

Discussion

Theoretical implications

The importance of self-determination is often underscored in the literature on development and entrepreneurship, yet few studies have measured self-determination or examined its antecedents or consequences empirically in a development context. Specifically, we are not familiar with any empirical studies of the relationships between religious beliefs and entrepreneurial self-determination. In this study we developed three measures of religious attitudes towards business activity and tested their effects on the self-determination of three hundred twenty-one small-scale entrepreneurs in the slum areas of Nairobi. Consistent with our predictions, we observed that calling orientation has a positive effect on both IM and IEM, the two motivational types with the highest level of self-determination (Ryan and Deci 2000). This is an important observation because higher levels of IM and IEM are likely associated with superior entrepreneurial performance. Reward orientation had no effect on IM, but a weak effect on IEM for females, whereas the fatalistic orientation had no effect on any of the motivational variables.

Our findings support the idea of religion as a resource in development efforts (Ter Haar and Ellis 2006). Religious resources have been divided into four categories (Ter Haar 2005): religious ideas, religious practices, religious organization and religious experiences. The religious orientations discussed and tested in the present research are related to the first and probably last categories of resources. Our analyses show that the idea of being called to use and gain from God-given talents for business stimulates the self-determination of entrepreneurs, which likely improves their performance. Although we did not test this proposition in our study, the calling orientation is probably reinforced by religious experiences, such as sensing the support, comfort or guidance of God in daily business operations. The role and impact of such experiences on the self-determination of entrepreneurs is a topic for future research.

The results also have implications for the historical debate of the Weber thesis: that Protestantism (more specifically, its Calvinist branches) promoted the rise of modern capitalism (Weber 1930). Calvinistic Protestantism had this facilitating effect, according to Weber, by affirming the doctrine of predestination—the notion that salvation had been decided for everyone from the beginning of time. Goodness and prosperity were seen as signs of being among the chosen ones and, thus, promoted diligence, persistence and pro-social behaviour. However, from the perspective of modern research on entrepreneurial activity, it is not very likely that belief in predestination has a positive effect on entrepreneurial activity. The many drawbacks entrepreneurs typically face before they eventually succeed would easily lead to the conclusion that they are not among the chosen ones. Whereas some historians reject the Weber thesis altogether (Tawney 1926), others maintain that Weber was right about the importance of religion, but wrong about the explanation of how it influenced economic activity. For example, Landes (1998) suggested that Protestantism generalized important virtues such as diligence and rationality among its adherents by means of "group pressure and mutual scrutiny in assuring performance—everybody looking at everyone else and minding one another's business" (p. 177). Our findings suggest another possibility: The leading role of Protestant merchants and manufacturers was caused by higher levels of calling orientation. Thus, we call for a reanalysis of the historic sources to test this proposition.

The positive effects of calling orientation we observed were due to the female entrepreneurs in our sample. No effects of religious orientations were observed for male entrepreneurs. The literature on entrepreneurship and gender shows that female entrepreneurs often have lower self-confidence than males (Verheul et al. 2006). Self-confidence and self-determination are highly correlated phenomena.

Thus, we can speculate that the potential of religious orientations to influence self-determination is higher for females than males. However, this explanation is rejected because the mean scores on both motivational variables (IM and IEM) were similar for males and females in our sample (see Table 1). Also, the extent to which the genders were influenced by the three religious orientations was about the same; mean scores are similar, with the exception of calling orientation, which in fact is somewhat higher for males than females. In addition, the two subsamples have a similar number of respondents, which means that the statistical power of the subsample analyses is comparable. Hence, the observed differences between males and females probably come from gender differences related to how calling orientation influences self-determination. Future research should delve deeper into the process of how calling orientation influences the thinking of male and female entrepreneurs.

Limitations and future research

The limitations of the study represent potential avenues for future research. First, a cautionary note is in place regarding the causal relationship between religious orientations and self-determination. Because our analyses are based on cross-sectional data, we are not in a position to conclude that calling orientation causes higher levels of self-determination (and not the other way around). In fact, we would expect a certain degree of mutual influence between the two phenomena: Calling-orientation increases the level of self-determination, which in turn confirms and reinforces the sense of calling. However it is not very likely that entrepreneurs "choose" religious orientations based on their level of self-determination. Rather, religious orientations are probably formed over time on the basis of religious teachings at local churches and on the social influence of significant peers. The sources of religious orientations towards business activity represent an interesting subject for future research. We also welcome studies on the effects of religious orientations based on longitudinal data. Such analyses would offer the opportunity to test causal relationships and examine how entrepreneurs with different religious orientations cope with drawbacks over time.

Three specific religious orientations towards business activity were developed and tested in this research. Other types of orientations and more elaborate measures should be developed and tested on other samples and in different African cultures. For example, there are different types of fatalism. The lack of significant (negative) effects of fatalism in this study could be due to the low levels of fatalism in our sample or low construct validity (e.g., wrong type of fatalism). Other types of religious orientations towards business activity could be relevant for Muslim or Hindu entrepreneurs. One important question is whether similar or other types of calling orientation can be found in other types of religious (non-Christian) contexts.

References

Burns, P. 2011. *Entrepreneurship and small-businesses: Start-up, growth, and maturity*, 3rd ed. Basingstoke: Palgrave.

Curran, C. E. 2002. *Catholic social teaching, 1891-present: A historical, theological, and ethical analysis.* Washington, DC: Georgetown University Press.

Dalgaard, B. and Supphellen, M. 2011. "Entrepreneurship in Norway's economic and religious nineteenth-century transformation." *Scandinavian Economic History Review* 59: 48–66.

Deci, E. L. and Ryan, R. M. 2000. "The "What" and "Why" of Goal Pursuits: Human Needs and the Self-Determination of Behavior." *Psychological Inquiry* 11: 227–268.

Gifford, P. 2009. *Christianity, politics, and public life in Kenya.* London: Hurst & Company.

Hagin, K. E. 1995. *Biblical Keys to Financial Prosperity.* Tulsa: Kenneth Hagin Ministries

Haynes, J. 1995. "Popular religion and politics in sub-Saharan Africa." *Third World Quarterly* 16, no. 1: 89–108.

Landes, D. 1998. *The wealth and poverty of nations.* London: Abacus, Time Warner Books.

Mersland, R., D'Espallier, B. and Supphellen, M. 2012. "The Effects of Religion on Development Efforts: Evidence from the Microfinance Industry and a Research Agenda." *World Development* 41: 145–156.

Paulhus, D. L., Harms, P. D., Bruce, N. and Lysy, D. C. 2003. "The Over-Claiming Technique: Measuring Self-Enhancement Independent of Ability." *Journal of Personality and Social Psychology* 84, no. 4: 890–904.

Ryan, R. M. and Deci, E. L. 2000. "Self-Determination Theory and the Facilitation of Intrinsic Motivation, Social Development, and Well-being." *American Psychologist* 55: 68–78.

Tawney, R. H. 1926. *Religion and the rise of capitalism.* London: John Murray.

Ter Haar, G. 2005. "Religion: source of conflict or source of peace?" In *Bridge or Barrier: Religion, Violence, and Visions for Peace*, ed. G. ter Haar and J. J. Busuttil, 3–34. Leiden and Boston, MA: Brill.

Ter Haar, G. and Ellis, S. 2006. "The role of religion in development: Towards a new relationship between the European Union and Africa." *The European Journal of Development Research* 18: 351–367.

Verheul, I., Van Stel, A. and Thurik, R. 2006. "Explaining female and male entrepreneurship at the country level." *Entrepreneurship and Regional Development* 18: 151–183.

Weber, M. 1930. *The protestant ethic and the spirit of capitalism.* New York: Scribner.

Wingren, G. 2004. *Luther on Vocation.* Eugene, OR: Wipf and Stock Publishers.

Wrzesniewski, A., McCauley, C., Rozin, P. and Schwartz, B. 1997. "Jobs, careers, and callings: People's relations to their work." *Journal of Research in Personality* 31: 21–33.

CHAPTER FIVE

Our Mission: Development

Comparative Perspectives on Development—David Livingstone and Finland's Development Policy Programme 2012

Mika Vähäkangas

Introduction

Western Christian mission has often been a target of harsh criticism concerning its political connections to the colonial project on one hand and its lack of interest in the political sphere on the other. Western mission has thus either been imperialistic or represented as a "pie-in-the-sky-when-you-die"[1] approach. Some of the criticism has been very one sided, maintaining that the Western Christian mission would be intrinsically one or the other. However, the reality of Western mission was extremely varied, with countless denominational, national, social, educational, linguistic, political and economic backgrounds enmeshing with different types of colonialisms that varied not only from one empire to another, but also within them depending on the time and the place.

Nordic governmental development cooperation sometimes acknowledges its historical dependence on the Nordic Christian missionary efforts in all corners of the world, but more often represents an approach labelled by radical lack of historical consciousness. When the missionary historical roots are taken up, one tends to strongly emphasize the socially active dimensions of Christian mission. In other contexts, one attempts to create a clear separation between the conversion-minded Christian imperialism and the benevolent and objectively founded governmental development cooperation. What is typical of Nordic governmental development institutions is an implicit denial of the colonial past. Development cooperation is considered post-colonial in the sense that it was launched after the colonial times and supposedly has neither historical nor ideological connections to the colonial project. This move is relatively easy in the Nordic contexts, where there is a widespread air of innocence vis-à-vis colonialism. The former and present colonial and imperial aspirations tend to be a blind spot of the neat Nordic states.[2]

In part, the more historically oriented part of the Christian missionary movement and studies revolving around it has almost become involved in self-flagellation or sharp criticism towards missions whereas the development section tends to criticize the colonial structures from a position of innocence.[3] Has the West finally learned how to distance itself from the colonial inheritance and start from a *tabula rasa*? Is there a radical discontinuity between the colonial Christian missionary development action and the post-colonial governmental development thought? This paper intends to compare very different types of documents in terms of development thought: David Livingstone's *African Journal* (AJ) and Finland's Development Policy Programme 2012 (FDP).

Livingstone's journals are an individual's diaries of a discovery journey through the continent and back. Although they provide an individual's views, Livingstone can be counted as one of the most influential persons in both the British colonial and Christian missionary projects. His views were widely distributed and read during his lifetime as well as throughout the colonial time and beyond. He can thus be counted as one of the central ideologists of both colonialism and mission, even though he was no deep philosopher, political scientist or theologian. *African Journal* was been selected for scrutiny because it was only posthumously published, without much editing, and thus represents Livingstone's private thoughts. Some of the more circulated versions of the journals or his other writings have been edited for a large readership and therefore could be seen to represent less original views having been modified to the publishers' demands. The differences, however, are very marginal.

FDP is taken as an example of a Nordic approach to development cooperation. It is very fresh as it was adopted by the government of Finland on 16 February 2012. Nordic countries often see themselves as a kind of avant-garde of development political though; therefore, one might expect this document to represent a view as post-colonial as would be available in the state sector.

General description of the positions

Livingstone can generally be seen as a representative of an idealistic or benevolent colonialism. He was a person who felt the white man's burden on his shoulders, and he was ready to sacrifice his life for carrying that burden (Livingstone 1963: 373). For Livingstone, Christian faith was the motivating factor behind his actions. Whether working as an ordinary missionary at the Kuruman missionary station in today's South Africa or as a discovery traveller, he did it as a Christian. For him, the Gospel, Western civilization, the British colonial empire and global commerce were all dimensions of God's good plan to uplift the world's suffering masses:

> The great thing in working for such people is to remember that we are forwarding that great movement which God is carrying on for the renovation of the world. We are parts of [the] machinery he employs, but not exclusive parts, for all who are engaged in ameliorating the condition of our race are fellow-workers, co-operators with God—sanitary reformers & clergy of all sorts, the soldiers at Sebastapol and sailors at the coast of Africa, inventors of telegraphs and steam engines, promoters of emigration and of prison reform. We shall not see the fruition of our hopes in any department, but we can work with the assurance that "the good time is coming yet". (Livingstone 1963: 243–244)

For Livingstone, Christian faith was a very practical and tangible reality that had to produce change in the living conditions of the people. In fact, Livingstone deeply despised other-worldly Christianity and considered it a result of a kind of parasitism as only parasites can afford not to be interested in the worldly:

> The Dutch ministers in the [Cape] Colony are mostly Scotchmen, and like such purchase of farms whereon to build a church. A good site is chosen, and then every effort made to obtain villagers. All the better parts are let to them, and as the village rises in importance the rents return a handsome revenue to the church. After thus making things snug, with from £200 to £400 per annum from the Government, they are in a position to preach total abstinence from politics, when the prevailing form is unsavoury, & pure spirituality as becoming in all the clergy. This is what deserves the name of worldly wisdom. Give me a £600 year, I think but little else but spirituality would be needed. For such, however, as are content to follow the mode pointed out by the saviour of the world, both spiritual and temporal must share their anxieties, and they never can come to the conclusion that the children of God ought to leave the affairs of the state entirely to the children of the devil. (Livingstone 1963: 444–445)

Livingstone was the colonial missionary par excellence. For him, however, the raison d'être of the colonial project was the common humanity and its betterment. Exploitation of the colonized populations was not acceptable, nor was it real colonialism. Livingstone's view of colonialism was very idealistic. The Livingstonian model included the transformation of the colonial state structures even in Britain. Such optimism was, beyond doubt, partly fed by the previous success of the "Clapham sect" in first banning British slave trade and then turning the British navy into a global anti-slavery fist (Tomkins 2010). The revivalist, politically active Christianity had thus already showed its teeth.

FDP is very immanent in its approach, as one may expect. It is, as the title proposes, a very practice-oriented paper. The document lacks any historical references, and the approach is very matter-of-fact in the sense of presenting one problem after another and how the Finnish government is supposed to tackle it. The document's view of society and human being seems to be quite mechanistic. The past does not play a greater role in how the present should be approached, and the intellectual and cultural dimensions of changes are also downplayed except when describing the importance of education. Education, in itself, is viewed very instrumentally and seemingly as a trading of objective truths. Development is not problematized, but rather seen as a given direction of change that the Western countries are obviously called to further. Human rights and ecological sustainability are the kingpins of the value system of the document.

Being practice oriented and proposing change, Livingstone and the Finnish government deal with views that can easily be compared. What has changed in the view of development in more than 150 years?

Comparing Livingstone and the Finnish government

In this section, I highlight a number of dimensions in the development views of the counterparts in comparison and evaluate them by juxtaposing them and viewing their similarities and differences *mutatis mutandis*. The historical context and the differing nature of the documents compared cause the comparison to be, in part, imprecise.

"The White Man's Burden" [4]

For most of his texts, it is implicitly clear that Livingstone is supposed to help the poor Africans as a white man and a Christian: "O Almighty God, help. Help & leave not this wretched people to the slave dealer and Satan . . . No land needs the gospel more than this miserable portion" (Livingstone 1963: 114). He describes, among others, how he returned war captives to their homes and tried to convince the local chiefs not to continue fighting among themselves (pp. 23–24), distributed plant seeds and seedlings (pp. 265; 266–267), helped with problematic wild animals (pp. 269–270), distributed Bibles (p. 300), fed undernourished local slaves (pp. 318–319) and benefitted the natives through his commerce with them (p. 256). This view of the whites' and the Christians'—or rather, white Christians'—responsibilities is so hegemonic that, for the most part, there is no need to mention it (Comaroff and Comaroff 1991: 18–30). The whole argumentation and planning are further permeated by this conviction.

However, this view of the white man's burden does not imply that the whites would always be the best in everything because every nation has its strengths:

> The population of the province of Angola called coloured are described as steeped in the grossest superstition, and yet with a general opinion they are wiser than their white neighbours. I think this good opinion of ourselves is very general in the world. Each tribe has a considerable consciousness of goodness, or following its own best interests in the best ways. (Livingstone 1963: 225)

For example, for Livingstone, Europeans appear to be overly greedy, and he emphatically states that he would rather trust an African than a European (p. 304). In spite of the fact that Livingstone at times believes that the blacks will permanently remain under the white domination (p. 243), much of his attention was geared to the uneven chances that people of various backgrounds have:

> a very good and attentive audience [to Livingstone's missionary preaching that he practiced in most villages]. Surely all will not be forgotten. How small their opportunity compared to ours, who have been carefully instructed in the knowledge of divine truth from our earliest infancy. The Judge is just and merciful. He will deal fairly and kindly with all. (Livingstone 1963: 288–289)

Therefore, it seems that, for him, given that the Africans would be have the same chances as, for example, the Britons, they would reach much higher in their capacities and strivings. Rather than a matter of race, Livingstone seems to consider Christian faith and civilization as the keys to improved humanity: "The natural man resembles the brute creation in abuse of those overtaken by misfortune" (Livingstone 1963: 289). This natural brute man is not at least purely defined by his racial characteristics because Livingstone also describes his own ancestors at times as "our rude forefathers" (p. 32).

Livingstone's view of colonialism is a kind of a Dr. Jekyll and Mr. Hyde perception. On one hand, he eagerly describes his ideals of Christian-motivated colonialism (e.g., Livingstone 1963: 243–244; 263; 265–266; 351; 373) while very strongly criticizing both Portuguese and British/Boer colonialism (pp. 207–208; 300–303). During those times when he defends Portuguese colonialism, the point is not that the Portuguese would be so good, but rather that the British—who so strongly criticize the Portuguese—are not any or at least much better.

> God grant that ere the ruthless [Cape?] Colonists advance so far the saving gospel be received as a solace for the soul in death. If they must perish, as certain races of animals, before others, by the decree of Heaven, we would seem to be under the (same) "terrible necessity" in our Caffre wars. . . . (Livingstone 1963: 324)

In his thoroughly religious worldview, mission sometimes serves as the umbrella term for all European activities to spread Christianity, commerce and civilization. This activity is God's in spite of the obvious shortcomings of the Europeans involved:

> No matter how great the outcry against the instrumentality which God employs for his purposes, whether French soldiery as in Tahiti or tawny Boers as in South Africa, our duty is onward, proclaiming God's word. . . . A few conversions shew whether God's spirit is in a mission or not. No mission which has his approbation is entirely unsuccessful. . . . All seek their own, not the things of Jesus Christ; and he knew that after his departure grievous wolves would spring up, not sparing the flock. Yet the cause of God is still carried on and on to more enlightened developments of his will and character, and the dominion is being given by the power of commerce and population unto the people of the saints of the most high. . . . May God accept our humble imperfect service. (Livingstone 1963: 58–59)

This picture mixes with his perception of the world where Christian views of the transcendental God compete with and partly complete evolutionist views. Evolution, however, is a process that God steers, according to Livingstone's theistic worldview. His activities show that the Christian is not supposed to be fatalistic, but rather an active political, economic and religious actor for the sake of the good to prevail. In Livingstone's world, the colonial actors—even if initiating many of the processes—would not be the sole agents, but he would rather see private entrepreneurs and local populations getting involved in civilizing or ameliorating the peoples' living conditions, or development in today's terminology (e.g., Livingstone 1963: 265–266).

Although Livingstone devoted most of his time and energy in palavers with the local chiefs, he does not consider them as any notable partners in development. Nowhere are they seen in his future plans. Here, he actually made a miscalculation as, for example, the Britons were able to strengthen these political entities through indirect rule, thereby making them a considerable power base for a century to come.

For Livingstone, there are three major avenues for development as mission: setting up an infrastructure for commercial purposes, preaching or teaching and setting a good example. Transportation infrastructure in particular facilitates the advancement of this Christianizing and civilizing mission:

> The sea after all is the great civilizer of nations. If Africa, instead of simple littoral outline, had been broken up by deep indentations of glorious old ocean, how different would have been the fate of its inhabitants. The waterfalls of Mosioatunyta, Kabompo, & others, explain why commercial enterprise never entered the interior of the continent except by foot travelers. (Livingstone 1963: 287)

Therefore, it is no surprise that he sketched how transport to the interior could be made more effective by building roads (Livingstone 1963: 117–119).

However, even the construction of proper infrastructure does not help if the local population is not ready to work for its own betterment. Therefore, civilizing the locals is the key to success in the endeavours to make their lives better. This readiness is reached through education and evangelism, whereby the pagan superstitions are overcome through good example:

> Instead of trying to carry civilization to the Interior, and thereby opening up Africa to the sympathies and succour of Christians . . . I am attempting to establish the system of the Africans proceeding on commercial speculations to the coast. There they learn in a short time to appreciate the power of Europeans, and the influence naturally flows: it those who have so much power and wisdom believe and value the truths of religion, how much more we. (Livingstone 1963: 265–266)

When a human being sees a more effective, more beneficial and humane way of organizing the society, he will take heed of it. Thus, a better society will follow almost automatically.

More than five generations later and after the end of the classical colonialism, the document produced by the Finnish government, which seems to consider itself clean of colonial guilt, should be very different. The context of development has changed drastically since Livingstone's times, the African countries' independence being one of the most notable changes. While FDP consistently emphasizes the need to cooperate with local governments and safeguard their independence from aid dependency (e.g., Ministry of Foreign Affairs of Finland 2012: 6; 12; 16), the primary actor seems to be the Finnish government. This is hardly surprising considering the nature of the document, which is supposed to steer the developmental activities of the Finnish government. However, what is striking is the almost complete lack of the idea of reciprocity and sharing. Although the list of the Finnish contributions to the world is endless, the document is happy to devote one general statement concerning mutual sharing: "Finland's development cooperation is implemented in a spirit of reciprocity and mutual learning that benefits development both in the South and in the North."[5] From the Finnish governmental perspective, the poor countries seem to have hardly anything to share with the affluent ones. In that sense, the white man's burden still weighs on Western shoulders.

The Finnish approach to development input are reminiscent of social engineering in that it sets up efficient state structures (Ministry of Foreign Affairs of Finland 2012: 14; 16; 28–29). Education plays an important role here (e.g., Ministry of Foreign Affairs of Finland 2012: 13). Compared to Livingstone, the Finnish approach seems more technocratic and sociological depending on the organizations whereas Livingstone is more individualistic and psychological—in a very religious sense.

Although the local ownership of development and local development planning are emphasized (Ministry of Foreign Affairs of Finland 2012: 12), one may wonder how well these principles augur for the quite strict Finnish expectations in terms of values and governance (Ministry of Foreign Affairs of Finland 2012: 14; 16). The governments that do not share the values and approaches of the Finnish government cannot expect to receive funds from Finland. One may wonder how independently some governments adopt these values and to which extent they retain jargon used for safeguarding the development funds. This problem is not discussed in the document.

Both Livingstone and the Finnish government view the white (wo)man as the primary activist in development. The Finnish government places much emphasis on the local state structures whereas Livingstone counts more on the local individuals. This major difference is due to the context, one may expect. The local ethnic political units were on the brink of collapse under the pressures from slave trade and colonialism during Livingstone's time, whereas today one still entertains high hopes of centralized strong African governments, although the fragility of a good number of countries has to be accepted as fact (Ministry of Foreign Affairs of Finland 2012: 30).

Both sides in the comparison also consider their positions to be so convincing that the expansion of the values of good governance and civil society spread almost automatically. Livingstone believes in the power of example whereas the Finnish government trusts in the democratic structures. Livingstone sees the profitability of slave trade as a serious threat to the advancement of the renewal of the societies (Livingstone 1963: 136), whereas the Finnish government seems to consider democracy to be the magic formula that will lead to better societies. The Arab Spring reminded us that a seemingly calm stability does not mean that citizens' rights will be safeguarded. What is left completely without consideration is the possibility that the majority of the population would actually opt for a "strong" leader and vote for a basically undemocratic person or ideology. Some of the worst dictators have been elected to power, and the Arab Spring does not necessarily mean the democratization of the countries involved—at least in the European sense (Ministry of Foreign Affairs of Finland 2012: 29).

Good governance and civil society

Both Livingstone and the Finnish government are eager proponents of good governance and civil society. Livingstone returns over and again to the adverse effects of corruption and unpredictable and evil rulers or civil servants (e.g., Livingstone 1963: 24; 104–105; 172; Ministry of Foreign Affairs of Finland 2012: 29–30; 33).

> The sway of the chief is absolute, and no voice dare be raised against any act, however outrageous or mad it may be. If another person gets possession of certain kinds of beads which may happen to be those which his fancy has dictated for his wives, he is in danger of being suddenly executed. On my asking if Matiamvo did not know he was a man & mortal as well as those he destroyed, and would be judged by God, who is no respecter of persons, he replied, "We do not go up to God, we are put into the ground." (Livingstone 1963: 81–82)

The Finnish government concentrates more on the positive side—namely, the goals concerning good governance—which is predictable, transparent, responsible and democratic (e.g., Ministry of Foreign Affairs of Finland 2012: 14). Nothing suggests that, *mutatis mutandis*, Livingstone would have had anything against such. He does not discuss democracy, but his ubiquitous argumentation against slavery can be interpreted as a struggle for more democratic societies (e.g., Livingstone 1963: 11–12; 56; 60; 72; 97.) In places like Tete in the Portuguese Mozambique, where 92% of the population were slaves according to Livingstone (1963: 439–440), slavery was the single important issue for democracy. Concentrating on anything else in relation to democracy would actually have been ridiculous.

Although the phrase *civil society* was lacking from the contemporary vocabulary, it is surprising how obvious Livingstone's thoughts hint towards that idea. One of the major adverse effects of slavery, according to Livingstone, was that society could not count on its members, thereby rendering the society weak. Freedom and equal opportunities would give rise to real citizenship, creating possibilities for development (Livingstone 1963: 119–120; 187–188; 428–429; 439–440).

The Finnish government approach reads much like an update of Livingstone's ideas. The emphasis is, in line with the difference in general approach, more on the side of organizational structures than on the individuals and changes in their patterns of thought (Ministry of Foreign Affairs of Finland 2012: 28–30). Ensuring every citizen's ability to participate in decision making is seen as the key to good governance and a properly just state (Ministry of Foreign Affairs of Finland 2012: 29). The right to participate could be described as today's struggle against slavery. In both cases, it is a matter of increasing individual freedom in the sense of both gaining control of one's life and being free from exploitation.

Livingstone and FDP serve as two examples of expressing the Enlightenment and Great Revolution ideals of freedom and equality, both tackling the burning issues of their time. The underlying set of values here would be human rights.

Human rights-based approach

The phrase *human rights* was not part of Livingstone's vocabulary even though the ideas of universal rights and human value had been in the making long before his time. They actually got their grand formulation and international acceptance (in principle, at least) in the United Nations Declaration of Human Rights of 1948.

Livingstone's journals are filled with compassionate descriptions of the fate of the unfortunate people suffering under all kinds of oppression and exploitation as well as his attempts to remedy the situation when he considered it possible. Naturally, most of his argumentation was directed against the main evil: slavery. At times, he highlighted the most abhorrent forms of exploitation, like the wilful starvation to death of slaves owned by Africans themselves (Livingstone 1963: 318–319; 299), human sacrifices or other killings due to local beliefs (pp. 81–82; 215–216), capital punishment for an escaped slave (p. 402) and oppression against women (p. 320). For him it appears to be self-evident that he as a Christian should fight against such evils. As such, one can maintain that Livingstone's program was human-rights oriented, but Christian values based. Naturally, one must remember that his interpretation of Christianity and its basic values was only one among many.

The Finnish government has committed itself strongly to human rights. In the argumentation, they can be seen as one of the focal points, almost as the Archimedean point where the rest of the argumentation is anchored, which is not properly reflected in the English translation from the Finnish original: "Finland pursues human rights-based approach to development."[6] The Finnish document is more outspoken than Livingstone concerning the attributes and contents of human rights as universal, the individual right to choose of way of life, equality and non-discrimination, among others. The specifically vulnerable groups are listed as women, children, ethnic/linguistic/religious minorities, aboriginal populations, disabled, people living with HIV/AIDS and sexual minorities (Ministry of Foreign Affairs of Finland 2012: 11–12).

Human rights are taken in FDP as given facts or starting points; using them as a point of departure is not argued for at all. Likewise, Livingstone's use of Christianity as the basis for his thoughts and actions goes without comparison or argument. It seems that, for the Finnish government, human rights play the role of the ideologically normative basis. In that sense, human rights seem to assume the role of a secular religion. They have become so commonly accepted in Western European societies that they no longer require any transcendental justification, as in the case of Livingstone. Livingstone made use of Christianity, the seldom questioned basis, in his argumentation for the rights of his fellow humans whereas no metaphysical arguments can claim a wider plausibility in today's European plausibility structures (Berger and Luckmann 1991: 110–121).

Attaching oneself to the global capitalism

Global capitalism is the way to happiness and prosperity for both Livingstone and today's Finnish government. While Livingstone gets lyrical about global free market, "[h]ow wonderful is commerce" (1963: 32), the Finnish government is more down to earth and indirect, yet still giving it full credit while defining more closely what kind of a global free market economy is desirable:

> Prosperity and well-being are generated by people's knowledge and skills as well as by work. Economic growth has lifted countries from poverty, but at the same time many have been left disadvantaged. Natural resources have been consumed unsustainably. Therefore economic growth alone is not enough. Economic growth should generate equal human development within the bounds of nature's carrying capacity. . . . The political will and policy performance of a government is of essential importance in creating and strengthening environment that is conducive to investment, entrepreneurship and responsible corporate activity. In its partner countries, Finland supports good governance that also promotes economic activity, equal distribution of economic benefits as well as the building of social capital. (Ministry of Foreign Affairs of Finland 2012: 32–33; see also pp. 5; 18–19)

Livingstone lived before communism while the Finnish government emerged after it. Liberal capitalist economy and ever-expanding and accelerating globalization are positive and mighty powers in the world to both, so it seems. Fair business enhances peace and prosperity and turns idle land and people into useful participants in the world order according to both of the compared development visions.

Livingstone's *African Journal* is actually a warehouse of facts, observations and ideas about how to engage that part of Africa between Angolan and Mozambican coasts in the global capitalistic order. His journals are filled with considerations on possible trade routes, agricultural potential of different areas and considerations for using different plants for commercial use. Nature appears to him to be a vast basket of resources awaiting exploitation: "The variety of wild fruits is astonishing. If these trees which now supply a pleasant refreshment to many had been subjected to culture for centuries, as our crab, sloe, &c, have been, what fine fruits they would have yielded. All the African thinks of is present gratification . . ." (1963: 21).

Livingstone observes everything—peoples, lands and nature—from the point of view of development in the sense of Christianity, civilization and commerce. The relationship among these three entities is such that, even though they can be considered separate, for Livingstone, the effective way forward for Africa seems to be to combine these three (1963: 243–244). On one hand, Christian civilization is the spiritual, moral and intellectual breeding ground for development. Unless people are civilized, the development efforts will turn into nothing, Livingstone seems to imply. On the other hand, commerce and the economic, infrastructural and other material developments facilitate the provision of intellectual and spiritual development. Poverty and diseases contribute to the intellectual and spiritual misery. In that sense, it seems that, for Livingstone, development could be seen as a positive spiral of ascending levels of material and immaterial improvements which support and even require each other.

The tone of FDP is surprisingly similar to that of Livingstone. FDP also considers commerce as the major way out of poverty and the best route to development. The document permeates the neoliberal spirit. This is evident not least in the way in which development is defined: "Development means sustainable and positive change as well as increased opportunities in people's lives."[7] That the focal point is freedom of choice (the original Finnish version "possibilities of choice" having been translated as "opportunities" in English) and not security connects this view of development to the liberal tradition. What is interesting is that "positive," despite its centrality in the definition, is not defined in any way; as such, it seems that it is supposed that there would be a universal conception about positive change.

Commerce is viewed in positive terms, and the harsh neoliberal capitalism is domesticated through democracy, human rights and ecological responsibility. However, nowhere is it discussed whether and how the capitalist logic and ideals of limitless growth and the conception of humanity as *homo oeconomicus* are actually in tension with democracy, human rights and the preservation of nature. How is one to resolve the tension between the commercial interest of the great foreign capital and the local poor populations? What should be done when the demand to improve people's living conditions and the ecological values of a certain area collide? It seems that FDP considers human rights, democracy and ecological awareness as such strong values that they will survive and, with a little governmental guidance, will even domesticate the beast of global capitalism.

In FDP, the way to bring about connection to the global markets and, thereby, economic growth and development seems to be that of setting up the proper governmental structures and good governance—free market economy will take care of the rest. Whereas Livingstone considered development to be a process that needs nurturing, FDP seems to start from the premise that the actions of *homo oeconomicus* are natural and thus follow almost automatically the creation of conducive environment through a kind of social and political engineering. But if humans are predominantly economical animals, what makes democracy, human rights and ecological awareness survive? Is it so uncontroversial that, by abiding to democratic rules, respecting human rights and preserving the nature, I or my company will make the greatest benefits? Colonial history, among others, would tell a different story. Here, Livingstone would possibly come to the help of the neoliberal. Livingstone argues against slavery by pointing out not only how unethical it is, but also how ineffective it is. The Portuguese, despite being involved in slavery, can in no way compete with the British products in the global market (Livingstone 1963: 147–149). One may wonder, though, how great a deal it was whether the nineteenth-century *Lumpenproletariat* in the British factories actually was much better off than some of the slaves on the plantations.

Whereas Livingstone emphasizes Christianization and education as tools of ideological, intellectual and moral change as the equal or perhaps even superior counterpart of economic growth, FDP relies much more on the economic side. Education is mentioned only in passing. Culture, traditions and religions are completely bypassed as factors contributing to development. One may wonder whether this is a matter of overly guarding political correctness in the post-Breivikian world or whether the FDP drafters really are as materialistic as they appear.

What is new under the sun?

Livingstone and the Finnish government's FDP document both pay plenty of attention to the material dimension of development. For Livingstone, this attention is completed with a similarly great emphasis on the spiritual and intellectual development as the counterpart of material. In this sense, Livingstone can be considered a representative of a holistic anthropology or an integral view of development. In this sense, FDP appears to differ, paying attention almost exclusively to the material dimension of development.

Development as a process is in both cases linked to integration to the global capitalist economy that will bring about well-being. How to bring this about are both similar and different in the views of Livingstone and the FDP. Both consider a conducive environment to play a crucial role. Livingstone sees it more as an intellectual and spiritual matter even if, for example, the transportation infrastructure plays a crucial role for his argumentation. FDP asserts that good governance and governmental mechanisms as well as other administrational and organizational improvements will play a crucial role in the creation of a conducive environment for development. Livingstone is much more individualistic and often turns his view on the individual rather than the organizations, even if he does not deny the role of the governments. For him, the power of example is the one that transforms the individual.

From today's perspective, Livingstone's zeal to convert the heathen and civilize the African might appear repulsive. Yet one can interpret that for Livingstone it was a matter of a humanization process whereby the Africans turned more into the image and likeness of what they were created for. That the Finnish government does not convert anyone but sets off from an acultural point of view where the differences in worldview are overlooked and launches its project of development from a supposedly objective scientific foundation is not much different, though. Western scientific worldview is a cultural product, too. The Western perceptions of human being are culturally defined, as well. To start from such premises does not make one objective because imagining having found the intellectual Archimedean point does not mean you really have found it. Just as Livingstone does not argue his Christian point of departure, considering it to be superior beyond doubt, the Finnish government does not question its cultural-philosophical premises, so hegemonic they are. Yet the result of projecting the Western worldview on the development thought is a matter of implicit proselytization into that worldview. The greatest difference between Livingstone and FDP, in addition to the difference in the worldviews they represent, is that Livingstone understands himself as a missionary whereas the modern development thought's missionary character often goes unnoticed by the stakeholders.

The white (wo)man is the *primus motor* for both Livingstone and FDP. The contemporary Finnish document emphasizes the need to cooperate with the local governments and other actors. Livingstone, in turn, probably saw how the local chiefdoms were on the brink of collapse in the pressures of colonialism, internal strife and slave trade. Therefore, he did not envision them to play a major role in the future. For both, however, the flow of skill and wisdom is one way: from the European to the African or the underdeveloped. A continuum of the colonial pattern is clearly visible, albeit turned into a more politically correct form through the emphasis on cooperation with the local governments.

Finally, the fundamental values behind the development views of Livingstone and FDP are Christianity for the former probably human rights from the latter's perspective. Democracy returns to human rights, and in some views ecological consciousness could be seen as an extension of human rights. A free market economy can also be anchored in the concept of freedom of choice, the core value in development for FDP. Freedom of choice is, in turn, one of the most basic human rights for the liberal mind.

Livingstone's thoughts and actions are anchored in tradition and transcendence, and he can refer to their unquestioned authority. FDP possibly anchors itself in human rights, which in turn are not anchored in transcendence; being of universal value, they cannot be anchored in any specific tradition either. Thus, the authority of the human rights lies in themselves, in their incontestable truthfulness or rightfulness. However, the credibility of anything is bound to the plausibility structures that are culturally conditioned. It is clear that not every culture and tradition respects human rights alike. We Europeans consider our concept of human rights as universal, thereby lifting our views as universally normative, to which the aid-receiving countries have to adhere if they are to receive support. In the final picture, the human rights as ultimate values have to gain their credentials from our cultural, political and social self-certainties and from society itself. Following Durkheim, one might claim that Livingstone based his convictions and values on religion and, thus, on society (Durkheim 1960: 3–6; 293–299). Livingstone's god and Christianity are a reflection of the values and power structures of his society, legitimizing his colonial penetration in the interior and the conversion and economical-political reordering of the people and societies in Africa. Today's Western European state structures seem to have reached such a hegemonic position and status that gods and religions are no longer needed as basic values can be anchored directly in society.

Livingstone's—and many other missionaries', merchants' and colonialists'—projects led to a world that is a tight web of commercial relations. Livingstone's and the missionaries' projects also led to the expansion of Christianity that made it a truly global religion (see, e.g., Johnson and Ross 2009). This globality also resulted in an unprecedented diversification, meaning that it is better to speak of Christianities. As a result, Livingstone's and others' attempts to convert were successful and unsuccessful at the same time. The African did not convert into a European but converted Christianity into an African religion (Ter Haar 2009). At the same time, Africa remains the poorest continent. Is this due to a failure of Christianity and civilization, a fault of the global capitalist order or a result of the brittleness of the Western governmental structures in Africa that never really took root in the tropics?

Only time will tell what will be the results of the Finnish and other Western governments' secular mission. Will the West be able to convert the African this time or will the African convert the Western scientific worldview? Does the removal of the gods and religions and direct linkage to the societies make this project unable to communicate and translate into the local cultures? Is the possibility of subversion thereby removed, leaving only rejection and rebellion as alternatives to submission? At any rate, the inheritance of benevolent colonialism as the European duty is alive and well in Western aid discourse, judged on the basis of the new Finnish development policy document.

References

Berger, Peter and Luckmann, Thomas. 1991. *The Social Construction of Reality: A Treatise in the Sociology of Knowledge.* London: Penguin Books. [Originally published in 1966]

Comaroff, Jean and Comaroff, John. 1991. *Of Revelation and Revolution, vol 1: Christianity, Colonialism, and Consciousness in South Africa.* Chicago IL: University of Chicago Press.

Durkheim, Émile. 1960. *Les formes élémentaires de la vie religieuse: Le système totémique en Australie.* 4th edition. Paris: Presses universitaires de France.

Hill, Joe. 1923. "The Preacher and the Slave." In *IWW Songs to Fan the Flames of Discontent,* 22–23. 19th edition. USA: IWW, 1923. [Originally published in 1911]

Johnson, Todd M. and Ross, Kenneth R. (eds.). 2009. *Atlas of Global Christianity 1910–2010.* Edinburgh: Edinburgh University Press.

Kipling, Rudyard. 1903. *The Five Nations.* Leipzig: Bernhard Tauchnitz.

Livingstone, David. 1963. *Livingstone's African Journal 1853–1856 2 vols.* Ed. I. Schapera. London: Chatto & Windus.

Ministry of Foreign Affairs of Finland. 2012. "Finland's Development Policy Programme (FDP)." Available from http://www.formin.fi/public/default.aspx?contentid=69859&nodeid=15319&contentlan=2&culture=en-US. Internet; accessed 7 November 2012.

Stockwell, Eugene L. 1990. "Mission Issues for Today and Tomorrow." In *The San Antonio Report, Your Will be Done: Mission in Christ's Way,* ed. Frederick R. Wilson, 114–128. Geneva: WCC Publications.

Ter Haar, Gerrie. 2009. *How God became African: African Spirituality and Western Secular Thought.* Philadelphia, PA: University of Pennsylvania Press.

Tomkins, Stephen. 2010. *The Clapham Sect: How Wilberforce's Circle Changed Britain.* London: Lion.

Ulkoasiainministeriö. 2012. "Suomen kehityspoliittinen toimenpideohjelma." Available from http://formin.finland.fi/public/default.aspx?contentid=47074&nodeid=15319&contentlan=1&culture=fi-FI. Internet; accessed 7 November 2012.

Notes

1 Hill 1923, chorus. The satirical reference to the transcendentally oriented Christianity is often heard in African theological discussions.

2 For Denmark, the colonial projects are obvious, ranging from India to Greenland. Sweden's long imperialistic history gradually faded as European colonialism peaked, making it easier for Sweden to dismiss its imperialistic past. Swedish colonialism was actually reduced to the same level as Finnish and Norwegian colonization of the northern areas and ethnic minorities. The plans of "Great Finland" until the end of World War II can also be viewed as colonizing towards the areas to be annexed in the east. The Nordic participation (e.g., through commerce, emigration, policies, individuals and mission societies) in the colonial enterprises of the greater empires is not insignificant either.

3 An example of such self-flagellation: Stockwell 1990: 115-116.

4 Kipling 1903: 99-101. Rudyard Kipling's poem "The White Man's Burden" (originally from 1899) popularized the expression referring to the Euro-American responsibility of civilizing the "half devil and half child" lower races of the colonies. It is a matter of interpretation whether this poem depicts Kipling's political views or is a satire.

5 FDP 20. The production of the document has probably not been very cooperative in direction to the southern partners as it was first produced only in Finnish and Swedish, after quite a bit of internal Finnish discussion. The English translation was available to the public only several months after the publication of the original versions in the national languages.

6 FDP, 7; cfr. original Suomen kehityspoliittinen toimenpideohjelma 7: "Suomen lähtökohtana on ihmisoikeusperustainen lähestymistapa kehitykseen."

7 FDP 13. SKT 13: "Kehitys merkitsee kestävää ja myönteistä muutosta sekä valinnanmahdollisuuksien lisääntymistä ihmisten elämässä."

CHAPTER SIX

Spiritual Gifts and Relations of Exchange among Congolese in Kampala, Uganda

Karen Lauterbach

Introduction

Rose B. is a Congolese woman and mother of three living in Kampala, Uganda. She and her children came to Uganda in 2009 as refugees. Here she was reunited with her husband. For the first one-and-a-half years in Kampala, they lived in a Congolese Pentecostal church. During a forty-day fasting and prayer meeting, Rose B. was touched by the Holy Spirit and had a spiritual gift revealed. Since then, she has used her gift of seeing visions about people and has received gifts and recognition in exchange.

In this chapter, I analyse spirituality (in the form of spiritual gifts) as a resource that can be part of relations of exchange. I discuss how spiritual gifts are perceived and used as an asset that can be exchanged for material objects (such as food or money) and other forms of support while simultaneously having symbolic value. Receiving a spiritual gift (e.g., healing and seeing visions) is both a way in which connection to the spiritual world is established and something that plays an important role in the everyday lives of people. Through an analysis of the manifestations and use of spiritual gifts, this chapter argues that spirituality is an asset that is largely drawn upon in relations of exchange and that takes on a specific meaning in a context of displacement. These relations of exchange form a spiritual economy that is drawn upon when refugees seek ways to make a living in a context of uncertainty, fluidity and lack of economic opportunities. However, as the analysis also shows, there are limitations as to how and in what ways spiritual gifts can be used. This indicates that these mechanisms of exchange are formed both by the material conditions that constitute the lives of refugees in Kampala and by religious and social norms (e.g., to what degree can one use spiritual gifts to make money?). Moreover, this chapter discusses how we can understand these relations of exchange as they are not rational relations of economic exchange, nor relations of reciprocity as in classical gift-giving theory. Spiritual economies involve relations of exchange between a giver and a receiver that can take the form of both a person and God—or both at the same time.[1]

In the academic literature on Pentecostalism and charismatic forms of Christianity, the ideology of prosperity gospel has received much attention, particularly as an explaining factor of the rise of this branch of Christianity in Africa over the last three decades (Gifford 2004; Lindhardt 2009; Maxwell 2012; Meyer 2004). In reviewing this literature, Coleman (2011) notes that the religious messages and practices on prosperity have been analysed as a reaction or response to economic needs. Religion has become instrumentalized in the sense that religious practices are understood as a way to obtain material gains. However, Coleman further points out that this literature importantly draws attention to the link between material conditions and religion (Coleman 2011: 29). Coleman also identifies a different direction within the scholarship that is less concerned with explaining the prosperity gospel as a response, but rather "with 'how' practices relating to Prosperity interact with wider aspects of believers' lives and self-understandings" (Coleman 2011: 36).

The aim of this chapter is to analyse how spiritual gifts can be seen as resources and, through this perspective, how religion is part of people's everyday lives and activities. Focusing on the link between religion and economic/commodity exchange does not imply that I approach religion only as a means to obtain something, as a strategic choice or in a reductionist way. As Soares underscores in an article on the prayer economy in a Malian town, there are limitations to understanding "religious practices within the frame of an economy" (Soares 1996: 741). He emphasizes that such an analysis can only be a partial analysis of religious practices and experiences. The approach of this chapter is based on the empirical observation that the religious sphere is closely connected to people's material lives and is seen as part and parcel of mundane everyday life. It builds on Fields' understanding of religion and belief as "routine common sense, [and] [. . .] how the supernatural was embedded in mundane social relations" (1985: 21). In this sense I seek to unfold the everydayness of religion through an analysis of the economy of spiritual gifts, which implies seeing the exchange of spiritual gifts as more than the exchange of different forms of capital, but also as a form of exchange that involves engagement in social relationships (Coleman 2011: 36).

My concern is therefore in the following to reflect upon how to grasp the daily functioning and practices of a spiritual gift economy as well as how we can approach these relations of exchange at the conceptual level. On the one hand, the concept of capital (economic, social, and cultural) has been widely used to describe how social relations and networks are drawn upon to the benefit of groups or individuals. As pointed out by Hämmerli (2011: 197–198), this line of analysis tends to rest on a utilitarian approach given that people are expected to exchange a number of resources to maximize their benefit and hence pursue an economic logic. On the other hand, relations of exchange have been conceptualized in terms of gift-giving, which were seen as having the overall aim of creating social relations of reciprocity (Mauss 1954). This builds on the understanding that there is no such thing as a free gift and that all gift-giving (or exchange) is based on a total system of reciprocity (Douglas 1990). Later work, for instance by Godbout and Caillé (2000), has developed this thinking to include the idea of freedom of giving and disinterestedness, but also to re-emphasize that "the gift is not a thing but a social connection" (2000: 7).

In the case of an economy of spiritual gifts, the relationships are extended as the spiritual (the non-material) is included (e.g., in the sense of receiving from or giving to God). How can we think of relations of exchange when spirituality is part of the exchange and when return is not necessarily thought of as coming from another person but from God? And what are the particularities of these relations in a context of displacement, where social relations have—at times—a fluid character and where people's lives are characterized by experiences of loss, violence and hyper mobility (Simone 2011)?

Context

Since the overthrow of President Mobutu in 1996, the Democratic Republic of Congo (DRC) has witnessed conflicts and mass displacement of people. Many Congolese have come to Uganda and other neighbouring countries to seek refuge. More recently, post-election violence (December 2011) and the continuing conflict in the Kivus have resulted in a growing number of Congolese refugees. In its 2013 country operations profile for Uganda, the UNHCR estimated that approximately 190,000 registered refugees and asylum seekers are in Uganda, of which 120,000 are from the DRC. In addition, 48,000 of the 190,000 refugees are considered to live in urban areas mainly in Kampala (UNHCR, 2013). The latest influx of Congolese refugees started in April 2012, with the creation in Eastern Congo of the rebel movement M23.

The official policy of the government of Uganda[2] has until recently been that all refugees should reside in refugee settlements (Bernstein 2005: 7; Lammers 2006). These settlements are located in rural areas, mainly in the north-western and western parts of the country. Refugees are allocated plots of land for agricultural activities, and the long-term aim is that they should become self-reliant. However, it has been unofficially accepted that refugees can live outside settlements if they are self-sufficient and can document this (Bernstein 2005), although they would have no rights to receiving assistance (Russell 2011: 295). With the passing of the Uganda Refugees Act by parliament in 2006, the legal rights of refugees to move, live and work outside settlements were acknowledged. Still, the provision of assistance has largely been restricted to those living in settlements (World Refugee Survey 2009).

A growing number of refugees are settling in Kampala and other urban areas (Omata 2012). Most refugees with whom I spoke had come directly to Kampala without passing through a camp. People come to Kampala for the better livelihood opportunities and better access to health and educational services. In addition, the refugee settlements are located close to the border with the DRC, which poses a security risk. For example, refugees living in settlements have been recruited to rebel groups operating in Rwanda and the DRC (Bernstein 2005; Murison 2002). People travel to Kampala either by bus or by getting a lift with a lorry or other people they meet on their way. Upon arrival in Kampala, they ask for the Congolese community or a Congolese church; many are referred to the Congolese churches that are known for helping refugees. Most refugees rent small rooms in the slum areas of Kampala (e.g., Katwe, Kisenyi, and Nsambya) if they can afford it. Some live in the streets or sleep at the premises of Old Kampala Police Station, where refugees register (Lammers 2006). Many refugees also find shelter in churches or in pastors' homes.

Urban refugees do not have access to assistance (food, shelter) and have to be self-reliant, which in practical terms mean that they depend on social networks and help from churches and small urban refugee associations. Urban refugees do in principle have access to the same basic social services as Ugandan nationals (education and health services), but due to a number of barriers (language, discrimination, lack of economic resources to pay fees, etc.), this is most often not the case. Some assistance is provided by the UNHCR and a number of NGOs, like medicine, access to medical treatment and counselling, but it is unclear to the refugees themselves who is entitled to this assistance and in what circumstances.

The difficulties refugees have making a living reflect the difficult living conditions in general in Kampala. Goodfellow (2010) argued that Kampala is in a situation of profound institutional crises (caused by a conflict between the national government and the city council, which is held by the opposition party), as reflected in the government's inability to address the growing problems of unemployment, inadequate housing, and conflicts over land. This has resulted in demonstrations in 2009 and again in spring 2011 (the walk-to-work campaign). However, certain obstacles are specific to the situation of refugees. Language and the translation of documents like diplomas pose a barrier to finding a job in the formal sector. In Kampala, Luganda and English are spoken by most, whereas Congolese mainly speak Lingala, Swahili and/or French.

Refugee churches

An important part of the Congolese community consists of religious institutions—more precisely, churches. According to the former leader of the Congolese Christian community in Kampala, the city is home to somewhere between thirty and fifty Congolese churches, many of which are registered with the Congolese Christian community. The churches differ in size, doctrinal orientation, history, identity and the composition of their membership. However, most are of a Pentecostal or Evangelical orientation. The number of churches is increasing due to both the continuing incoming of Congolese refugees and the splitting up of already existing churches. Most, but not all, churches would identify themselves as refugee churches—an identification that was also explained as a barrier for having a stable and growing church because of the high degree of mobility among members and because people did not have any income and therefore could not contribute to the work of the church or the income of the pastors.

I conducted fieldwork in two churches that were different in terms of size, membership composition and activities aimed at refugees. The first church had been founded by a Congolese refugee, but was now headed by a Congolese pastor who had come to Kampala from Kisangani in the DRC specifically to lead the church. Between one hundred and two hundred people attended the Sunday services I observed. According to the leading pastor, about 40 per cent of these were "real" members (*membres effectives*). The membership consisted of a group of Congolese who had been in Kampala for five to ten years, including some who were well-established (had houses, jobs, cars, etc.). A large proportion of the church members were young people. The head branch of the church was located in the DRC. The second church had a church membership of about thirty to forty people. The church had been founded in Kampala by a Congolese who had since moved to Canada. The church was now headed by three Congolese pastors who had all come to Kampala as refugees (two women and a man). The church had been situated at three different premises during 2011, which had resulted in the loss of many of its members (according to the pastors). This church was known (among refugees and NGOs) for assisting refugees, and many asked specifically for the location of the church upon arrival in Kampala. The church membership seemed to be less well-established, changing a lot, and the church as well as its members had few economic resources.

Spiritual gifts

In Pentecostalism there is an emphasis on spiritual gifts. A spiritual gift can have different meanings; it can symbolize what people offer to God (through paying tithes or offerings) and what God gives in return, but it can also take the form of charismatic gifts, which is the capacity to do certain things that demand divine influence (e.g., healing, preaching, speaking in tongues) The latter is not restricted to religious leaders, but can also be manifested in laypeople. In this section, I focus on how charismatic gifts become part of a spiritual economy, which is different from the ways in which spiritual economies or relations of gift-giving have been seen in the literature, as the focus has merely been on the giving of gifts (often in the form of money) and the relationship between the giver and receiver/God, often mediated through a spiritual leader (Coleman 2004; Lindhardt 2009; Soares 1996). My focus is on how charismatic gifts (in the sense of having the gift of healing, prophesizing, seeing visions, etc.) can be exchanged and become part of a spiritual economy.

In the two churches I studied in Kampala, several church members had had spiritual gifts revealed. It was often seen as a way to rise in the church hierarchy, for instance by becoming an evangelist or a missionary. Several pastors explained how they observe church members and then discern their spiritual gifts. When a spiritual gift has been discovered, it is the task of the pastors to train and guide the person. This implies that a spiritual gift is often translated and confirmed by a church leader. Thus, receiving a spiritual gift also is a social process that involves the recognition of someone in a position of authority (Lauterbach 2010: 269). One pastor explained the process like this:

> We start by initiating him, we approach him. If he is approachable we approach him and we start to make him work. We could tell him to do this or that. Then he starts to practice what he has in him. You equip them and train them and they fly with their own wings.[3]

A spiritual gift can also be revealed to a person, such as during a prayer program; in such cases, the person is thought of as being directly influenced by the Holy Spirit. Receiving a spiritual gift could lead to an increased social standing in church as well as become part of relations of exchange, as will be discussed later in this chapter. Someone with a spiritual gift is seen as someone mediating the word and the power of God, whether it is a pastor or a church member.

An economy of spiritual gifts

When a pastor or a church member is practicing and performing a spiritual or charismatic gift to the benefit of another person (e.g., praying, healing, or seeing visions), the receiver will show appreciation or gratitude either in the form of giving things or money or simply by expressing gratitude verbally. When I asked pastors how they made a living, I often got the reply that they got their blessings if they had helped someone through spiritual means. This implied that gifts in return or gifts of gratitude constituted an important part of their livelihoods. For example, one pastor explained how he had healed different people and that one person had afterwards helped him and supported him financially so that he could pay for his children's school fees.[4] This return can be seen both as a way of returning something (reciprocity) and as an expression of gratitude. It is moreover a way to recognize the performance and act of a person and in this case to show recognition of a position as pastor.

Stated in more economic language, one could say that there is an exchange of spiritual services for other commodities. However, it is important to note the aspect of showing gratitude as the return gift is intended not only for the person having performed a spiritual gift, but also for God. Gifts of gratitude are not to be taken for granted. One pastor explained how he had promised in church to pay for the shoes and school books for a young boy so that he could go to school. When making the promise, the pastor did not know how to pay for it, as he did not have any money. The pastor, being himself a refugee, did not have a regular income, so I asked him how he had managed to find the money to buy the items for the boy. He explained that by coincidence he had met a former church member and his son at a bus station in central Kampala the day before. The pastor had prayed for the son earlier and the son's problem had been solved. The father therefore gave the pastor money as a sign of recognition and gratitude. This money then enabled the pastor to provide material help to the young boy in church. This is a form of chain of economic and spiritual exchange that is thought of in terms of providing help, giving something in return and showing gratitude. At the same time, when talking about spiritual gifts and signs of gratitude, the voluntary aspect was emphasized. One pastor said, "You cannot force someone, because it is God who gives."[5]

The classical anthropological ideas of gift-giving as reciprocal and non-free stand in contrast to (theological) ideas of the gift as a pure gift that only can be given without return and of gift-giving to the undeserved or unworthy who cannot give in return (Barclay 2012). The idea of the pure gift (as a non-reciprocal relationship, and perhaps rather as a form of displaced reciprocity as it is God who gives the returns) was referred to many times by the Congolese pastors with whom I spoke, as was the idea of giving to the undeserved.

The case of Rose B.

The following case is an example of a woman who received a spiritual gift and how this gift became part of the exchange relationship.[6] Rose B., whom I briefly mentioned in the beginning of this chapter, and her family were refugees from the DRC. During their first one-and-a-half years in Kampala, they lived in a Congolese church. Later they lived for a while with a church member, and then they moved to a small house with two rooms, as Rose B. had managed to put aside 140,000 Ugandan Shilling (approximately 55 USD) to pay for the first month's rent. In January 2013, they moved again to a one-room house a bit outside of Kampala. The rent was cheaper, and Rose B. found that the place was better for her children as it was quieter. Her husband was educated as an engineer. He did not work when I first met the family in 2012, but in 2013 he was carrying cement at a construction site, earning 5,000 Ugandan Shilling (approximately 1.90 USD) per day. The children did not attend school. The family was mainly living from the income Rose B. got from petty trading, small collections in church and gifts from other church members (food, clothes).

Rose B. got a spiritual gift that was revealed to her during a 40-day prayer and fasting meeting. This meeting was initiated by a female preacher (called a prophetess) from the US. The prophetess herself was present during the first part of the program; she then travelled on to Nairobi. She had come along with a book she had authored on revelation by fire. Every day a text from the book was read in church, and a special sermon and prayer related to that were delivered. Many church members were full of hope that this would change their situation in Kampala and help them find a job so they could send their children to school, get enough money to get medical treatment or be accepted for resettlement by the UNHCR.

Rose B. and a pastor from church explained to me how this revelation had helped her. At the end of the 40 days of prayer and fasting, the pastors had called upon the Holy Spirit to descend. Rose B. was touched by the spirit and fell to the ground in church. She had a vision where she saw herself dressed in special clothes, wearing sandals and getting onto a horse. When she confessed, the preacher (prophetess) confirmed that what she had seen in the vision was all written in her book. This was seen as approval of the vision as genuine, and her spiritual gift was thereby legitimized by the religious leaders. The fact that Rose B. had had her spiritual gift revealed in church was important because it was exposed publically and recognized by the pastors.

Rose B. explained how God had started to use her after that. The first experience was in her house. She and her husband started to hear dogs barking; the husband could only hear barking, but she could understand what the dogs were saying, which related to an incidence of a thief who had stolen their clothes. The thief returned after a few days, admitted what he had done and returned their belongings. Both Rose B. and her husband saw this as a gift from God. A while later she had a vision about a woman. The woman had been a housemaid in the past. She and the man of the house had fallen in love, and the wife of the man had left. The housemaid and the man lived together in the house but could not have children. One day Rose B. was walking in the street and passed this woman. She turned around called the woman and started talking to her although they had never met before. Rose B. was able to reveal things from her past. The woman was surprised and affected and said that everything in the dream was true. It was seen as if God had spoken to her through Rose B. The woman offered Rose B. sugar and bread as a sign of appreciation. In the same way, Rose B. had received other gifts, such as soap and food for her children. One person who was moving abroad had given Rose her furniture, TV and refrigerator.

A third incident happened (all within a few weeks) in which Rose B. witnessed someone stealing a cell phone in a restaurant. She prayed that the phone would be given back; the next day, the phone was returned. The rumour spread that she had the ability to get stolen things back, and she was contacted by people who had lost their phones and memory cards and wanted her to use her spiritual gift to get the things back. She was also offered money to render this service. However, at this point, Rose B. refused. She explained that she was aware enough not to "misuse" the gift she had received from God and that it was not God's purpose that she should get paid or use it deliberately to make money. Thus, there is a distinction between getting paid for offering a service and receiving gifts (material and money) as a sign of gratitude.

A year later I met Rose B. and the pastors from her church again. Rose B. had moved to a new house and no longer attended church on a regular basis. She explained that she did not pray a lot at this time and, therefore, her spiritual gift did not manifest itself. She would receive visions about other people only when she was in deep prayer. She was occupied with moving to a new house and finding the daily bread. However, she also said "This is a grace that God has given me and God does not take away his gifts."

The revelation of having a spiritual talent had given Rose B. a special position in church and had drawn the pastors' attention to her for other reasons than the problems she was suffering (and for which she would receive counselling and spiritual guidance). With this gift from God and the knowledge that God had a purpose with her and was using her, she created some hope in life. She found herself in a position where she had something to offer that had value to other people. At the same time there were limitations to the ways in which the spiritual gifts could be used, guided by social norms related to not exploiting a spiritual gift. There were also limitations related to the material conditions in which the person was living. Using a spiritual gift demanded time devoted to praying; therefore, the role of a spiritual gift could change according to a person's general life conditions.

Complementary to this, many church members would reward a pastor on an individual basis as an acknowledgement for a particular service and also as recognition of the spiritual strength of the pastor. Yet gifts were also sometimes given in a more unilateral sense (or were explained in this way). One pastor for instance talked about how a lady he knew felt pity (in the sense of feeling sorrow for someone) for him and therefore helped him ("*elle a eu pitié de moi*"). This was a common way of explaining why unknown people would provide assistance (e.g., helping someone come to Kampala, helping with food and accepting delay in the paying of rent). These forms of assistance were not confined to the church, but more widely to people's neighbourhoods.

Concluding remarks

These ways of thinking about help, assistance, rewards and material goods, are different from what is normally known as the prosperity gospel. In these churches, there was not a lot of focus on being rich in terms of money and goods; when tithes were collected, it was the norm that no one would pay (people would rather pay a little at church offerings) because their income was so irregular and small. We are seeing a different way of relating and conceptualizing material and spiritual forms of exchange and how this is related to wealth. It takes form as relations of exchange that are not necessarily utilitarian in approach and not only reciprocal in a classical gift-giving sense. The relations of exchange are reciprocal, but in the sense that they include more than the giver and receiver: They also include God (as both giver and receiver), which has implications for the expectations people place on each other. These relationships of exchange are also understood around ideas of gratitude and pity—ideas that somehow also dissolve or transform some of the social mechanisms of gift-giving. One could say that there is a combination of motivations and rationales behind the form of spiritual economy discussed here, as they include both altruism and material interest (Godbout and Caillé 2000).

It is important to point out is that materiality and the limits of one's material life conditions matter with regard to one's involvement in a spiritual economy. The spiritual economy feeds into people's everyday lives, but is also restrained by the material limitations of these lives in a context of displacement and uncertainty.

References

Barclay, John. 2012. *What do we mean by grace? A fresh reading of Romans from the perspective of ancient gift-reciprocity*. Lecture at Faculty of Theology, University of Copenhagen, 9 October 2012.

Bernstein, Jesse. 2005. "*'A drop in the ocean': Assistance and protection for forced migrants in Kampala.*" Refugee Law Project Working Paper No. 16. Makerere University, Kampala.

Coleman, Simon. 2011. "Prosperity Unbound? Debating the "Sacrificial Economy."" In *The Economics of Religion: Anthropological Approaches* (Research in Economic Anthropology, vol. 31), ed. Lionel Obadia and Donald C. Wood, 23–45. Bingley: Emerald Group Publishing Limited.

Douglas, Mary. 1990. "Foreword. No free gifts." In *The Gift. The form and reason for exchange in archaic societies*, M. Mauss, ix-xxiii. London and New York: Routledge.

Fields, Karen. 1985. *Revival and rebellion in colonial Central Africa*. Princeton: Princeton University Press.

Gifford, Paul. 2004. *Ghana's new Christianity: Pentecostalism in a globalizing African economy*. London: Hurst and Company.

Godbout, Jacques T. and Caillé, Alain. 2000. *The World of Gift*. London: McGill.

Goodfellow, Tom. 2010. "*'The bastard child of nobody'?: Anti-planning and the institutional crisis in contemporary Kampala.*" Working paper no. 67, Crisis States Working Paper Series no. 2. London: LSE.

Hämmerli, Maria. 2011. "Religion and Spirituality between Capital and Gift." *Religion and Theology* 18: 195–210.

Lammers, Ellen. 2006. War, Refugee and Self. Soldiers, Students and Artists in Kampala, Uganda. Ph.D. thesis, University of Amsterdam.

Lauterbach, Karen. 2010. "Becoming a pastor: Youth and social aspirations in Ghana." *Young* 18, no. 3: 259–278.

Lindhardt, Martin. 2009. "More Than Just Money: The Faith Gospel and Occult Economies in Contemporary Tanzania." *Nova Religio: The Journal of Alternative and Emergent Religions* 13, no. 1: 41–67.

Maxwell, David. 2012. "What makes a Christian?: Perspectives from studies of pneumatic Christianity." *Africa* 82, no. 3: 479–491.

Mauss, Marcel. 1954 [1990]. *The Gift. The form and reason for exchange in archaic societies*. London and New York: Routledge.

Meyer, Birgit. 2004. "Christianity in Africa: From African Independent to Pentecostal-Charismatic Churches." *Annual Review of Anthropology* 33: 447–474.

Murison, Jude. 2002. "The Politics of Refugees and Internally Displaced Persons in the Congo War." In *African Stakes of the Congo War*, ed. John F. Clark, New York: Palgrave Macmillan.

Omata, Naohiko. 2012. "Refugee livelihoods and the private sector: Ugandan case study." Working paper series no. 86. Refugee Studies Centre. Oxford: University of Oxford.

Russell, Adrian. 2011. "Home, music and memory for the Congolese in Kampala." *Journal of Eastern African Studies* 5, no. 2: 294–312.

Simone, AbdouMaliq. 2011. "The Urbanity of Movement: Dynamic Frontiers in Contemporary Africa." *Journal of Planning Education and Research* 31, no. 4: 379–391.

Soares, Benjamin. 1996. "The Prayer Economy in a Malian Town." *Cahiers d'Études Africaines* 36, no. 144: 739–753.

UNHCR. 2013. "2013 UNHCR country operations profile—Uganda." Available from http://www.unhcr.org/pages/49e483c06.html. Internet; accessed 13 February 2013.

World Refugee Survey. 2009. "U.S. Committee for refugees and immigrants, Uganda report." Available from http://www.refugees.org/resources/refugee-warehousing/archived-world-refugee-surveys/2009-wrs-country-updates/uganda.html. Internet; accessed 13 February 2013.

Notes

1 The chapter is part of a postdoctoral project funded by the Danish Council of Independent Research | Social Sciences. It is based on recent fieldwork in Kampala (two months in 2012 and one month in 2013) in Congolese congregations. I conducted a little more than eighty interviews with Congolese pastors and church members, most of whom were refugees. I also participated in church services and other church-related activities. All names used in the text are pseudonyms, and names of specific churches do not appear. I would like to thank the participants of the NOS-HS funded explorative workshop in religion and development held in Helsinki in December 2012 for their insightful comments, particularly Tomas Sundness Drønen and Päivi Hasu for organizing the event. I would also like to thank my colleagues at the Centre of African Studies, University of Copenhagen for their comments on earlier drafts of the paper.

2 Based on the Control of Alien Refugees Act from 1960.

3 Interview with Congolese pastor, Kampala, 5 January 2013, translated from French.

4 Interview, Kampala, 16 January 2012.

5 Interview, Kampala, 11 January 2013.

6 Interviews Kampala, 31 January 2012, 2 February 2012, 7 January 2013 and 9 January 2013.

CHAPTER SEVEN

Reinventing "Tradition"

Social Reconstruction and Development in Post-Genocide Rwanda

Anne Kubai

Introduction

In this chapter, I will explore how Rwanda has turned to its indigenous cultural beliefs and practices in search of social reconstruction and development models for a deeply wounded post-genocide society. The data on which this chapter is based were collected during fieldwork for a larger study in 2010. It must be borne in mind that, in Rwanda's post-genocide context, reconciliation at different levels—namely, individual, inter-community, intra-community and national—as well as social reconstruction and economic development have to go hand-in-hand. I will explore the appropriation of cultural values and social institutions (practices and social institutions which derive from the Rwandan worldview and, therefore, are part of the indigenous spirituality[1]) which have been reinvented and revitalized to provide both the logistical framework and the fundamental principles for social, political and economic reconstruction. Here I will use the term *tradition* to refer to the indigenous cultural beliefs and practices of Rwandan society.

We must also take note of how the government of Rwanda defines poverty reduction and development. According to the Ministry of Local Government and Social Affairs (MINALOC), it is all about change: social, economic and political change. Change is also about people—individuals who together form the relationships, systems and processes that need to be altered. It is about improving individuals' ability to access and control resources of all sorts, whether financial, physical, natural, human or social. Rebuilding the social capital, the relationships and interdependencies so horrifically destroyed during the war and genocide is a key part of this approach. Another challenge identified by the government was the situation described as the "negative mindset" of many Rwandans, which was considered to be an impediment to development, coupled with the loss of values "that were an integral part of the Rwanda culture."[2] Furthermore, according to the government of Rwanda's National Unity and Reconciliation Commission, between 1998 and 1999 the government decided to "reshape Rwanda to encourage values that can help to build a good Rwandan citizen."[3] This implied the use of cultural values in practical ways to alleviate the governance, economic and social problems arising from the genocide. To legitimize this approach, it was embedded by law: Article 8 of the preamble to the 2003 Rwanda Constitution provides the evidence that Rwandans consider "it [to be] necessary to draw from our centuries-old history the positive values which characterized our ancestors that must be the basis for the existence and flourishing of our nation."[4]

Kelsall (2008, cited in Schatzberg 2002: 37; 70) warns "that most studies of Africa are 'out of focus' with local political realities, and urges that '[u]nless we begin to take indigenous understandings of concepts and categories more seriously than we do currently, we shall continue to miss vital and living elements of politics in this part of the world.'" Kelsall goes on to say that "Schatzberg demonstrates convincingly that a common cultural logic informs political experience in countries as outwardly diverse as Nigeria and Tanzania, while remaining sensitive to differences in volume and style. And here he is surely correct" (p. 9). Rwanda is no exception to this common cultural logic, and the government evidently turned to traditional cultural norms for "solutions" to difficult post-genocide problems. In the interim *Poverty Reduction Strategy Paper* (PRSP) from November 2000, the government reckoned that:

> Traditional Rwandese society had positive features, which were eroded by colonialism and subsequent poor governance. These included traditional judicial institutions, safety nets and solidarity. Modernizing the economy will therefore be pursued in tandem with the revival of these positive features. In some cases, traditional cultural norms act as a constraint. Economic innovation will be nurtured by the development of a more questioning and independent-minded culture throughout Rwandese society . . . social capital and solidarity. Rwanda has a strong tradition of mutual assistance . . . and voluntary contributions. . . . Given the low resource base and high expenditure needs, we need to mobilize such voluntary contributions for specific poverty reduction measures. (p. 9)

This is an important statement which explains the government's decision to turn to cultural practices in search of ideas that could inspire poverty eradication policies. Let us go through it step by step: First, there is recognition of the erosion of positive cultural values. Second, change and modernization of the economy are inseparable from the revival of positive traditional values, while at the same time it is acknowledged that certain traditional norms can be a hindrance to social change and also hamper development process. Third, the society needs to develop an independent-minded culture while encouraging solidarity and social capital for the mobilization of communities for poverty reduction.

In order to appreciate the link between Rwanda's indigenous values and practices as well as the current development policies, it is important to situate the latter within the society's worldview. Here I rely on Magesa's rich contribution to the study of African traditional religious system to elucidate some basic elements of the African religious thought, of which Rwanda is a part. Magesa says that "the economic organization of Africa [is such that] community and not association is the underlying principle. One cannot separate the economic sphere from other spheres of life for the African" (1997: 42). Furthermore, he notes that essentially:

> African Traditional Religion emphasizes community wellbeing. It is only when a community is healthy and strong that the welfare of members of the community is assured. In this regard, it is considered to be in the best interest of all to promote the welfare of individual group members. (p. 42)

This is also echoed by Alolo who says that "ethics in Africa encompasses every aspect of life–individuals' understanding of themselves and their relationship with others" (2007: 30). To this, Dalton (cited by Magesa) adds that

> production process and the disposition of goods and services—in short production and distribution—are expressions of underlying kinship obligation, tribal affiliation and religious morality. There is no economic system to be analyzed independently of social organization. Labour, land services and produced goods are allocated, exchanged or appropriated through transactional modes of reciprocity and redistribution. (Dalton 1967: 157)

Therefore, poverty reduction or "inequalities are compensated for by such mutual supplementation" (Magesa 1997: 42).

Rwandan society, like any other African society, is traditionally communal in its orientation. In my analysis of how Rwanda has re-invented these beliefs and practices to inspire the theory and practice of poverty eradication, social and economic development of its citizens, I take as my point of departure Rakodi's idea that "the meanings attached to symbols, rituals and myths are constantly re-interpreted, reflecting characteristics of and tension within social contexts, as well as people's imaginings about how they would like their world to be" (2011: 64). It must therefore be borne in mind that, as culture is not static, Rwanda like any other society is constantly innovating and reinventing its culture. In addition, religion provides a cosmological lens that people use to understand the world and their place in it: "It is also an important source of values—the morals and principles that inform a sense of right social ordering and personal attitude" (p. 17).

From this perspective, we can understand the government's recourse to the familiar realm of indigenous culture as the driving force behind social and economic development as well as the means to bring about "desirable change" and a "change of mind-set," creating a "new national narrative" and "a new moral order in which there is no fear and mistrust." The latter are the two elements said to have largely contributed to the genocide (Kubai 2005). It seems that the same culture that nurtured the ideology of the immutable difference between the Tutsi and Hutu groups should now be used in reverse to foster unity and reconciliation—what in Rwanda is referred to as "culture-based development" (Kubai 2010). Given that development as either an analytical category or societal goal has many strands and meanings, this chapter examines the cultural practices that Rwanda has turned to in search of development models.

Rwanda has a total land area of twenty-six thousand square kilometres and a population of ten million, nine hundred forty-two thousand, nine hundred fifty (World Bank 2011), making it the most densely populated country in Africa. Before the genocide, Rwanda was the darling of aid agencies. Uvin (1998), in his brilliant study fittingly titled *Aiding Violence: The Development Enterprise in Rwanda*, thoroughly scrutinized development politics and trends in Rwanda before the genocide in 1994. Uvin informs us that, during Habyariman's regime, the image of Rwanda created by the international development community was "'an idyllic one'—a country of subsistence farmers faced by daunting economic and democratic challenges and endowed with a government" (1998: 42) that was considered to be following the right path to development as defined by the donors. This "rosy image of Rwanda was shared by NGOs as well as bilateral and multilateral aid agencies" (p. 46), including the World Bank.

According to the donors, despite a number of handicaps, the hard-working population enjoyed the benefits of government policies. As early as 1976, the World Bank—in its memorandum on the economy of Rwanda—noted that, "despite these handicaps [that is, low income and embryonic modern sector, a land shortage, rapid population growth, and its inland position,] the present government . . . has made perceptible progress in developing a strategy to lift the economy from its present low level" (World Bank 1976, cited in Uvin 1998: 42). Uvin further points out that the challenges as well as the government's success in addressing them "are repeated over and over in all descriptions of Rwanda, like an endless prayer, a ritual in the development religion: although 'the task was forbidding . . . Rwanda's approach to economic and social development could be considered as successful'" (world Bank 1989b: 3, cited in Uvin 1998: 43). To quote Uvin yet again, many academics who subscribed to this ideology of development picked up from where the agencies stopped and paid glowing tribute to what they believed to be a model developing country.

It is not my intension to examine the impact of what became known as the structural adjustment programs or other development projects supported by the donor agencies in pre-genocide Rwanda; the point here is to sum up the development rhetoric during Habyariman's regime, under whose watch the society accelerated towards genocide in order to connect the past with present development policy in post-genocide Rwanda. For instance, I shall illustrate how the traditional practice of *umuganda,* obligatory community labour, which was part of Rwanda's much-vaunted development machinery during the Second Republic under Habyarimana, has also become an important aspect of the current development policy and politics. This background to the rosy image of Rwanda created at that time by the donor community is also necessary for our understanding of the similarly rosy current picture that has been painted by the same donor agencies, perhaps as a way of saying "mea culpa" for their failure during the genocide. Rwanda is once again hailed as the best user of IT in Africa, the easiest place to start a business and the least corrupt country in the continent: "Rwanda is the top business friendly destination in East Africa, the third in Africa and the second top reformer globally according to the World Bank" (*New Times* 2011).

Development politics and trends after the genocide

Rwanda's current social, political and economic situation is shaped by the post-genocide context, which makes Rwanda different from other post-conflict African countries. In the aftermath of the 1994 genocide, recovery was complicated by the loss of resources, devastated economy, crashed social fabric and decimated human and social capital, coupled with a dire need for resettlement and rehabilitation of large numbers of people in many parts of the country. To address these challenges, the government started by articulating justice, reconciliation and economic development and poverty reduction strategies (EDPRS). Medium-term strategies for the attainment of Vision 2020, the government development scheme to propel Rwanda to a middle-income country by year 2020, were put in place. According to the

Minister of Finance and Economic Planning, the first strategy was elaborated towards the end of the emergency period, when the country was:

> still recovering from the effects of the war and genocide of 1994. Our main concerns were for securing (sic) the nation, rebuilding the economy, growing enough food, building roads, providing housing, educating our children, providing health care and ensuring justices was done. It is now 2007 and Rwanda has come a long way. We are a stable nation, on the path to achieving better lives for each and every one of our citizens. We have made great achievements in human development, particularly in the areas of health and education. We are making strides towards improving economic governance through decentralization of public service delivery. (2007: i)

Nineteen years after the horrific 1994 genocide, the effects are still clearly visible, and Rwanda faces monumental challenges of rebuilding the country's infrastructure, social fabric, and administrative, economic and political systems that lay crushed. Rwanda remains one of the poorest and least developed countries (LDCs), and the government has acknowledged the fact that—despite concerted efforts—rates of poverty reduction "have been modest and not fast enough to meet either the targets set in Vision 2020 or the Millennium Development Goals (MDGs)" (MINECOFIN 2008). In its 2008 community development policy, the government articulated the country's development challenges as follows:

> High population density, combined with Rwanda's steep terrain and a lack of intensive farming practices, have all served to create immense pressure on the country's land and natural resources. Inadequate food is a problem with the majority of poor Rwandans living in rural areas. Poverty still prevails, although at a decreasing rate, and Rwanda remains one of Africa's poorest countries. Per capital income was estimated at $US 281 in 2006 and 56% of the Rwandan population are still poor, while 36.9% survive in conditions of extreme poverty. Multiple factors contribute to this situation . . .
>
> Rwanda still faces enormous challenges stemming from its turbulent history and the 1994 genocide. The genocide swelled the ranks of vulnerable groups such as widows or women whose husbands are in prison; recently freed prisoners, unskilled and unemployed youth and people with disabilities; and created new ones, such as households headed by children, landless farmers, elderly people taking care of their surviving relatives who are minors. The four decades leading up to the genocide saw much of Rwanda's social-cultural capital destroyed. A culture of deference to authority was fostered, mistrust between communities took hold and individual or collective entrepreneurship had very limited space in which to express itself. These are all areas where community development policy can make a real difference. (MINALOC 2008: 5–6)

With a strong resolve not only to find a balance between justice and reconciliation or between retribution and forgiveness for both survivors and perpetrators as well as to bring about social, political and economic transformation, the government has endeavoured to create a collective identity (over and above the Tutsi and Hutu identities) to bring about "desirable change" and a "change of mind-set," ultimately creating a "new national narrative" and "a new moral order in which there is no fear and mistrust." In the search for viable solutions to these problems, Rwanda (once known as "the most Catholic country in Africa") turned for inspiration to its indigenous cultural resources: traditional social institutions embodying the principles of justice, sharing, communalism, truth-telling, forgiveness and reconciliation, which are considered the prerequisites for social-economic development of this deeply wounded society. The most well-known of these indigenous institutions that has been used to adjudicate hundreds of thousands of genocide cases is the *Gacaca*, a traditional justice system that has attracted much research attention—most of it critical in terms of what it was likely to achieve. However, after the closure of the tribunals in June 2012, researchers have assessed its achievements, and there is no doubt that the novelty of the *Gacaca* will be presented in a different light in future research.

It is against this backdrop that this chapter will examine the appropriation of indigenous culture concepts and practices, what others would call African Traditional Religion, for the social transformation and economic development of the Rwandan society. This chapter examines the ways in which Rwanda is tapping into its traditional thought system by focusing on how the traditional concepts of *Ingando*, (solidarity camps) *Itorero ry'igihugu*, national civic education program, *ududehe,* (sharing), *imihigo* (performance contracts), *umuganda* ("voluntary" community work) and *Girinka* (one cow per poor family) have been re-invented and are now being used to bring about social, political and economic development in a society ravaged by genocide. I take as a starting point the unequivocal belief of the Rwanda people in the potential of their traditional cultural concepts and ideals to solve modern post-genocide social and economic problems. Therefore, I shall give a brief explanation of each of these concepts and illustrate how they have been innovatively applied in this rather unusual situation where victims and perpetrators live side by side, without choice, but to find ways and means of reconciling with their individual situations and with each other. Here I argue that, although it is possible to find traditional values and religious concepts in many African countries, Rwanda's recourse to traditional cultural resources to address complex modern challenges is not only different in important respects, but is also the first serious experiment of this kind and its novelty and ingenuity are thus far unparalleled on the continent.

Choice of indigenous culture-based models of social and economic development

In post-genocide Rwanda, communities must be mobilized for social, political and economic reconstruction. The immediate major problem for Rwanda is how to do just that. For our purposes here, Ellis and Ter Haar provide a starting point for the "future debates on development in Africa" in their brilliant article entitled "Religion and development in Africa." They observe that:

> First, that neither economic growth nor even state-building should be thought of as goals in themselves, although both are crucial aspects of a better future for Africans. Any development enterprise must begin by considering how people's full range of resources, including their spiritual or religious resources, can be used for their general well-being. Religious resources do not consist only of networks of people who relate to each other through religious practice or adherence. Religious resources can be considered under four headings: ideas; practices; organizations or institutions; and experiences. It is quite feasible to think of development in the future in terms of spiritual empowerment, in a similar sense as has been considered in regard, for example, to women's empowerment. (2006: 2)

The Commission for Africa also picks up the debate on the role of cultural resources in the development of the continent and urges that culture should

> become an inherent component of all development strategies–not just in terms of cultural products, but also in defining the terms of the development debate and the actions that follow. Culture becomes a way of working as well as an end in itself . . . a culturally determined sense of shared identity and responsibility is needed to underpin effective local, national and international governance. . . . (Commission for Africa Report 2005: 130)

This is the notion that seems to be gaining currency in post-conflict societies: South Africa's Truth Commission was the first to break the ground, but Rwanda's reliance on its cultural values and their potential to provide the logical framework and models for social, political and economic reconstruction of the nation after the horrific genocide is unique, not the least because the development context in Rwanda is inextricably linked to the processes of justice, healing and reconciliation, if not dependent on them. I shall illustrate this in the following section.

Ubudehe and the decentralization development strategy

Traditionally, *ubudehe* was a practice that brought members of the same community together in a combined effort to work on each other's farms to make them ready for the planting season. Thus, *ubudehe* usually took place sometime at the beginning of the dry season, when members of the community would prepare banana beer and sorghum beer and invite their peers for *ubudehe*. While the function involved working the land, it was also an occasion for conviviality, the celebration of harvest (not to be confused with *umuganura*), sharing and spreading harmony in the community.[5] The post-genocide government of Rwanda revived the concept—its full name in Kinyarwanda is *ubudehe mu kurwanya ubukene*, which can be rendered as *ubudehe* to fight poverty—and now uses it in community-oriented development projects, with support from the government, NGOs and donors.

Because the *ubudehe* "system had always been useful and effective, the government revived it to serve as a model for a program designed to alleviate poverty and provide for community rebuilding in the wake of Rwanda genocide and civil war in the early 1990s" (Andekunle 2007: 13). Habiyonizeye and Mugunga also reiterate the role of the new *ubudehe* as follows:

> The government has resurrected this traditional cooperative mechanism as a model for a program designed to foster collective action at the community level, rebuild trust and alleviate poverty . . . This innovative use of neo-traditional cultural institutions as operational tools to support the implementation of the country's poverty reduction and development strategies was born out of the national dialogue which took place at the end of the nineties. (2012: 5–6)

The *ubudehe* approach is participatory as it involves the entire community horizontally in local-level activities aimed at reducing extreme poverty. The activities are identified by local communities with the support of the central government working through the local government, but the underpinning idea is that collective participation in the activities rooted in the Rwandan culture is harnessed to build and strengthen community participation in local governance, accountability, transparency and empowerment at the grassroots level. This new approach to *ubudehe* was first piloted for a five-year period in the Butare region in the southern part of the country, before it was expanded to other regions in 2006.

In principle, through this approach, the community should be able to identify the most needy in their midst at the village level (two families in each village). Those who are identified as such are expected to be able to analyse their situation, including their skills and existing opportunities. Through community mapping facilitated by local government, villagers analyse their poverty following official classification of poverty levels articulated in the Poverty Reduction Strategy Paper of 2002 and rank their priorities. Households have been classified into six categories: first are those in extreme poverty (*umutindi nyakujya*), who do not own any property or adequate clothing and survive on begging; second are the very poor (*umutindi*) who do not own any land or livestock but are capable of working on land owned by others; third are the poor (*umukene*) who have some land and housing, live on their own labour and produce, but have no savings and are often undernourished, have no access to healthcare, and their children do not go to school; fourth are *umukene wifashije*, who have some livestock and other items from which they can generate some money to send their children to primary school; fifth are *umukungu*, who own land with fertile soil and therefore have enough food and are often employed in salaried jobs, meaning they can access healthcare; finally, sixth are those who have money, *umukire*, with land and livestock and often salaried jobs, good housing, a car and enough money to lend and collateral to get bank loans and they can migrate to the urban centres. The household or individuals who belong to *umutindi nyakujya* and *umutindi* are considered to be the most in need of assistance; therefore *ubudehe* allows the community to reach a consensus in identifying such cases. The chosen family is given a maximum amount of sixty thousand FRW (equivalent to 75 USD) in financial support for a project of their choice, but of course the project is identified with the help of local community leaders. The beneficiary is expected to pass on the profits to the next person in line; thus, the refund scheme is also managed by the community.

In the words of the leaders, *ubudehe* is now used as a traditional cultural tool to solve modern-day challenges. Although it is horizontal in as much as it involves the community participation, it is also top-down from the administration to the *imidugudu,* village level. It is also said to provide a link with national planning and budgeting system, financial and political decentralization as well as unity and reconciliation. In their evaluation of *ubudehe*, Habiyonizeye and Mugunga concluded that:

> Ubudehe is relevant and consistent with the "Vision 2020 Umurenge Programme" (VUP), the Poverty Reduction Strategy Paper (PRSP—2002–2005), the Economic Development and Poverty Reduction Strategy (EDPRS—2008–2012) and the Millennium Development Goals, which are guiding all the reform initiatives being undertaken by the government of Rwanda. In particular, Vision 2020 includes a specific objective to achieve "Rural economic transformation", while the PRSP and EDPRS identified the key priorities as rural development and agricultural transformation, as well as the need to intensify small-scale agriculture, livestock and skills development. (2012: 146)

Thus, *ubudehe* was reinvented and harnessed to serve the goals of the decentralization strategy, which is expected to tackle Rwanda's post-genocide social problems (unity, justice and reconciliation), drive change and contribute to growth and development. In his explanation of the function of *ubudehe*, a senior official of MINALOC once said that the country Rwanda needs standard infrastructures, health and education facilities, security and so forth as well as addressing all these required combined efforts, as was the case "in the past when *ubudehe* provided a good solution." In addition, one cannot but note that—in recognition of its efforts to reduce extreme poverty as well as adhere to principles of collective participation, accountability and transparency in its implementation—*ubudehe* was awarded by the UN prize that recognizes global excellence in public service in countries around the world in 2012.

Ingando: Learning about citizenship

Here, I shall argue that the use of *ingando*, which is seen by its critics as a platform for indoctrination, is an important element of the process of changing the Rwandan mindset, bringing about the "desired change," "creating a new moral order" and a "new national narrative." It is not my intention to pursue the strand in the debate about the usefulness and the purpose of *ingando* as a government indoctrination tool; instead, I will illustrate how it is used with the express aim of imparting a sense of national citizenship in an attempt to eradicate the historical dichotomy between the Hutu and Tutsi identity groups.

Traditionally, *ingando* fell under the military domain. Traditional Rwanda being an expansionist monarchy, the dynasty called on able men now and then to prepare for war. Warriors would gather for military drill and preparations for war. The place where they assembled before and after the war was called *ingando*, and the action was called *kugaandiika*. In ancient Rwanda, *ingando* was organized by the military; when faced by national disasters, the king would mobilize the population through *ingando*. In post-genocide Rwanda, the new *ingando* has been re-invented and adapted to the current needs; it has been used to mobilise the youth, public servants, demobilised soldiers and returnees (from refugee camps in Congo, etc.) who are gathered in specific *ingando* and solidarity camps and taught about government programs. They are updated on the new orientation in the life of the country, including citizen duties, rights and obligations. The National Unity and Reconciliation Commission (NURC) revived and formally developed *ingando* as a method of reintegrating and rebuilding communities. However, it is important to note that the first to undergo *ingando* training were demobilized ex-combatants; it was subsequently expanded to include community leaders, youth, survivors, released prisoners and pre-university students. *Ingando* is carried out throughout the country; it entails residential camps bringing together 300 to 400 participants per program for a period of three weeks to two months. The topics covered during this residential training include obligations and duties of leadership, human rights and the history of Rwanda. The extent to which *ingando* has contributed to changing the Rwanda mindset offers an interesting subject of inquiry, but judged by the intensity of involvement of groups from different social sectors and its countrywide coverage, it is an important activity of NURC.

Here we shall illustrate how the *ingando* utilizes various concepts drawn from indigenous spirituality in order to impart new ideas and ideals of Rwandan citizenship. NURC, established by law in 1999, is the institution that is charged with work of organizing *ingando* for various categories of citizens, including former combatants and students. The evaluation and impact assessment report of the activities of the commission points out that "NURC has contributed tremendously towards promoting culture as a tool of reconciliation," by incorporating cultural concepts. The report further notes that the:

> use of culture to achieve justice that is reconciliatory and restorative is at the heart of the transitional justice debate in several African countries today. Culture makes justice more accessible and participatory, thus helping to build greater ownership, confidence and legitimacy. Rwanda is regularly cited as an example in this regard. (Report 2005: 6)

As I have mentioned elsewhere (Kubai 2010), *itorero* and *ingando* concepts have been streamlined in the government development and governance programs. The Ministry of Local Government developed the Rwanda Decentralization Implementation Program (DIP), 2008–2012, which is an integral part of the government's national development strategy as articulated in the Vision 2020 and the Economic Development and Poverty Reduction Strategy (EDPRS). One of the five objectives of the National Decentralization Policy (NDP) adopted in May 2000 is "developing sustainable economic planning and management capacity at local levels that would serve as the engine for planning, people and resource mobilization, and implementation of social, political and economic development to alleviate poverty." In order to achieve this goal, the ministry developed a rather illustrative model of culture-based governance and development.[6] This model has inclusiveness as its foundation at the *umudugudu*, village level, in which the concepts of *itorero* (cultural civic education) and *umuganda* (public free labour) are embedded.

Itorero ry'igihugu: Inculcating "good cultural values" for nation-building

The background to the introduction of the national civic (re-)education program can be summed up thus: In February 2007, a high-level retreat at Kagera Game lodge mandated the Ministry of Local Government, Ministry of Education, Ministry of Sport and Culture and the National Unity and Reconciliation Commission to establish strategies to make the Vision 2020, the Development Millennium Goals and the Economic Development and Poverty Reduction Strategy understandable to Rwandans. They were also mandated to encourage the active participation of the Rwandan people in order to achieve these strategies through changes in mindset and ways of working. The a meeting on 12 November 2007, the Cabinet approved the creation of *Itorero ry'igihugu* as the main vehicle for accelerating the change in mindset and, through this change, achieving the objectives of Vision 2020. Thus, nation-building, with which the National Unity and Reconciliation Commission was tasked, became a key element of social and economic reconstruction in Rwanda.

The National Unity and Reconciliation Commission, which also worked closely with the *Gacaca* tribunals, launched cultural education centres, *itorero*, on 19 November 2007 to provide a forum for various stakeholders to discuss different problems facing the country. In the past, *itorero* was the traditional culture school where the youth would gather and be taught traditional values of "good culture," such as language (eloquence), social relations, sport, dances and songs, the defence of the nation and patriotism. *Itorero* equipped the participants with such important skills as hunting and provided the formative training for leaders of the nation. The only aspect of *itorero* that survived the colonial and missionary onslaught was the traditional dance. Today, it is used in the same spirit, albeit in different social and political circumstances shaped by the genocide and other forces of globalization. After the launch of the indigenous national education initiative (i.e., *Itorero ry'igihugu*), at least twenty-four thousand trainers were reported to have participated in the training in order to help train others on a number of national issues, including the Rwandan culture at the grassroots level.

This cultural education initiative aims to promote traditional culture and foster unity and reconciliation among the masses. The president of NURC was quoted as saying that:

> Teachers and leaders are key stakeholders in social and economic development of our country, we want them to use the Rwandan culture to discuss and find solutions to national problems . . . *Itorero* for teachers was necessary since they are involved in train-

> ing the young generation in the good practices that would help in molding and brightening their future based on culture. It would give teachers a platform based on our culture to solve problems, promote national unity, instill discipline and fight genocide ideology in their respective schools. (Staff reporter 2008)

The president of NURC argued that not only would *Itorero ry'igihugu* permeate all administrative levels from the lowest village level, sector and district up to the national level in order to enable all citizens to participate in finding their own solutions to their problems, but it would also promote government development programs. In the words of NURC leadership, *Itorero ry'igihugu* provides a culture-based channel for mentoring and re-educating Rwandans in good cultural values that should characterize a Rwandan citizen. Through *Itorero*, the government has redefined concepts and values, with the result that new taboos have emerged "to help achieve Vision 2020" as outlined by NURC (2009:7). According to the leadership of *Itorero*, such values (*indanga-gaciro*) include unity, patriotism, heroism, humanity, the culture of work based on *imihigo* (performance contracts) and Rwandan spirit. Taboos (*kirazira*) include bloodshed, betrayal of the nation, discrimination and cowardice.[7]

Umuganda: Voluntary community work for development, unity and reconciliation

In the traditional setting, *umuganda* referred to timber used in the construction of thatched houses in Rwanda. When it was time for a man to start a family, and therefore to build a house, he went around in the community asking for *umuganda*. All those who had a forest provided one piece or more of timber so that a house could be erected. The timber was not used to build a timber house in the Scandinavian style, for example. The *imiganda* (plural) were erected as pillars to support the roof. Beyond the construction aspect of the concept of *umuganda*, the term had an additional, perhaps even more important meaning. When a man preparing to get married went around asking for *umuganda,* he also meant to ask for solidarity—not help, not support, but solidarity—from his community. It must be stressed that, even if one would have the necessary *imiganda* in their family's forest(s), they would still go around asking for the *umuganda*[8] for solidarity. Marriage was not entirely an individual affair; it also involved some degree of community participation. This communal aspect is probably where the modern meaning of *umuganda* derives from. Today, the term implies community work for public interest, which means that members of the community in a given administrative unit, usually a village or cell, also get together to construct roads, schools and any other infrastructure that they deem necessary for the community.

According to Uvin (1998: 131), during Habyarimana's time,

> [the] system of obligatory community labour, *umuganda*, was part of Rwanda's much-vaunted development machinery. Every Saturday, one adult per family had to participate in community labour on projects chosen by the state. . . . Even though absence could lead to fines and even imprisonment, discontent with and resistance to these obligatory work programs were strong, for people often saw no benefit in these works . . . and resented their obligatory nature. . . . When democratization started, *umuganda* was stopped all together.

During the genocide, the same idea of the obligation to do public work was used to mobilize the killers. Many of those who were unwilling to participate in the killing were coerced to do *muganda* (i.e., to "work").

After the genocide, *umuganda* was revived, but this time it was dubbed "voluntary community work"—namely, community participation for the common good. It was positively linked to *imihigo*, the newly introduced performance contracts for public servants to create an efficient public service delivery system in Rwanda. In defence of the new *umuganda*, it was said that traditional culture always had communal work as a way of solving various problems facing society.

Current *umuganda* activities, performed on the last Saturday of the month, are usually reported in the local media, showing where the country's top leadership—including the president—spent the morning working to clear drainage systems, dig roadside trenches, or do other work. *Umuganda* is coordinated at the lowest administrative units (i.e., the village and cell), and mobilizing people to participate is the responsibility of the local leaders, with the requirement that all busineses be closed during *umuganda* hours and that all take part in the voluntary community work. For each *umuganda*, a theme is selected by local leaders, and the topic for discussion to encourage public discourse on pertinent issues is selected. It is understood that, through *umuganda*, there is a common perception of development and a shared sense of "Rwandanness" that is promoted through community labour. It supplements national resources by executing specific activities and instils a culture of collective effort in the population. Hence, the other function of *umuganda* is to engender unity and reconciliation as people of all classes and identity groups work together for the common good. Although *umuganda* retained much of its institutional characteristics, after the genocide "it shifted its purpose to reflect the new state's values, with reconciliation and unity playing larger, more emphasized roles" (Barnhart n.d.: 7).

Girinka: Eradicating Poverty One Cow At A Time

In the olden days, Rwandans greeted each other and expressed good wishes for well-being and the good things of life. One of these expressions was *gira inka umunyarwanda* ("may you get cows"). One of today's poverty eradication programs—"One Cow per Poor Family," or *Girinka*—is based on this expression. The *Girinka* program was approved by the Cabinet in April 2006 as part of the government strategy to reduce extreme poverty and empower vulnerable groups in society (Ombudsman Report n.d.: 11). It is included in the government's economic development and poverty eradication strategies geared for the achievement of Vision 2020. The "one cow per poor family" program, targeting three hundred fifty thousand families, aims to produce a chain effect in social and economic development by 2017: a wide-ranging social transformation by improving soil fertility through manure or organic fertilizer from the cow, which in turn will increase food production, leading to improved health of communities, reduced malnutrition in children and hence improved school enrolment, ultimately improving individual and community livelihoods.

"Why the cow?", some might ask. It is often quipped that two of the most discussed aspects of society in Rwanda are women and cattle. I do not wish to test the veracity of this contention; my intention is to illustrate the importance of cattle in the Rwandan tradition. In Rwanda in the past—and even today—cattle were not only the highest priced commodity, but were also a symbol of both status and culture. According to Kimenyi, (n.d.), cow metaphors are "found in all components of the Rwandan culture, namely concepts, values, customs, symbols, rituals, art, dance, music, sports and social organization" (p. 1). He adds that "Kinyarwanda cow vocabulary is used very extensively in everyday language to refer to objects, states and events which don't have anything to do with cows" (p. 1). Therefore, by turning to this traditional commodity of both social and economic significance, as a model for poverty eradication for the "very poor" in society, the government not only appeals to the familiar realm of culture, but by investing new meanings into what cattle symbolized in the traditional society, it also lays the foundation for the process of eventual social change.

In this program a poor family is identified by the local government authorities and receives a cow. When it calves, the calf is donated to the neighbour, who gives the next calf to another neighbour, and so on. The program lays special emphasis on those identified as "vulnerable groups," which include child- and female-headed households. Significantly, 34 per cent of all households are female-headed, and 60.8 per cent of these are widows of genocide (Hamilton 2009), who "make up more that 40% of all women" (Schindler 2009: 8).

By focusing on the most vulnerable populations in society, the program has noble intentions to improve their lives. However, we must point out that the program has its challenges. In many cases it is circumscribed by the prevailing social norms which place a high premium on cows while making it taboo for women to perform the important task of milking cows. Therefore, some genocide widows and young girls living in child-headed households are forced to rely on the good will of male friends and neighbours to come in the morning and evening to milk the cows for them.

In addition, as with all other issues touching on social reconstruction and economic development in Rwanda, the distribution of cows to poor families is laced with ideological undertones. A cow is expected to engender reconciliation in Rwanda's deeply wounded post-genocide society. It is believed that the act of donating a calf to a neighbour promotes not only good neighbourliness, but also the much-desired unity and inter-ethnic reconciliation—namely, "unity and social cohesion among Rwandans in their respective communities thereby mitigating the ideology that led to genocide in 1994" (MINAGRI Report, n.d.). It is also expected to lead to an "improved mindset" because the government traces the genocide to:

> . . . bad governance and the impact of divisive policies (and therefore) responds by promoting good governance and inclusive policies. The focus on citizenship has become a vehicle for unity. Arguably, Rwandan citizenship assists in dissolving the hostile perceptions of the identity groups since it neutralises the weight of fear and of differences over historic developments which lie at the heart of the conflict. Due to its inclusive and egalitarian nature, it has the potential to erase the injustices of the past. This is based on a legalistic understanding of citizenship as having equal rights, most prominently the right to life. Central to this strategy is thus to move from ethnic to national identity. (Burckley-Zistel 2006: 4)

Regarding social transformation, "improved mindset" is defined as a "departure from looking at cattle as a status symbol (the more cows one has the better) to a source of income and livelihood" (MINAGRI n.d.). The government also includes in the objective of the program an aspect of eradicating hostile perceptions of different ethnic identities in Rwanda. Here, I venture that it is a veiled reference to the traditional idea that cattle keeping defined the identities of Tutsi and Hutu.[9] The underlying idea is that cattle should no longer be a mark of ethnicity or high or low social status in a society that is struggling to bridge its historical divisions and eradicate social stratification. The government believes that this can be achieved through a process of de-ethnicization of the society by transposing traditional norms, rituals and practices and infusing them with new meanings and symbolism.

Concluding remarks

In this chapter, I have sought to demonstrate that, with a firm belief in the potential of the cultural resources for mobilization for change and development, the Rwanda government made a conscious effort to identify and reinvent some traditional institutions and practices that have been used to provide both the inspiration and framework for community participation in development programs. The success and the real potential of concepts based on the traditional beliefs and practices to change Rwanda society and bring about development that will move the country from the list of LCDs to middle income by 2020 are not the focus of this essay. Their use is my main interest, and I have illustrated both the rationale for and methods of reinventing traditional concepts and practices as articulated by government officials and ordinary Rwandans who are mobilized for community participation in development programs.

Admittedly, it is logical for the government to seek to change the way people in Rwanda think and feel because it is only through a change of mindset that such practices as "*umuganda*, the dreaded obligatory communal labour[,] and *umusanzu*—obligatory financial participation in the construction and maintenances of infrastructures" (Uvin 1998: 133)—can now find acceptance among the people. It requires a change of mindset for people who know that *imihigo* was traditionally a form of gathering to test individuals' valour and must now accept the reinvention of *imihigo* as the all-important performance contracts signed between the president of the republic and the mayors of the districts as well as between individual families and the state through the local government. Indeed, it requires a change of mindset to create a new moral order as the government is determined to do in order to move the country forward. In this case, it looks as if the means justifies the end.

Through *ingando*, the state can publicly articulate the discourse of patriotism and heroism. It is not by accident that heroism and patriotism are accorded an important place in public discourse. Rwandans are acutely aware of their history, even though it is contested. This history is what they are re-writing through the creation of a new national narrative, and all the traditional practices that have been revived for this purpose are well coordinated to make them into a whole system of interdependent elements. *Ingando* and *itorero* complement each other because *itorero* resonates more with the public discourse on morality (e.g., learning the values of integrity, ethical behaviour).

It is also helpful to remember that critics of Rwanda's culture-based development models have raised some important questions regarding some of the programs presented here. They see the return to indigenous culture for development models as a resuscitation of an idealized past which glosses over the country's troubled history, the true nature of the traditional social stratification and the expansionist nature of the ancient kingdom of Rwanda. Johann Pottier, in his book *Re-imagining Rwanda. Conflict, Survival and Disinformation in the Late Twentieth Century*, says that "the resuscitated functionalist narrative on Rwandan society and history is also 'at work' in the design of policy initiatives for rural restructuring" and that "the aim of land reform . . . may well be to rationalize existing practices and boost production, as officials and experts claim, yet the discourse of reform also acts as an instrument which, through its representation of the past, helps to legitimate the present" (2002: 179).

Nevertheless, according to a senior government official in the Ministry of Local Government and Social Affairs, the current economic growth and social development can be attributed to the employment of some cultural practices, such as *ubudehe*, *umushikirano* (Annual National Dialogue) and *Itorero ry'igihugu* (national civic education), where issues affecting communities are discussed and important solutions are determined. The veracity of such claims can only be reasonably challenged through extensive evaluation of the various development programs, but perhaps this is also unnecessary because Rwanda does not owe anyone an explanation for its recourse to cultural beliefs and practice in the search for models for sustainable development, especially when development, like democracy, is said to elude the African continent. The concept of homemade solutions is perhaps taken more seriously in Rwanda than elsewhere in Africa.

In their call for African epistemologies to be taken seriously, Ellis and Ter Haar (2007) advise that "a religious mode of apprehending reality . . . constitutes an epistemology that is simultaneously traditional and modern, capable of updating and renewing itself as times change" (p. 394). This cannot be truer for Rwanda, where traditional concepts are reinvented and infused with new meanings to provide solutions to modern problems. Ellis and Ter Haar further note that "there are signs of a growing acceptance of the possibility of different paths to political and economic development" (p. 396). Rwanda has boldly chosen to walk this path.

References

"Rwanda still among best reformers—World Bank," *New Times*, 21 October 2011.

Adekunle, Julius. 2007. Culture and customs of Rwanda. Westport: Greenwood press.

Alolo, Alhassan. 2007. "African Traditional Religion and concepts of development: A background paper". Working Paper 17. Africa Development Bank.

Barnhart, Jaclyn. n.d. "Umuganda: The ultimate nation-building project?" Pursuit: The Journal of Undergraduate Research at the University of Tennessee. Available from http://trace.tennessee.edu/cgi/viewcontent.cgi?article=1055&context=pursuit. Internet; accessed 10 March 2012.

Buckley-Zistel, Susanne. 2006. "Dividing and uniting: The use of citizenship discourses in conflict and reconciliation in Rwanda." Global Society 20, no. 1: 101–113.

Ellis, Stephen and Ter Haar, Gerrie. 2007. "Religion and politics in Africa." *Journal of Modern African Studies* 45, no. 3: 385–400.

Ellis, Stephen and Ter Haar, Gerrie. 2006. "Religion and development in Africa." Paper obtained from Gerrie ter Haar.

Government of Rwanda. Ministry of Agriculture (MINAGRI) Report. n.d. "Girinka munyarwanda", Available from http://www.africaplatform.org/sites/default/files/resources/cd_case_story_rwanda_that_has_transformed_the_lives_of_the_poor_rwandans.pdf. Internet; accessed 20 April 2011.

Government of Rwanda, Ministry of Local Government (MINALOC). 2008. "Community Development Policy, Kigali, 2008." Available from www.minaloc.gov.rw. Internet; accessed 20 December 2010.

Government of Rwanda, Ministry of Local Government (MINALOC). 2007. "Economic development and poverty reduction strategy". Report, Kigali.

Government of Rwanda. 2000. "An Approach to the poverty reduction action plan for Rwanda." Kigali: The Interim PRSP.

Habiyonizeye, Yvonne and Mugunga, Jean Claude. 2012. "A case study of citizen engagement in fostering democratic governance in Rwanda." Paper presented at the international conference on democratic governance and corruption in Africa, Pennsylvania University.

Hamilton, Heather. 2001. "Rwanda's women: The key to reconstruction." *The Journal of Humanitarian Assistance*. Available from http://www.jha.ac/greatlakes/b001.htm. Internet; accessed 14 February 2011.

Kelsall, Tim. 2008. "Going with the Grain in African development?" Discussion Paper, no. 1. Available from http://www.institutions-africa.org/filestream/20080623-discussion-paper-1-going-with-the-grain-in-african-development-tim-kelsall-june. Internet; accessed 15 March 2013.

Kimenyi, Alexandre. n.d. "Cow metaphors." Available from http://www.kimenyi.com/cow-metaphors.php. Internet; accessed 12 October 2012.

Kubai, Anne. 2005. Being Church in Post-genocide Rwanda: The Challenges of Forgiveness and Reconciliation. Uppsala: Life & Peace Institute.

Kubai, Anne. 2010. "Gacaca and post-genocide Reconstruction in Rwanda." In *Indigenous Voices in sustainability discourse. Spirituality and the struggle for a better quality of life*, ed. Frans Wijsen and Sylvia Marcos, 261–280. Berlin: LIT VERLAG.

Magesa, Laurenti. 1997. *African Religion: The Moral Traditions of Abundant Life*. Nairobi: Paulines Publications Africa.

Niringiye, Aggrey and Ayebale, Chris. 2012. "Impact evaluation of the *ubudehe* programme in Rwanda: an examination of the sustainability of the *ubudehe* programme." *Journal of Sustainable Development in Africa* 14, no. 3: 141–154.

Pottier, J. 2002. *Re-imagining Rwanda. Conflict, Survival and Disinformation in the Late Twentieth Century*. Cambridge: Cambridge University Press.

Rakodi, Carole. 2011. "Inspirational, inhibiting, institutionalized: exploring the links between religion and development." Working Paper 66. International Development Department, University of Birmingham.

Republic of Rwanda. (n.d.). Ombudsman Office Report on "One Cow per Poor Family" and construction of shelters. Available from http://www.ombudsman.gov.rw/Documents/GIRINKA ENGLISH.pdf. Internet; accessed 20 November 2011.

Republic of Rwanda, National Unity and Reconciliation Commission (NURC). 2005 "The role of Women in reconciliation and peace building in Rwanda: Ten years after genocide". Kigali

Republic of Rwanda. 2007. "Economic Development and Poverty Reduction Strategy 2008 - 2012." Ministry of Finance and Economic Planning (MINECOFIN) Kigali.

Schindler, Kati. 2009. "Time allocation, gender and norms: evidence from post-genocide Rwanda." German Institute for Economic Research (DIW Berlin). Available from http://www.socialpolitik.ovgu.de/sozialpolitik_media/paper_update/Schindler_Kati_uid595_pid532-p-525.pdf. Internet; accessed 4 March 2012.

Uvin, Peter. 1998. Aiding Violence: The Development Enterprise in Rwanda. West Hartford: Kumarian Press.

World Bank. 1976. Memorandum on the economy of Rwanda. Washington, DC: East African Country Programs II.

Notes

1 Here I use the phrase indigenous spirituality in lieu of African traditional religion.

2 See Itorero Ry'igihugu "Policy Note and Strategic Plan." The Republic of Rwanda National Unity and Reconciliation Commission, Kigali 2009: 3.

3 Itorero Ry'igihugu "Policy Note and Strategic Plan." The Republic of Rwanda National Unity and Reconciliation Commission, Kigali 2009: 3.

4 Itorero Ry'igihugu "Policy Note and Strategic Plan." The Republic of Rwanda National Unity and Reconciliation Commission, Kigali 2009: 3.

5 Personal communication, Ubaldo Rafiki, Uppsala, March 2013.

6 See "Assessing and improving governance for results-based management: ensuring good governance for effective service delivery." Ministry of Local Government, Kigali, 2007.

7 Presentation of Itorero by Chairman/TF, Kigali, 2009.

8 Personal communication, Ubaldo Rafiki, Uppsala, March 2013.

9 Colonial administrators defined a Tutsi as anyone who had ten or more cows; however flawed this definition was, it served the intended administrative purposes of ethnic distinction.

CHAPTER EIGHT

Fragile Health Justice
Cooperation with Faith Organizations

Ville Päivänsalo

> [T]he principal aims and objects of TANU shall be as follows: . . . To see that the Government mobilizes all the resources of this country towards the elimination of poverty, ignorance and disease.
>
> *The Arusha Declaration* (1967) FOR THE TANGANYIKA AFRICAN NATIONAL UNION [TANU] BY J. NYERERE

The need for cooperative health justice

The United Nations' *Universal Declaration of Human Rights* (UDHR 1948), in article 25(1), describes "the right to a standard of living adequate for . . . health and well-being." Another salient text in the human rights tradition, *The International Covenant on Economic, Social and Cultural Rights*, affirms the right to "the highest attainable standard of physical and mental health" for all (The United Nations / ICESCR 1966: Art 12(1)).[1] Numerous other statements by non-confessional official or semi-official organizations and faith-based organizations (FBOs) alike have espoused the human right to health and demanded that corresponding action be taken. While the literature on health justice has grown rather abundant (e.g. Daniels 2008; Ruger 2010; Venkatapuram 2011; Wolff 2012), the roles of FBOs in the cooperation for health justice have not always been fully recognized in mainstream development thought.

High-level declarations have not remained mere words; development assistance for health has ballooned since the 1970s (Rosenberg et al. 2010; Murray et al. 2011). Many developing countries have also mobilized their national resources for health on a broad front. For example, Julius Nyerere (1967: Part 1, Art. 1e), the first president of the United Republic of Tanzania (from 1964 to 1985), called for the mobilization of no less than "all the resources of this country towards the elimination of poverty, ignorance and disease."

Despite greatly increased medical knowledge and public funding as well as an improved average standard of living world-wide the right to health has remained a dream in many regions. In Sub-Saharan Africa (SSA) the HIV/AIDS pandemic, and, for example, maternal ill health and mortality are still huge challenges, and out-of-pocket payments for health services have driven millions to catastrophic health spending. It indeed seems that public health agencies and leading development organizations need collaboration with voluntary health organizations to be able to bring about better health justice results (Garrett 2000; Easterly 2006; Crisp 2010; UNICEF 2010; Rees 2011).

Two models of transitional health justice

In this paper I will first analyze two models of transitional health justice, i.e., models for taking steps towards health justice in non-ideal circumstances. In Model 1, or the *priority of public health* model, the public sector non-confessional agencies are clearly the primary responsible agencies. Only when they fail to provide adequate health justice for all, must the secondary responsible agencies such as FBOs be ready to step in. Model 2, in turn, is the *pluralist cooperation for health* configuration. It includes the assumption that FBOs and other secondarily responsible health agencies can play a significant role in non-ideal as well as comparatively ideal circumstances. This implies that the transition from non-ideal circumstances towards more ideal ones need not lead to the marginalization of faith-based health organizations. In general, faith-based organizations are in a more subjected position in Model 1 and a more collaborative position in Model 2.

The idea of a foundational level in health justice, distinct from the corresponding practical considerations, plays a salient role in my argument for the plausibility of the pluralist cooperation model. In order to achieve effective, stable, and dialogically practical cooperation for health justice, there needs to be a sufficient consensus at the relevant practical levels (including high-level principles and goals, mid-level policies, and low-level practices). Once this condition is satisfied, there is room for a relatively broad variety of foundational understandings. There must, however, be reasonable limits to the diversity of foundational understandings as well.

Wildly diverse foundational views on health justice can hardly translate into fruitful dialogues about collaborative practices and fairness, for example regarding fair salaries for health professionals in both the public and faith-based sectors.

My second objective is to shed light on these theoretical models with reference to the situation in Tanzania, where at least 15 percent of all health facilities and almost 40 percent of hospitals on the country's mainland are owned by FBOs, predominantly Christian ones (Makawia et al. 2010: 12; The United Republic of Tanzania 2010: 53–59; Boulanger and Criel 2012: 81–82). Resembling Model 1, the World Bank study *Making Health Financing Work for Poor People in Tanzania* by Dominic Haazen (2012) builds its future scenarios on the basis of strengthening public health institutions. This approach seems promising indeed and, being more predictive than normative, it probably could be complemented by rather keen collaboration with the faith-based sector. As such, however, it does not make much of the comparatively beneficial character of the FBO health services for the poor, which appears evident at least on the basis of a recent study (Makawia et al. 2010) also referred to by Haazen (2012).

Model 2, in turn, has its roots in the longstanding appreciation of Christian health work in Tanzania. President Nyerere was willing to cooperate with faith-based health organizations in the 1960s and 1970s, and closer to today more formalized types of partnerships have become more common. Although this cooperation has not always functioned smoothly, the government has taken steps to address many essential challenges, particularly since the turn of the millennium (Ministry of Foreign Affairs of Denmark 2007: 105–109). As well, the government's *Health Sector Strategic Plan III* (The United Republic of Tanzania 2008) for July 2009–June 2015 emphasizes the importance of collaboration with the FBO sector.

When discussing these models, I will highlight certain theoretical approaches to health justice (mainly Rosenberg et al. 2010 and Ruger 2011) and argue that they do not imply the marginalization of faith-based health services. They only need to be fine-tuned to be sensitive to collaboration with religious agencies such as the Evangelical Lutheran Church in Tanzania (ELCT), which broadly shares the objectives of non-confessional health agencies (ELCT 2010). Similarly, thinking in terms of pluralist collaboration, with its foundational and practical levels, could be encouraged in any context where the contextual preconditions for collaboration are being met.[2]

I do not assume in my analysis that ideal health justice can be achieved in Tanzania, or anywhere else for that matter. I instead assume that (1) the goals and principles of health justice are fragile, (2) its means are fragile, and (3) the motivation of its agents is fragile. For example, the motivational basis of a health worker can include a faith factor, a community factor, and a humanitarian factor as well as personal financial concerns (Flessa 2005; Boulanger & Criel 2012; ELCT 2010).

But insofar as the faith factor includes a calling for health work, it actually functions as a resource for health justice.

A quest for dialogical cooperation

One of the more elaborate theories of cooperation for development in the health sector has been put forward by Mark L. Rosenberg et al. in their *Real Collaboration* (2010). They pointed out that in the late twentieth century the major development agencies somehow managed to coordinate health sector development, but there is no single telephone number to call if one wants to know what the development guidelines and strategies for today are. While new actors have emerged, for example in HIV/AIDS work in Tanzania, the WHO's relative significance has decreased. (Rosenberg et al. 2010: 23–30)

Rosenberg et al. (2010: 5–6) do not assume that close collaboration is always the ideal to strive for. The degrees of partnership integration they depict are *coordination*, *cooperation* and *close collaboration*. In general, they propose that coordination is appropriate when there is a proper authority available and the effort is suitably limited, as in the case of disaster aid. Cooperation involves a broader degree of sharing goals and information. Close collaboration is a more integrated form of collective action still, involving years of joint efforts towards ambitious goals directed by a willing and able core team.

Beyond what Rosenberg and company have to say, I would like to call further attention to the possibility of long-term collaboration under circumstances where *high-level practical goals and principles* are broadly shared (e.g. "health for all" as an internationally endorsed norm) but where the *foundational premises* and *low-level practices* of the partnering agencies clearly differ from each other. By foundational premises I basically refer to the faith premises of FBOs, which are premises not shared by non-confessional partner organizations.

Differing foundational premises can make the emerging collaboration schemes unstable, inefficient, and perhaps unfair, but not necessarily so. *Explicit agreements at relevant mediating levels* can serve as means to stabilize the collaboration schemes in question. *Genuine dialogue*, in turn, can help resolve the impasses faced in attempts to work on the basis of broadly shared practical goals and explicit treaties.

Incomplete goals and principles

Rarely is it fully possible to identify the underlying differences concerning the goals and principles of collaboration between the various approaches to health justice, not to mention precisely defining what universally acceptable reasonable health justice is. Jennifer Ruger, representing the capability approach to health, has addressed the challenge of disagreement systematically in her *Health and Social Justice* (2011) by introducing an account of "incompletely theorized arguments" (ITA) in the context of health justice thought. Within the ITA theory, which has been used by constitutional lawyers, she distinguishes three models to be explored further.

In the first model, there is *agreement about high-level goals or principles*, but disagreement about their application both at the mid-level and low-level. In the second, the *agreement prevails at the mid-level.* Ruger's example is that a group of people agree about the importance of universal health insurance coverage, although they disagree about the high-level principles of health justice and specific policies in the implementation of the mid-level goal in question. In the third model, the disagreements lie in the middle but the parties involved *agree about both the high-level goals and the low-level practical issues.* (Ruger 2011: 72–73)[3]

The ITA framework helps us see that collaborators need not always agree upon high-level principles in practice. Complete high-level disagreement, however, is bound to make the collaboration scheme drastically unstable. In the case of practical conflict the collaboration partners would then have no joint premises that could be used to adjudicate their case. True, collaborators can often have partially different goals, but there must be reasonable limits for this partiality if the collaborative scheme is to be at all stable. Mediating grounds must be sought out to bridge the opposite positions.

Differing from Ruger's account, I will employ a four-level rather than three-level framework. The first level in my emerging framework concerns (1) the *foundations of health justice*, whether non-confessional or faith-based, which is then followed by (2) *high-level goals and principles of justice*. The idea of the distinction here is that people with different understandings of the very basis of health justice can nevertheless endorse virtually the same practical high-level goals and principles. For example, there could be a strong consensus about the goal of fighting HIV/AIDS, although non-confessional and faith-based organizations understand this misery differently at the foundational level (e.g. the theologies of *imago Dei* and a wounded body are not shared). Insofar as the parties ultimately promote different means to tackle the pandemic at lower levels, they could nevertheless enter into a meaningful dialogue about balanced and suitably distanced cooperation in the light of the high-level practical principles and goals they share (beginning with human dignity).

At the lower levels, i.e. (3) *mid-level policies* and (4) *grassroots-level practices*, there can prevail either consensus or disagreement quite as Ruger has depicted. And at all levels, indeed, we must be ready to take into account non-ideal conditions.

Responding to non-ideal conditions

Many shortcomings in health standards can be explained in terms of individual factors ranging from each individual's genetic outlook to life-style choices, but other shortcomings are essentially socio-political. The United Nations Committee on Economic, Social and Cultural Rights (UNCESCR) has expressed its awareness of the individual and socio-political factors within the context of health rights, for example, in its General Comment 14 (The United Nations / UNCESCR 2000: Art. 9), in which it nevertheless maintains that "the right to health must be understood as a right to the enjoyment of a variety of facilities, goods, and services." Adopting the UNCESCR approach, I take it for granted that, *prima facie*, various agencies can enhance health justice at least by (1) *providing health facilities, goods, and services.* In addition, (2) *improving the conditions of individuals to make use of available health services* and (3) *influencing the individual's health-related behavior* can stand as other, less direct ways of promoting health justice.

In the *priority of public health* model, the ideal for the public sector should be to provide the health services, i.e. (1) above. In this case, the primary response of an FBO to health injustice would be essentially limited to (2) improving the conditions of health justice and (3) supporting individual health-related behavior. In the *pluralist collaboration for health* model, on the other hand, FBOs could be fully and stably integrated partners in the provision of health services as well. They could respond to health justice concerns either by fully adopting the goals and principles of health justice as laid out by the public authorities, or by operating partly according to their own standards and trying to establish a dialogical consensus at each level of practical health justice.

Poor financial conditions are a major issue in most contexts of non-ideal health justice. Whereas poverty is often conducive to ill health, ill health also often pushes individuals and households into poverty (Sachs 2006; Flessa 2007). According to the *World Health Report* 2010, in 33 mostly low-income countries "direct out-of-pocket payments represented more than 50% of total health expenditures in 2007" (WHO 2010: xiv). Haazen's (2012: 2; 20–23; 53–58) World Bank study recognizes this problem very clearly in Tanzania. Haazen supports improving the provision of health services and expanding and harmonizing the insurance schemes already operating in the country. These suggestions seem plausible, for they would expectedly reduce the share of direct out-of-pocket payments in particular and thus catastrophic health spending. Money alone, however, can hardly serve as the key response to the shortcomings of health justice. Individuals should also be able to use it wisely to support their health. And if health services are being provided for free, the significance of money as a determinant of health justice for an individual decreases.

The connections between economics and health are highly relevant at organizational, national, and international levels as well. For a developing country as a whole, for instance, dependency on *foreign* public money can also be a burden (Easterly 2006; Moyo 2010). President Julius Nyerere already warned Tanzanians about this in *The Arusha Declaration*. Nyerere (1967: Part 3(1)) rebuked those leaders in TANU and the Tanzanian government who "speak as if the most important thing to depend upon is MONEY" (emphasis Nyerere's). He continues on the subject of foreign assistance in particular, saying that its amounts will inevitably be limited, and it tends to sap Tanzanians' self-reliance. Nyerere's (1967: Part 3 (9–10)) recipe for development instead stresses hard and well-planned work, not least in agriculture. Directly as a matter of health justice, Nyerere (1967: Part 3(6)) worries about the poor health services available to productive peasants in the countryside.

Whatever the overall merits of Nyerere's 'African Socialism' (or *Ujamaa* policy), in the health sector it meant a request for the churches to do their part in the people-centered reform for the development and well-being of the country. Boulanger and Criel (2012: 78) depict the climate of this collaboration which emerged as harmonious and dialogical. They go on to point out, however, that the *Ujamaa*-inspired management of the health sector remained notoriously centralized until 1982, when a decentralization process was initiated under circumstances of severe economic difficulty. Subsequently the partnership agreements between the Ministry of Health (MoH), the churches, and individual hospitals (Boulenger and Criel 2012: 17; 83–86) became increasingly formalized. Hence it has been affirmed as part of the status quo that church-owned health facilities—as they indeed have responded to the non-ideal health condition in that country in a thorough way—are an integral part of Tanzania's system of health service provision.

Although financial assets are usually of high importance for individuals, organizations, and governments alike in their aspirations for health justice, we must also be aware that financing alone rarely provides a sustainable solution in this regard. A look at the *Arusha Declaration* helps us to see the importance of people as a resource for development. Haazen's (2012) study affirms that the lack of human resources still remains a key challenge for the development of the Tanzanian health sector. Stressing the importance of people, however, has its limits in terms of promoting justice: people cannot be expected to work for the common good for free, at least not as a matter of ideal justice. This assumption brings us a step back to the search for a balanced view: maintaining sustainable health justice requires both financial assets and capable people. And in both of these respects, the Tanzanian public sector has been dependent on foreign assistance as well as on FBOs.

Trust-based practices with agreements

In 1961, missionaries ran half of the hospitals in Tanzania. Today, under the auspices of The Christian Social Service Commission (CSSC), the umbrella organization for Christian social and health work in the country, there are almost 90 operating hospitals. This equals almost 40 percent of hospitals on the Tanzanian mainland. Most of these belong to the Catholic Church, followed by the ELCT with its 23 hospitals. There is also a wide network of Christian health centres—ca. 21 percent of health centres on the Tanzanian mainland—in addition to many Christian and Muslim dispensaries all over the country. (ELCT 2010: ELCT Health 2013; CSSC 2012; Boulanger and Criel 2012: 81–82; The United Republic of Tanzania 2010: 53–59; The United Republic of Tanzania 2012)[4] The Kilimanjaro Christian Medical Centre (KCMC) and Bugano Medical Centre (BMC), both owned by Christian organizations, are two of the four national referred hospitals (The United Republic of Tanzania 2012; Boulanger and Criel 2012: 86).[5]

When the CSSC was founded in 1992, the roles of FBOs in the health sector became cleared and more decentralized. The government of Tanzania, the Christian Council of Tanzania (CCT), and the Tanzania Episcopal Conference (TEC, Catholic) negotiated a *Memorandum of Understanding* (MoU) to provide a formal framework for CSSC-related health service collaboration. The collaboration among public authorities and Christian health organizations below the principled and national level, however, relied in large part on trust-based relationships—as it still does in several respects. (Boulanger and Criel 2012: 85–87; 91–93) But insofar as the relationships have been trustful, the increased formalization has not necessarily disrupted them. At least in the case of Karagwe hospital, Boulanger and Criel (2012: 87) report that the shift towards a more comprehensive formalization of its cooperation with public authorities has nurtured mutual trust among the key collaboration partners.

The Government of Tanzania has also signed *Memorandum of Understanding* documents with international donors, such as the MoU with five foreign official donors for the July 2003 to June 2008 period. This document sets terms for pooled funding, or basket funding, that is "intended to complement the Tanzanian Government efforts in the health sector" (MoU 2003, A.3.) Basket funds have also been regularly channelled to faith-based health organizations.

Since 2007, so-called Service Agreement (SA) documents have been used to specify the forms of collaboration between the MoH and individual hospitals. If a voluntary agency (VA), characteristically a faith-based health organization, does not have an SA, basket funding is not fully available to it (Boulanger and Criel 2012: 86). SAs aim at clearly describing the responsibilities of the parties of the agreement, including the details of the services to be provided, and their expected costs, and also the financing of the hospital by the state as well as from other sources. The SA approach also involves a more thorough monitoring of practices than previously, which has mainly been regarded as a welcome development within the CSSC. Overall, public funding for the faith sector has increased. (Boulanger and Criel 2012: 79–99) In the official ideal scenario projected to 2015, the allocation of health funds "to public and private health providers [would be] based on competence and performance, using service contract mechanisms" (The United Republic of Tanzania 2008: 59). This vision accords with the *pluralist cooperation for health* model.

When it comes to the intermediate and peripheral levels, health sector public-private partnerships (PPPs) have still been problematic (Ministry of Foreign Affairs of Denmark 2007: 106–110; Boulanger and Criel 2012: 99–102). In the case of Nyakahanga, Boulanger and Criel (2012: 99–102) point out that the contracting document for this hospital has not been updated since 1992 and it is incomplete in both form and content. The human resource problem has not been adequately addressed. In particular, there is no requirement to pay an equal salary to civil servants and the not-for-profit health organization's staff. As a result, Nyakahanga and many other faith-based health organizations have lost personnel to the public sector. At the same time, faith-sector representatives in Nyakahanga did not generally regard the monitoring practices as useful: it seemed that the public sector authorities did not really hear their concerns. The problems of the FBOs' loss of personnel due to unequal salaries and the fragility of trust in the related partnerships have also been more broadly recognized (Ministry of Foreign Affairs of Denmark 2007: 109–110).

Further, updated studies are needed about the dynamics of the inherent trust and fairness as well as the incentive structures of the country's transforming health system. But first, attaining a level of public funding for faith-based health organizations that enables the *equal salary principle* to be realized appears to be one advisable step towards the above-delineated *pluralistic cooperation for health* model. This could provide a clear baseline for fair cooperation between public and faith-based hospitals. *Improved dialogue*, in which the concerns of all parties come to be heard, recognized, and understood, would be another step towards such a model. It could also generate trust under circumstances where understandings of the terms of justice differ.

A diminishing role for the FBOs?

Dominic Haazen's (2012) study understandably focuses on improving the public sector opportunities to implement health justice in Tanzania. In a country where population growth will be rapid in the decades to come, it is of essential importance that public health care and publicly administered insurance schemes be continuously developed. Haazen (2012: viv-vx; 4–9) asserts that, assuming robust economic growth and increased public spending on health care, this is a quite realistic objective. What is more worrying to Haazen (2012: 16–17), however, is that measurable health outcomes have not been as impressive as the increased funding levels. This indicates that much will have to be improved in the efficiency of the system.

In Haazen's future Option 1 the number of public hospital beds is to be increased from 26,000 to 52,000, and in Option 2 to 63,200, by 2020. The number of faith-based and private hospital beds, in turn, would increase from 17,000 to 22,700 in Option 1, but only to 19,700 in Option 2. In the latter case the percentage of faith-based and private hospital beds would decrease from 39.8 to 23.7 percent of the total.[6] Haazen (2012: 63) bases this on the assumption that the Community Health Funds (CHF) and their urban equivalents would be coordinated with the public health facilities only. It is reasonable to ask, however, why he does not introduce any scenario in which the FBO sector might also be growing substantially? Referring to Suzan Makawia et al. (2010), Haazen (2012: 24–25) indeed notes that faith-based health services have been advantageous for the poor when compared with both public and private health service providers. This could be interpreted as indicating that it is worthwhile, especially in a health justice programme focusing on the poor, to pay particular attention to partnerships with the FBO sector.

Within the World Bank at large, collaboration with faith organizations have received increasing attention. John A. Rees (2010) has developed a particular dialogical approach on this front. Yet it takes a special effort to bring about initiatives in concrete terms in each context. Haazen may well have a sound view about the scenarios he represents, and not every future possibility needs to be addressed in a single report. But perhaps it would now be time for quite detailed scenarios as well that aim at taking the best advantage of the FBOs for the public health in a focused way.

The theories of health justice discussed above do not imply that the role of faith-based health services should be marginalized in any particular country. The case is rather that FBOs easily become neglected by theorists working within non-confessional paradigms. From faith perspectives, in turn, strengthening public health facilities is a desirable development indeed, for it promotes health justice. But insofar as faith organizations nevertheless are partners in health justice implementation, major studies on health justice should properly recognize their efforts and to seek ways to integrate them into the big picture in a fair manner.

One Lutheran hospital's perspective

Although Haazen's report suggests that the share of faith-based hospitals in Tanzania's health system is likely to decrease, the increased funding for health has helped FBOs to expand their health facilities in absolute terms. The 2011 annual report of the Nkoaranga Lutheran Hospital, in the Meru Diocese, supports this impression—as well as clarifies the current challenges this hospital has to face.

The number of staff at the Nkoaranga Lutheran Hospital (2012: 21–23) in December 2011 was 59, of which 11 had been hired in 2011. Simultaneously, government grants to the hospital—for medical staff salaries, drugs, and basket fund support—increased from 138.5 million Tz. in 2010 to 184.3 million Tz. in 2011 (Nkoaranga Lutheran Hospital 2012: 2; 21–22; 27). Hence the trend in this case has clearly been towards greater public funding, and thus at least in this respect towards a deeper integration of this faith-based hospital into the health system of the country.

The reported challenges which the Nkoaranga Lutheran Hospital (2012: 2–3; 24) still faces include a lack of staff, but also, for example, rising costs for drugs which patients are entitled to, a lack of ambulances, poor electrical system, and inadequate staff housing. Funds for the hospital are acquired in part through patient fees—which actually comprise the largest source of income for the hospital—in addition to being raised from different donors. The report does not give details of salary costs, but it does mention increased government resources for this purpose, and the hospital's continuous efforts to find additional funding from various sources. For the purposes of the current study, this illustrates the model of pluralist collaboration with increased government funding as a sign of a viable partnership between the MoH and a faith-based health organization.

One way in which the basis of faith comes forth in the case of the Nkoaranga Lutheran Hospital (2012: 2, 4) is that its annual report begins with a quote from Luke 10:9: "Heal the sick who are there and tell them, the Kingdom of God is near you." A couple of pages later, it is stated that the mission of the hospital is "to provide quality health care to our people so as to alleviate disease burden within our community ultimately glorifying GOD" (emphasis in the source). So the basis of the care work in Christian faith is explicit. This does not imply that the health services of the hospital are in any way less needed from the standpoint of the government or from that of the ill. For a reasonable collaboration, however, the faith should be expressed reasonably, and not in ways that could disrupt the care provided.

Foundational insights and the question of motivation

In FBOs, a standard theological assumption is that at the most foundational level the motivation for action is faith—whatever 'faith' refers to. FBOs typically explicate their understanding of faith in their official documents in terms of a vision, a mission, and values. The *Health Service Charter* of the ELCT (2010: 3) begins with a reference to the mission of the ELCT, being centered on Jesus Christ, and it then depicts the health sector work as "the healing arm of the church" that "aims to demonstrate Christ's love in offering healing and compassion for those people in need." The subsequent, more definitive formulation of the mission of the ELCT's (2010: 4) health work is, first of all, "[t]o witness and glorify God through [the] provision of holistic affordable and accessible quality health care supported by [the] community and other stakeholders."

During colonial times a major problem with medical missions was that they often focused more on the health needs of white people. Today, however, it is quintessential for Christian health work that it is for all people. According to the *Health Service Charter* of the ELCT (2010: 4), in particular, the church is to "[p]rovide health care to all people irrespective of creed, status or social inclination." This is understood to be perfectly compatible with faith in God and respecting life as sacred, and, for example, "Biblical teachings on caring for the body (or temple of God) and adhering to conditions that enable individuals and communities to improve their health status" (ELCT 2010: 4–5).

I would not say that health service thus understood is perfectly neutral in terms of faith and ideology, but it appears to be as reasonable as non-confessional agencies can hope for—insofar as they are willing to encounter FBOs dialogically at all. President Nyerere, for instance, promoted *Ujamaa*, or African Socialism. His vision, mission, and values, ideological as they were, nevertheless made cooperation with Christian health services on reasonable practical terms possible. Nor are business-based health services ideologically neutral, though their ideological intentions are usually not unreasonable when they conduct their business in a lawful way.

In the *pluralist cooperation for health* model it is perfectly acceptable for collaborators to have different views about the foundations of health justice. The related ideological and faith factors, however, must be reasonably compatible with broadly agreed practical health justice goals and principles. I see the ELCT health service mission as an example of this type of a confessional and at the same time reasonable understanding of health justice. It is not religiously neutral and it hardly can provide the sole basis of motivation for health work for most professionals in the field. As with health justice in general, Lutheran health justice is fragile. Yet it includes its own type of motivational resources for a broadly collaborative promotion of health justice.

German health economist Steffen Flessa has complained about the relative lack of a profound understanding of the impact of Christian religious motives on health economics in developing countries—particularly in East Africa, where church-related health services are highly prominent. Flessa (2005: 236) maintains that such an understanding should extend to the Biblical roots of Christian health work:

> Without a profound knowledge of the biblical value systems, health economists and public health specialists will not understand church-related health care and will lose opportunities to understand, cooperate and integrate in order to achieve a better health situation in developing countries.

Flessa (2005: 238) moves on to identify love, dignity, communication, stewardship, realism, and justice as Christian values. Health economics, which is often concerned with efficiency, comes close to the Christian value of stewardship. Christian stewardship, however, mostly complies with other Christian values such as justice as a "fundamental value," and love, which "must be the main motive of all church-related services" (Flessa 2005: 239). In the language of health economics, in addition to efficiency, the above-mentioned Christian values translate into affordability, sustainability, high quality, and participation. In Flessa's model, the main target groups of Christian diaconal work are the vulnerable, the poor, and the unhealthy (Flessa 2005: 238–240).

Flessa (2005: 243–244) points out that in Tanzania his approach would suggest less funding for high-cost treatments such as surgery in the biggest ELCT hospitals and more for comparatively cheap basic health services and preventive work. However, he reminds us that the values of Christian health work can also be conflicting and hard to explain in terms of health economics. Christians do this work because they are called to it. This motivational basis needs to be integrated into the dialogues with health economists and public health authorities, even though it does not fully translate into their language.

Yet according to the pluralist collaboration model the prevalence of a calling-centered motivation should not be seen as a justification for lower salaries. If, under non-ideal circumstances, employers simply cannot afford to pay full wages, then Christian health workers might choose to follow their calling anyway. In the model of pluralist collaboration all workers are equally recognized and dialogically integrated partners in a common effort to reach jointly endorsed high-level practical goals.

Concluding remarks

The idea of double-digit percentages of a nation's health services being provided by FBOs may sound odd to Europeans, and especially those in the Nordic region, who are accustomed to relying on broad public sector health services. Wide and affordable accessibility to health services, together with their high quality and stability, has been used to justify the *priority of public health* model of health care provision. From this perspective it might be tempting to assume that insofar as a public health system does not function ideally somewhere else, the recommendation should always be to work towards the primacy of the public sector model. In this approach, the role of faith-based health services would be to provide supportive health services in hard times, and in better times promote health justice mainly through relieving poverty and encouraging behavioral change.

In Tanzania, however, faith-based health organizations have been an integral part of the health system for generations. In my analysis I have found no reason to regard such an approach as particularly non-ideal. What is non-ideal is the prevalence of curable illness that still remains in this country, despite several health reforms backed by forceful national leaders and international donors alike. The World Bank study by Dominic Haazen (2012), while recognizing the positive impact of faith-based health work for the poor, focuses on the public sector reforms. As promising as this approach may be, it could be complemented with another scenario that takes more profoundly into account the possible benefits for health justice from partnerships between public authorities and faith-based health organizations. In fact, the current governmental health strategy of the country already includes promising initiatives on this front.

In our non-ideal world, any model of health justice is bound to be fragile. In virtually any context, there will be illness, lack of funding, lack of personnel, and mixed motivations to do health work. But likewise there will always be a need for health workers with a steadfast calling to help others, faith-based or not. Within the health justice discourse, dialogue must continue about the reasonableness of faith-based as well as non-religious ideological callings to health work. But there are reasons to beware of taking for granted a characteristically European approach to health justice, which might at least in some African contexts emphasize the secular public sector too straightforwardly and thus fail to be optimally collaborative and fair.

References

Boulanger, Delphine, and Criel, Bart. 2012. *The Difficult Relationship between Faith-Based Health Care Organizations and the Public Sector in Sub-Saharan Africa: The Case of Contracting Experiences in Cameroon, Tanzania, Chad and Uganda*. Antwerp: ITGPress.

Crisp, Nigel. 2010. *Turning the World Upside Down: The Search for Global Health in the 21st Century*. London: Royal Society of Medicine Press Ltd.

Daniels, Norman. 2008. *Just Health: Meeting Health Needs Fairly*. Cambridge: Cambridge University Press.

Easterly, William. 2006. *The White Man's Burden: Why the West's Efforts to Aid the Rest Have Done So Much Ill and So Little Good*. New York: Penguin Books.

ELCT. 2010. *The Health Charter*. Arusha: The Evangelical Lutheran Church in Tanzania (ELCT).

ELCT Health. 2013. Arusha: The Evangelical Lutheran Church in Tanzania (ELCT). http://health.elct.org, Internet; accessed 31 Oct 2013.

Flessa, Steffen. 2005. "Why Do Christians Care? Values and Objectives of Church-Related Health Services in Developing Countries." *Journal of Public Health* 13: 236–247.

Flessa, Steffen. 2007. "Investing in Health: Overcoming the Poverty Trap by Effective and Efficient Health Care. *Journal of Public Health*. DOI 10.1007/s10389–007–0115–3.

Garrett, Laurie. 2000. *Betrayal of Trust: The Collapse of Global Public Health*. New York: Hyperion.

Haazen, Dominic. 2012. *Making Health Financing Work for Poor People in Tanzania*. Washington, D.C.: The World Bank.

Makawia, Suzan, Machal, Jane, Ally, Mariam and Borghi, Josephine. 2010. *An Assessment of the Distribution of Health Service Benefits in Tanzania*. Ifakara: Ifakara Health Institute.

Memorandum of Understanding between the Partners (Government of Tanzania and Donors) Participating in the Pooled Funding ("Basket Funding") of the Health Sector. 2008. MOU FY03/04-FY0708.

The Ministry of Foreign Affairs of Denmark. 2007. *Joint External Evaluation of the Health Sector in Tanzania, 1999–2006*. http://www.evaluation.dk. Internet; accessed 7 February 2013.

Moyo, Dambisa. 2010. *Dead Aid: Why Aid Is Not Working and How There Is a Better Way for Africa*. New York: Farrar, Straus and Giroux.

Murray, Christopher J.L. et al. 2011. "Development Assistance for Health: Trends and Prospects." *The Lancet* 378, no. 9785 (2 July 2011): 8–10.

Nkoaranga Lutheran Hospital. 2012. *Annual Report for the Year 2011*. Usa River, Meru Diocese: Evangelical Lutheran Church in Tanzania.

Nyerere, Julius. 1967. *The Arusha Declaration, 5 February 1967*. Transcribed by Ayanda Madyibi. http://www.marxists.org/subject/africa/nyerere/1967/arusha-declaration.htm, Internet; accessed 21 Jan 2013.

Rees, John A. 2011. *Religion in International Politics and Development: The World Bank and Faith Institutions*. Cheltenham, UK: Edward Elgar.

Rosenberg, Mark L., Hayes, Elisabeth S., Macintyre, Margaret H. and Neill, Nancy. 2012. *Real Collaboration: What it Takes for Global Health to Succeed*. Berkley: University of California Press.

Ruger, Jennifer Prah. 2010. *Health and Social Justice*. Oxford: Oxford University Press.

Sachs, Jeffrey. 2006. *The End of Poverty: Economic Possibilities for Our Time*. New York: Penguin Books.

United Nations. 1948. *The Universal Declaration of Human Rights* (UDHR). http://www.un.org/en/documents/udhr. Internet; accessed 27 Dec 2012.

United Nations. 1966. *The International Covenant on Economic, Social and Cultural Rights* (ICESCR). http://www2.ohchr.org/english/law/cescr.htm. Internet; accessed 27 Dec 2012.

United Nations (2000). *The Right to the Highest Attainable Standard of Health E/C.12/2000/4: Substantive Issues Arising in the Implementation of ICESCR: General Comment No. 14*. http://www.unhchr.ch/tbs/doc.nsf/(symbol)/E.C.12.2000.4.En. Internet; accessed 27 December 2012.

United Nations Children's Fund. 2012. *Partnering with Religious Communities for Children*. New York: UNICEF. http://www.unicef.org/eapro/Partnering_with_Religious_Communities_for_Children.pdf. Internet; accessed 12 June 2012.

The United Republic of Tanzania. 2006. Annual Health Statistical Abstract. Dar-es-Salaam: Ministry of Health and Social Welfare. http://www.moh.go.tz/documents/Abstract_2006_Version 3.pdf. Internet; accessed 8 February 2012.

The United Republic of Tanzania. 2008. *Health Sector Strategic Plan III: July 2009–June 2015: "Partnership for Developing the MDGs."* Ministry of Health and Social Welfare. http://ihi.eprints.org/970/1/HealthSectorStrategicPlan.pdf. Internet; accessed 8 February 2013.

The United Republic of Tanzania. 2010. *Basic Facts and Figures on Human Settlement: Tanzania Mainland 2009*. Dar-es-Salaam: National Bureau of Statistics. http://www.nbs.go.tz/takwimu/references/Basic_Facts_and_Figures_on_Human_Settlements_2009.pdf. Internet; accessed 8 February 2013.

The United Republic of Tanzania. 2013. "National Website: Health." http://www.tanzania.go.tz/healthf.html. Internet; accessed 24 Nov 2013.

Venkatapuram, Sridhar. 2011. *Health Justice: An Argument from the Capabilities Approach*. Cambridge: Polity.

Wolff, Jonathan. 2012. *The Human Right to Health*. New York: W. W. Norton & Company.

World Health Organization. 1946. *The Constitution of the World Health Organization*. http://www.who.int/governance/eb/who_constitution_en.pdf. Internet; accessed 27 December 2012.

World Health Organization. 2010. *Health Systems Financing: The Path to Universal Coverage*. The World Health Report. http://whqlibdoc.who.int/whr/2010/9789241564021_eng.pdf. Internet; accessed 27 Dec 2012.

Notes

1 ICESCR follows here The Constitution of the World Health Organization (WHO 1946, Preamble).

2 My own perceptions and informal interviews during my trip to Tanzania in June 2012 have helped me to put such documents into context. I am most thankful to all those who helped me during this visit, especially to my most important guides Mauri and Ritva Niemi (the Finnish Evangelical Lutheran Mission) and Dr. Gwamaka Mwankenja (the Evangelical Lutheran Church in Tanzania).

3 Ruger argues that the capabilities approach is more plausible than its usual rivals at the level of goals. The ITA approach that Ruger defends, however, can be adopted without the presumption of the moral priority for the capability approach.

4 Different sources give slightly different numbers.

5 KCMC is an institution of the Good Samaritan Foundation of Tanzania and BMC of the Tanzania Episcopal Conference (TEC) of the Catholic Church.

6 According to the United Republic of Tanzania (2006: 12-14), the number of beds in government hospitals in 2006 was only 12,349, in voluntary/FBO hospitals 9,880, and in private ones 1,081 on the Tanzanian mainland, which works out to the percentages of 52, 41, and five, respectively, with the remaining ca. two percent as beds in parastatal hospitals.

CHAPTER NINE

Transformative Masculinity

Religion, Development and Gender in an Ecumenical Context

Kjetil Fretheim

Introduction

As the linkages between religion and development receive renewed attention from the scholarly community, the complexities of this relationship are being discovered. This has led some to challenge the understanding of religion as an obstacle to development, while others explore new ways of viewing religion as an integral part of development. Yet some tensions between the development agenda and religious identities and worldviews seem to remain. One such field of tension concerns gender—namely, women's rights and gender equality. Often these issues are interpreted as clashes between Western, liberal and secular values on the one hand and traditional, conservative and religious values on the other.

In the context of development studies, the concept of gender has become an important approach to studying and understanding development processes. Gender relations are seen as "an organising dimension within households, communities and public policies" (Pearson 2006: 189) and, thus, an integral part of the society where development takes place. The role of women and gender issues has also been highlighted in development policies during recent decades. Almost forty years ago, the year 1975 was declared International Women's Year and saw the first World Conference on Women (in Mexico). The decade that followed, from 1976 to 1985, was the UN Decade for Women, with follow-up conferences in Copenhagen

(1980), Nairobi (1985) and Beijing (1995). This international focus on women and gender issues has had an impact in the sense that a relatively broad consensus has been reached on several issues, expressed in both the Declaration on the Elimination of Violence against Women (DEVAW) and the Convention on the Elimination of All Forms of Discrimination against Women (CEDAW; see Parekh 2009). Nordic development policies in particular have had a noticeable gender focus, reflecting the emphasis on gender equality in Nordic domestic policies.

Today a wide range of national and international donors—both governmental and non-governmental—allocate substantial funds towards women's rights organizations. Often this is given an instrumental justification. UN WOMEN, for example, argues that gender-based violence must end because it "not only violates human rights, but also hampers productivity, reduces human capital and undermines economic growth."[1] However, in its recent World Development Report 2012, the World Bank challenged this understanding, emphasized the intrinsic value of ending gender-based violence, and discussed gender equality as a matter in its own right (World Bank 2011). Nordic and international donors have increasingly integrated religion and faith-based partners in their development policies. In fact, religion is now deployed by a wide range of international actors (donor states, non-governmental organizations, feminists, development practitioners and human rights activists) in their engagement with gender issues. Often their approach to religion is as instrumental as the understanding of gender issues in relation to productivity and economic growth has been.

Gender issues have also been addressed by religious groups themselves. One such example is the work done by various international ecumenical Christian organizations, which will be my focus as I describe and discuss recent gender initiatives by the World Council of Churches (WCC) and the Young Men's Christian Association (YMCA) movement. I will focus on their shared commitment to transformative masculinity as this is expressed in the WCC publication *Created in God's Image. From Hegemony to Partnership. A Church Manual on Men as Partners: Promoting Positive Masculinities* (Sheerattan-Bisnauth and Peacock 2010) and the on-going *transformative masculinity* program of the YMCA. The discussion focused on the latter will be based on documents from the African Alliance of YMCAs (AAY) and its Norwegian partner organization KFUK-KFUM Global. I will highlight key features of these initiatives and argue that they represent self-reflective, participatory and partnership-oriented faith-based gender-development projects. First, however, I will clarify what I mean by *religion* in this context and how the term *masculinity* relates to religion, development and gender.

Religion, development and gender

Political scientist Jeffrey Haynes distinguishes between two senses of the concept of religion. In a spiritual sense, religion relates to models of social and individual behaviour. Religion has to do with *transcendence* (supernatural realities), *sacredness* (a notion of the holy) and *ultimacy* (the ultimate concerns and conditions in people's lives). In the material sense, on the other hand, religious beliefs motivate "individuals and groups to act in pursuit of social or political goals" (Haynes 2011: 147). Against this background, especially considering the material dimension, it comes as no surprise that religion can play an important role in development processes. The question is rather what role religion does play in this context. As there are different kinds of religion, this is a complex matter; accordingly, it is necessary to speak of them in the plural: religions. In addition, religions are always interpreted in their contextual settings, and what is labelled Christianity might come across as quite different religious practices and worldviews—indeed, quite different religions—according to their contextual expressions.

The academic study of religion in society and development processes acknowledges this variation, but approaches and conceptualizes it in different ways. Sociologists of religion Paul Heelas and Linda Woodhead have suggested one typology as they distinguish among three main varieties of religion and spirituality: religions of difference, religions of humanity and spiritualties of life (Heelas and Woodhead 2000; Heelas and Woodhead 2005). Whereas the first emphasizes the authority of a transcendent reality external to the self, this authority is in the second variety located in the human or in humanity, while in the latter it is located in the self.

The same pluralism applies to faith-based organizations (FBOs) engaged in development work. At a superficial level, one can readily distinguish between FBOs: Some are conservative, others progressive, still others liberal organizations. Some are high church, others low church, etc. Drawing on discussions during Oxfam GB workshops Cassandra Balchin makes a distinction among progressive religious groups, conservative religious groups, fundamentalist religious groups and finally "extremists" or "the hate brigades" (Balchin 2011: 27–29). Such labels might lack analytical strength, but they still indicate the futility of lumping all these organizations together, assuming that they all carry the same added value, understanding of and approach to development. Yet in the typology offered by Heelas and Woodhead, the WCC and the YMCA would largely belong to the category "religions of humanity" as they both seem to emphasize a close connection between the work of God and the work of man, as well as the unity and fellowship of all human beings regardless of gender, sexual preference, ethnicity, political stance or religious affiliations (although this might not apply to all their member groups).

Regarding the crossroads among religion, development and gender, this is a field receiving growing attention from both development scholars and practitioners (Carroll 1983; Nussbaum 2000; Bradley 2006; Tomalin 2011). In 1998 Oxfam GB issued *Gender, Religion and Spirituality* which aimed to "analyse the complex relationship between culture, religion, and feminism, and how this is played out in gender and development work in countries of the South" (Sweetman 1998: 2). This complexity has also been the starting point for similar analysis within gender and development studies, although there seems to have been a stronger emphasis on gender issues in relation to fundamentalism and radical religion or religious movements (i.e., Hawley 1994; Howland 2001) than to mainline and mainstream churches. By focusing on WCC and the YMCA, this paper seeks to resist this bias and broaden the horizon of this field of research.

It seems one can find some degree of patriarchy, meaning a system based on and sustaining male privilege and domination and female subordination, in most—if not all—cultures and religions (Alkire 2006: 506–7; Staudt 2011: 165). However, religions and religious settings tend to be contradictory in relation to women's rights and gender issues. On the one hand, religion can be a source of violence against women, and religious teachings are frequently used to justify women's inequality in society. In the Christian context, one can note that already the first pages of the Bible can be used to underscore differences. In Genesis 2 (Adam and Eve), man is created first; this has been interpreted as reflecting man's superiority over woman. In Genesis 3:6, a woman is portrayed as the source of sin and consequential suffering. With support from Corinthians 11 (women covering the head in worship), this has been interpreted as legitimizing male domination over females.

On the other hand, religion can benefit women and give them an arena in which to mobilize forces, reform and resist: "The transcendent aspects of religious discourse can serve as a source of social change and political criticism, motivating women to make claims for equality, empowerment, and emancipation" (Jakobsen 2011: 129; see also Mahmood 2005). Support for gender equality in religious texts is also at hand (Tuyizere 2007), including in the Christian Bible. In Genesis 1:27, both man and woman are created in the same image of God. In 2. King 4:8–37, women are portrayed in roles equal to men, as is the case in several of Paul's letters in the New Testament (e.g., Gal 3:28).

This positive potential of religion with respect to gender issues has made faith-based actors attractive as development partners. However, in a report from the United Nations Research Institute for Social Development (UNRISD), Mariz Tadros identified what she refers to as a series of conundrums relating to the emerging understanding of FBOs as driving forces in the struggle for gender equality. She notes four such conundrums:

> The first conundrum is the difficulty in sometimes determining the nature of an FBO's gender agenda, because often a single organization takes different standpoints on various gender issues. The second conundrum is the complex way in which some FBOs provide women with a range of spiritual and social activities while at the same time delineating the ways in which they are expected to exercise their agency. The third conundrum lies in the fact that, while many FBOs may indeed be working successfully at the grassroots level, this does not necessarily mean that they all emerge from within the community or that they are necessarily "indigenous". The fourth conundrum has to do with the dilemmas women face when the extension of services and assistance is conditional on their conforming to the FBOs' interpretation of religiously appropriate gender roles and behaviour. (Tadros 2010: iii)

Thus, including gender in the analysis of the relationship between religion and development seems to only add to the complexity of this relationship, suggesting the need for more in-depth and empirical studies into this field. This chapter is one contribution towards achieving this goal.

The masculine and the feminine

A key task within gender studies is the inquiry into the stereotypes of men and women. Similarly, much of the focus on women and gender issues in development policies and studies—though often focusing on the role of women in development and the empowerment of women—have relied on the contrast between the masculine and the feminine. Yet the reality is much more complex than the simplified understanding of men as the strong and dominant and women as the weak and manipulated. First, there are several notions of women: They are the victims of war, but are also the survivors of conflict. They can be soldiers as well as caretakers. Second, the notions of men are as many and as varied. Men are corrupt and violent, breadwinners, indifferent and activists.

One of the main insights from gender studies is that, although the identities of men and women tend to be seen as natural and thus inevitable, these categories are socially constructed and dynamic (Parekh 2009: 233). This insight implies that what is in fact fluid and in flux is made static and fixed. Consequently, power is a key concept in the field of gender studies. Another implication is that gender studies not only have a political interest, but also come across as a normative field (McElroy 2002). There is a dedicated focus on women as an oppressed and marginalized group, but also on inquiries into ways of ending such oppression and on women's empowerment.

Considering these characteristics of gender studies, it comes as no surprise that gender studies have been integrated into the field of development studies (Young

1988; Cornwall, Harrison and Whitehead 2007). A key publication in this respect is Ester Boserup's *Women's Role in Economic development* (Boserup 1970), in which Boserup highlighted the role of women in development processes and prepared the ground for the "women in development" approach (WID) in gender and development studies. An important political and normative concern in this approach was to include women as both participators and beneficiaries of development programs, and it was argued that women should have equal access to education, technology and commercial markets (Pearson 2006: 191–192).

WID reflected a modernist approach to development issues, but since this was increasingly being questioned towards the end of the 1970s, new approaches to understanding the role of women in development were called for. One proposal was coined the "women and development" approach (WAD; see, for example, Sen and Grown 1985). At this point, it was argued that "the problem was not women [being] marginalized from development but the development model itself and the terms on which women were integrated" (Pearson 2006: 192).

Both WID and WAD are characterized by an explicit focus on women, women's rights and women's living conditions. Over time this led to a questioning of the lack of focus on men in both theory and practice, and as a result the development field has been opened up to include an interest in both men and women. This led to a third approach: gender and development (GAD). GAD highlights "not the identities of women as opposed to men in developing countries, but the gender ideologies, structures and norms which construct the different positioning of both men and women" (Pearson 2006: 192).[2] In other words, GAD relied on the previously mentioned constructivist notion of gender. This approach also opened up a renewed study of how notions of masculinity are constructed in relation and opposition to notions of the feminine and vice versa. Accordingly, masculinity and masculinity studies have become part of the agenda in both gender and development studies (Cornwall, Edström and Greig 2011).

The focus on masculinity has led to a new take on the familiar issue of patriarchy. Referring to the African context, Jeanette Malherbe pointed out how an "analysis of the masculine stereotype for instance (assertive, physically strong, self-willed, rational and logical, authoritative, etc.) shows that to be a man in our society is to be in a very privileged position" (Malherbe 2000: 6). This privileged position is also a relational position. She asserted:

> The feminine condition is determined in large part by the masculine condition. Women broadly speaking can be self-sacrificing and subservient only if men are self-willed and dominating. That is, the masculine gender is the complement of the feminine; to understand or change the one involves understand and changing the other. [. . .], the male sex and the masculine gender (the two are not the same) do in fact feature in any

> discussion of gender. Men are always present by implication, as those whom women are to serve and nurture, heed and obey; they are present as the background for the feminine condition. (Malherbe 2000: 6)

The term *masculinity* refers here to the notion of manhood, the typical traits and characteristics, and the roles and kind of behaviour associated with men. However, being a social construction, masculinity is also closely related to context-specific conditions (see Connell 2000; Kimmel, Hearn and Connell 2005). Accordingly, as there are many contexts and thus versions of masculinity, this term is often used in its plural as well: masculinities. Even within specified contexts, there might be a number of such masculinities. The general point that gender must be understood as relational and dynamic also applies to masculinity. Masculinities are created in contrast to notions of womanhood, but as they are created, change and intervention are also possible.

One example of masculinity is the machismo common in Latin America, which refers to a kind of excessive masculinity with a strong element of bravado, fierceness and domineering (Sheerattan-Bisnauth and Peacock 2010: 206). Such masculinity is not limited to Latin America; similar masculinities can be found elsewhere. Writing from and about the African context, and more specifically reflecting on the HIV and AIDS epidemic, Ezra Chitando identified three aspects of dominant masculinities in southern Africa: 1) particular constructions of male sexuality that lead men into risky sexual behaviours, 2) men being prevented from engaging in the provision of care to people living with HIV, and 3) dominant masculinities contributing to the stigmatization of women living with HIV (according to van Klinken 2011: 278; see also Morrell 2001; Cornwall 2005; Ouzgane and Morrell 2005).

When explaining this kind of masculinity, Chitando makes the contextual character of masculinity his starting point. However, in contrast to other scholars, he noted the religious factor and argued that the dominant masculinities in Southern Africa are closely linked to patriarchal religious gender ideologies (according to van Klinken 2011: 278). It is against this background that various church bodies have begun to address masculinity specifically as part of their work with gender. I will now discuss two ecumenical examples of this: one from the context of the WCC and one from the YMCA movement.

WCC: Partnership and bible study

The WCC is an umbrella organization for most mainline Christian churches, the most prominent exemption being the Catholic Church. WCC was founded in

1948 and is involved in both inter-denominational and inter-religious dialogue, development and advocacy work. It works in close cooperation with other international church organizations, such as the Lutheran World Federation (LWF) and the World Communion of Reformed Churches (WCRC), and through the ACT Alliance and the Ecumenical Advocacy Alliance (EAA). Regarding gender, and inspired by the UN's Decade against Violence against Women, the WCC called for an Ecumenical Decade of the Churches: In Solidarity with Women from 1988 to 1998. The ecumenical decade was designed to keep the concerns of the UN decade alive. Key topics were violence against women, women's full participation in the life of the church, the global economic crisis and its effects on women and racism and xenophobia and their effects on women.

In 2010, WCC and WCRC jointly published *Created in God's Image. From Hegemony to Partnership*, presented as *A Church Manual on Men as Partners: Promoting Positive Masculinities* (Sheerattan-Bisnauth and Peacock 2010). This publication follows the *Created in God's Image: From hierarchy to partnership* (WARC 2003), a gender manual that focused on women, and a process where the World Alliance of Reformed Churches (WARC, later WCRC) and partners began to self-critically reconsider the way they engaged in addressing gender issues. This implied that they began:

> . . . a process of gender conscientization for men to promote positive masculinities and men's empowerment for partnership of women and men. This process is aimed at unravelling various forms of manhood from a faith perspective. It takes various approaches, which examine and question hegemonic masculinity and provide space for creating enabling environments in which men and women work towards re-defining, re-ordering, re-orienting and thus transforming dominant masculinity. Re-reading and studying the Bible with the perspective of gender justice is essential in the process. (Sheerattan-Bisnauth 2010: 3)

The specific focus on men and masculinities is, in other words, quite explicit. However, important distinctions are made among hegemonic masculinity, dominant masculinity and not least positive masculinities. As the overall aim is to change hegemonic or dominant masculinity and to promote different and more positive kinds of masculinity, it seems the WCC here relies on the same constructivist notions of gender and masculinity favoured in recent academic discussions on the topic. This focus on men and masculinities does not seem to imply a disregard of women or the relationships between men and women. To the contrary, the process of gender conscientization implies both promoting positive masculinities and a partnership of women and men.

This latter dimension of the WCC publication can be read as a continuation of earlier efforts to focus on women and women's rights, but it is also in line with the constructivist understanding of masculinity as a relational concept and something which must be understood in relation and contrast to notions of who women are, what they do and the roles they play. It is made clear that the publication is "based on the understanding that gender includes both men and women and any attempt to transform gender relations must be inclusive of both" (Sheerattan-Bisnauth 2010: 4). The constructivist take on gender and masculinity is equally explicit: "The approach is not to demonize men or to instil feelings of guilt and powerlessness but to peel away the layers of gender construction which are key to understanding manhood within specific cultural, economic, political and social contexts" (Sheerattan-Bisnauth 2010: 5).

This concern "not to demonize men" is worth noting. On several occasions in the document, various contributors are eager to explain and justify this specific focus on men while being equally eager to avoid misunderstandings or alternative interpretations of the underlying agenda when adopting such an approach. The bishop of the Anglican Diocese of Southern Malawi James Tengatenga contextualizes the focus on men against the background of gender conflict:

> There is a battle raging: men against women. The solution for a long time has been to talk to women and empower them for the struggle. There is no doubt that when bringing groups from the margins it is necessary to have them apart for empowerment without the dominant lot. However, the dominant lot always reads such action as ganging up against them and, in reaction, either sneer at the programme or work out rightly against it. This is what has happened with gender work. It has been construed as women trying to work against men to emasculate them. Mutuality, interdependence and partnership envisaged by advocates for gender equality and justice are missed. With their masculinity considered to be at stake, men feel threatened and see the world rising up against them and this causes them to become defensive. (Tengatenga 2010: 7)

The WCRC general secretary, Rev. Dr. Setri Nyomi, is less backward looking, but reflects the same analysis when he underscores sensitivity and a will to dialogue. He argued that *Created in God's Image:*

> . . . has been developed with sensitivity to invite men into dialogue and critical examination of what it means to be man in today's society. It is neither confrontational nor prescriptive, but takes into consideration that gender analysis needs to be contextual and must be done with gender justice perspectives. (Sheerattan-Bisnauth and Peacock 2010: preface)

Against this background, it is not surprising that the concept of partnership receives such a prominent position throughout this WCC publication (most explicitly in Peacock 2010).

The other key feature of the process leading up to this WCC/WCRC publication and of the publication itself is that it seeks to address the issue of masculinity and partnerships between men and women from a faith-based perspective. This is not surprising, given the Christian identity of the contributors and the publisher, but it also highlights the specific contribution the churches see themselves as able to offer when addressing these issues. Bible studies and the re-reading of biblical texts is specified as "essential in the process" (Sheerattan-Bisnauth 2010: 3).

Revisiting religious sources of authority is a well-known strategy amongst those seeking to change religious and/or social practices. In the context of the evangelical Christian development organization World Vision, this has been a key strategy: "Giving biblical evidence of Jesus' positive attitude to women's status and needs is a key strategy in promoting our policy on gender with our own staff, partner organisations and with communities in the countries where we work" (Tripp 1998: 62). One way of providing such "biblical evidence" could be to refer to those texts and biblical passages that seem to give support to women's rights and gender equality. However, and as previously noted, religions are contradictory; this applies to Christianity as well. As noted earlier, the Bible itself is ambivalent about the role of women in relation to men and the use of violence (see also Prior 1997; Davies 2010).

A more comprehensive strategy compared to the one adopted by World Vision, and the one advocated in this WCC publication, is to deal with even the difficult parts of the biblical tradition. According to Bishop Tengatenga:

> The patriarchy of the Old Testament and some of the Pauline corpus will need to be reviewed in the light of partnership and gender justice. Not only is biblical hermeneutics at issue here but also a hermeneutic of suspicion needs to be applied to our cultural and social contexts together with the changing dynamics of our societies that have led to calling into question gender role stereotypes. (Tengatenga 2010: 8–9)

Bible studies in this context become an instrument for the liberation of masculinities. Texts addressed in the WCC publication include Genesis 19 (Sodom and Gomorrah destroyed) and 39 (Joseph and Potiphar's wife), Ruth 2 (Ruth meets Boaz in the grain field), Galatians 3 (children of God), Ephesians 5 (instructions for Christian households) and Luke 8 (Jesus raises a dead girl and heals a sick woman); these are made the normative starting point in search for alternative masculinities. Another text frequently used in this context and for such purposes is the text about Tamar, a young woman who is raped by her half-brother in 2. Samuel 13 (Ackerman 2004; Nyabera and Montgomery 2007), which was used as a starting point for a campaign to combat gender-based violence.

To summarize, a key feature of this WCC publication is a return to traditional, religious and normative sources and the attempt to reinterpret, contextualize and apply insights in or from these texts to the current situation of patriarchy and in the (re)construction of masculinity. It is at the same time a reaffirming, reclaiming and reinterpretation of the Christian faith and a reinterpretation and reconstruction of masculinity through a reading of religious texts. The publication is also characterized by a strong focus on the close links between notions of the masculine and the feminine and the need for, and importance of, male–female partnerships in the struggle for gender equality and justice.

YMCA: Participation and transformation

The YMCA is an ecumenical movement present in more than 125 countries. The international World Alliance of YMCAs was founded in 1855 following the adoption of the Paris Basis stating the guiding principles for national YMCAs and the relationship between them. The movement has roots in Evangelical and so-called Muscular Christianity, but is today known more for its open program and membership policy, community development programs and children and youth work. With regard to gender, the YMCA has focused on gender issues on their own and in partnership with their sister organization, the Young Women's Christian Organization (YWCA). Their joint Bible reading plan for 2010–11, *Women Creating a Safe World* (World YWCA and World Alliance of YMCAs 2010), is only one example of their shared commitment to gender issues. The YMCA was also part of the Tamar campaign (in 2007) addressing gender-based violence.

The transformative masculinity program is a recent and on-going example of YMCA involvement in addressing gender issues. It was initiated by the regional African Alliance of YMCAs (AAY) in 2009 and involves national YMCA movements in several countries in Southern Africa: Madagascar, South Africa, Zambia and Zimbabwe. It is presented as part of a wider agenda of the AAY and its larger vision of an African Renaissance. Moses Malunda, Chair of the Southern Zone of AAY, explained that the program is "designed to bring about renewal and transformation. This impact will be our contribution to the realisation of our shared African YMCA vision of empowering young people for the African Renaissance."[3] The African Renaissance is claimed to be "based on a core identity of ecumenism, youth focus and African-ness" and a commitment to redefining a future for "African YMCAs which involves self-determination."[4] The program is also part of a larger program entitled *From Subject to Citizen: Building the Civic Competence of Youth in Africa* which seeks to empower youth to demand their rights and influence decision makers around them.

The transformative masculinity program is a three-year project which relies on a highly participatory methodology as it is argued that "the only way forward is to now begin to focus on transformative masculinity for boys and young men and work from a partnership approach."[5] The activities include participatory research, regional workshops and group work, although emphasis is on the establishment of Y-Clubs for youths between 13 and 19 years (with four specific activities and different types of mentoring and dialogue activities) and Renaissance-clubs (R-clubs) for youth between the ages of 20 and 35 (with vertical mentoring, where older youths mentor younger ones on re-defining masculinity; see NORAD application form 2009). Three "change objectives" are identified:

> The first is to reorient youth masculinity from a hegemonic to a transformative state. [. . .] The second change objective is to transform male identity and roles by engaging the structures that disempower men. [. . .] The third identified change objective is to establish a power understanding that produces mutually enhancing relationships between the two genders. (Ngunyi 2009: 8)

The YMCA also presents the program as a step away from former and more traditional approaches to gender issues and, thus, a result of a self-critical assessment of earlier commitments. As in the example from WCC, this implies a new and explicit emphasis on the role of men. Carlos Sanvee, the general secretary of Africa Alliance of YMCAs, wrote: "Without compromising our quest for dignity for young girls, we have decided to go a step further—to address the root causes and perpetrators of violence and exploitation of our sisters and mothers in Africa" (Sanvee 2009: 1).

The program was initiated against the backdrop of "the dire need in Southern Africa for gender transformation" and the explicit intention to "specifically address young boys in their developmental phase."[6] In an initial application for financial funding to The Norwegian Agency for Development Cooperation (NORAD), the problem the YMCA seeks to address is described as a two-fold crisis: a material and a moral crisis. The material crisis is characterized by a lack of and poor education, unemployment and "the invasion of foreign capital and its impact on young people" (NORAD application form 2009: 4). All of this leads to what is termed "economic inertia." Regarding the moral crisis, it is claimed that this has multiple manifestations:

> Critical amongst these is the prevalence of a "subjugated masculinity." Under this, young men are socialised to indignify others in order to gain significance and social relevance, Rape, crime and banditism are obvious outcomes. [. . .] Most of the rape cases are done by young men. And a majority of them are gang rapes. The boys argue that this is a form of male bonding. This distorted masculinity is also about hegemony, dominance and power. We expect to tackle the root-causes of these symptoms by re-ordering youth masculinity. (NORAD application form 2009: 2)

Against this background, the stated intention is, in line with the WCC publication, to "re-define, re-order and re-orient youth masculinity" which together is referred to as "transformative masculinity" (NORAD application form 2009: 3). This is understood in contrast to "hegemonic masculinity," which is understood to be dominant in the African context:

> In Africa, the male gender is socially constructed to be hegemonic. If it is not dominant, it is not male. As a result, even male weakness is understood to be superior to femaleness. The female has to be caricatured for the male to "happen." And this is why in Southern Africa, rape is seen as a way of asserting male hegemony. Similarly, the young man is socialised to believe that having multiple sex partners is a symbol of "hegemonic power." To establish hegemony in some places, a young man has to kill as a sign of masculinity. (NORAD application form 2009: 3)

It is interesting to note how the roots of this kind of masculinity are described. In the same document, it is explained that:

> In Southern Africa, this hobbled notion of masculinity has a basis in the history of white rule. Because the system dominated the male gender, the man found himself in need of hegemonic space at home. As a result, he sought to dominate the woman in return. But there was a complication. The woman, especially in the "mining countries," was financially independent and tended to tease the dominated man. In retaliation, the male folk established hegemony through rape, GBV and other forms of discrimination. Unfortunately, the social construction of this hegemony has now been transferred to the next generation despite the shift from white domination to the new republics. This cultural misnomer is what we seek to address. (NORAD application form 2009: 3)

To summarize, the YMCA's transformative masculinity program addresses gender equality and gender-based violence in much the same way as WCC. It also has a clear focus on the role of boys and men and related notions of masculinity. It includes the same emphasis on partnership and joint action between men and women. The main difference is perhaps the return to biblical texts found in the WCC publication and the much more participatory approach advocated by the YMCA. This difference can, at least in part, be explained by referring to the differences between a publication and a program, but also indicates the range of approaches and strategies that can be found among international ecumenical organizations. The social and structural analysis and focus on root causes are also stronger in the presentation of the YMCA program and show how some religious actors do not limit themselves to a religious field separate from the wider society. On the contrary, YMCA clearly bases the transformative masculinity program on a postcolonial social analysis that goes beyond the borders of the religious group or setting.

Conclusion

International and ecumenical Christian organizations represent important FBOs involved in the development field. Their size in terms of both human and financial resources makes them an obvious object of research interest for scholars in the field of religion and development. They also largely represent mainline churches and Christian organizations as well as what can be seen as a spirituality of humanity. Finally, these organizations are often involved in addressing gender issues, such as gender equality and gender-based violence. Thus, studying these organizations fills an important research gap at the crossroads among religion, development and gender.

The two cases highlighted herein, the WCC publication *Created in God's Image* and the transformative masculinity program of the African Alliance of YMCAs, demonstrate key features of how these organizations address gender issues. They share a focus on masculinity and partnership between men and women, but emphasize in different ways the use of religious sources (biblical texts) and popular participation. This indicates their shared commitment to addressing social and development issues from a faith-based perspective, but also the range of approaches adopted by these organizations. In both cases the commitment to addressing gender issues comes across as an integral part of their work and activities.

When studying religion, development and gender, scholars need to adopt a critical approach to religion and FBOs, but it is also necessary to understand the self-critical dimension of religion and spirituality noted in this discussion. Religion is not only ambiguous, but can also be both self-reflective and self-critical, as noted in both cases discussed in this paper. This reflexivity is an important resource for both religious and development actors, as it prepares the foundation for a process that might change patriarchal structures and gender-based violence—indeed, FBOs and religions themselves.

References

Ackerman, Denise. 2004. "Tamar's Cry: Re-Reading an Ancient Text in the Midst of an HIV and AIDS pandemic." In Grant me justice!: *HIV/AIDS & gender readings of the Bible*, ed. Musa. W. Dube and Rachel A. Kanyoro, 27-59. Pietermaritzburg: Cluster Publications.

Alkire, Sabine. 2006. "Religion and Development." In *The Elgar Companion to Development Studies*, ed. David A. Clark, 502-510. Cheltenham: Edward Elgar.

Balchin, Cassandra. 2011. *Avoiding Some Deadly Sins. Oxfam learnings and analysis about religion, culture, diversity, and development*. Oxford: Oxfam GB.

Boserup, Ester. 1970. *Woman's Role in Economic Developmen*. New York: St. Martin's Press.

Bradley, Tamsin. 2006. *Challenging the NGOs: Women, religion, and western dialogues in India.* London: Tauris Academic Studies.

Carroll, Theodora F. 1983. *Women, Religion, and Development in the Third World.* New York: Praeger.

Connell, Raewyn W. 2000. *The men and the boys.* Cambridge: Polity.

Cornwall, Andrea. 2005. *Readings in Gender in Africa.* London: International African Institute in association with Indiana University Press.

Cornwall, Andrea, Edström, Jerker and Greig, Alan. 2011. *Men and Development: Politicizing masculinities.* London: Zed Books.

Cornwall, Andrea, Harrison, Elisabeth and Whitehead, Ann. 2007. *Feminisms in Development: Contradictions, contestations and challenges.* London: Zed Books.

Davies, Eryl W. 2010. *The Immoral Bible: Approaches to biblical ethics.* London: T&T Clark.

Hawley, John S. 1994. *Fundamentalism and Gender.* New York: Oxford University Press.

Haynes, Jeffrey. 2011. "Religion." *In Politics in the Developing World,* ed. Peter Burnell, Vicky Randall and Lise Rakner, 145-163. Oxford: Oxford University Press.

Heelas, Paul and Woodhead, Linda. 2000. *Religion in Modern Times: An interpretive anthology.* Oxford: Blackwell.

Heelas, Paul and Woodhead, Linda. 2005. The Spiritual Revolution: *Why religion is giving way to spirituality.* Malden, MA: Blackwell Publ.

Howland, Courtney W. 2001. *Religious Fundamentalisms and the Human Rights of Women.* New York: Palgrave.

Jakobsen, Janet R. 2011. "Gender in the Production of Religious and Secular Violence." In *The Blackwell Companion to Religion and Violence*, ed. Andrew R. Murphy, 125-136. Chichester: Wiley-Blackwell.

Kimmel, Micheal S., Hearn, Jeff and Connell, Raewyn W. 2005. *Handbook of Studies on Men & Masculinities.* Thousand Oaks, CA: Sage.

Mahmood, Saba. 2005. *Politics of Piety: The Islamic revival and the feminist subject. Princeton*, NJ: Princeton University Press.

Malherbe, Jeanette. 2000. "Gender Studies and Transformation." In *Women, Society and Constraints*, ed. Jeanette Malherbe, Marc Kleijwegt and Elize Koen, 1-11. Pretoria: Unisa Press.

McElroy, Wendy. 2002. *Liberty for Women. Freedom and Feminism in the Twenty-First Century.* Chicago: Ivan R. Dee.

Morrell, Robert. 2001. *Changing Men in Southern Africa.* Pietermaritzburg: University of Natal Press.

Ngunyi, Mutahi. 2009. "YMCA transformative masculinity approach." In *Siyahamba*, African Alliance of YMCAs Newsletter, Issue 14 July.

NORAD application form. 2009. *Individual agreements 2009.* March 14.

Nussbaum, Martha C. 2000. *Women and Human Development. The Capabilities Approach.* Cambridge: Cambridge University Press.

Nyabera, Fred and Montgomery, Taryn (ed.). 2007. *Tamar Campaign. Contextual Bible Study Manual on Gender-Based Violence. Nairobi*: The Fellowship of Christian Councils and Churches in the Great Lakes and The Horn of Africa (FECCLAHA).

Ouzgane, Lahoucine and Morrell, Robert. 2005. *African Masculinities: Men in Africa from the late nineteenth century to the present*. New York: Palgrave Macmillan.

Parekh, Serena. 2009. "Gender and Human Rights." In *The Ashgate Research Companion to Ethics and International Relations*, ed. Patrich Hayden, 233-246. Farnham: Ashgate.

Payne, Anthony and Phillips, Nicola. 2010. *Development*. Cambridge: Polity.

Peacock, Phillip. V. 2010. "Towards a Theology of Partnership of Women and Men." In *Created in God's Image: From Hegemony to Partnership. A Church Manual on Men as Partners: Promoting Positive Masculinities*, ed. Patricia Sheerattan-Bisnauth and Phillip V. Peacock, 36-42. Geneva: World Communion of Reformed Churches/World Council of Churces.

Pearson, Ruth. 2006. "Gender and Development." In *The Elgar Companion to Development Studies*, ed. David A. Clark, 189-196. Cheltenham, UK: Edward Elgar.

Prior, Michael. 1997. *The Bible and Colonialism: A moral critique*. Sheffield: Sheffield Academic Press.

Sanvee, Carlos. 2009. "Greetings YMCA family and friends." In *Siyahamba*, Africa Alliance of YMCAs Newsletter, Issue 14 July.

Sen, Gita and Grown, Caren. 1985. *Development, Crisis, and Alternative Visions: Third World women's perspectives*. New Delhi: DAWN.

Sheerattan-Bisnauth, Patricia. 2010. "Introduction." In *Created in God's Image: From Hegemony to Partnership. A Church Manual on Men as Partners: Promoting Positive Masculinities*, ed. Patricia Sheerattan-Bisnauth and Phillip V. Peacock, 2-6. Geneva: World Communion of Reformed Churches/World Council of Churces.

Sheerattan-Bisnauth, Patricia and Peacock, Phillip V. (ed.). 2010. *Created in God's Image: From Hegemony to Partnership. A Church Manual On Men as Partners: Promoting Positive Masculinities*. Geneva: World Communion of Reformed Churches/World Council of Churches.

Staudt, Kathleen. 2011. "Women and Gender." In *Politics in the Developing World*, ed. Peter Burnell, Vicky Randall and Lise Rakner, 164-181. Oxford: Oxford University Press.

Sweetman, Caroline (ed.). 1998. *Gender, Religion and Spirituality*. Oxford: Oxfam GB.

Tadros, Mariz. 2010. *Faith-Based Organizations and Service Delivery*. Geneva: United Nations Research Institute for Social Development (UNRISD).

Tengatenga, James. 2010. "Transformative Masculinities in Partnership for Gender Justice." In *Created in God's Image: From Hegemony to Partnership. A Church Manual on Men as Partners: Promoting Positive Masculinities*, ed. Patricia Sheerattan-Bisnauth and Phillip V. Peacock, 7-9. Geneva: World Communion of Reformed Churches/World Council of Churches.

Tomalin, Emma (ed.). 2011. *Gender, Faith and Development*. Bourton on Dunsmore, Rugby: Practical Action Publishing.

Tripp, Linda. 1998. "Gender and development from a Christian perspective: Experience from World Vision." In *Gender, Religion and Spirituality*, ed. Caroline Sweetman, 62-68. Oxford: Oxfam GB.

Tuyizere, Alice P. 2007. *Gender and Development: The role of religion and culture*. Kampala: Makerere University.

van Klinken, Adriaan. 2011. "Transforming masculinities towards gender justice in the era of HIV and AIDS. Plotting the pathways." In *Religion and HIV and AIDS; charting the terrain*, ed. Beverley Haddad, 275-296. Scotsville: University of KwaZulu-Natal Press.

World Bank. 2011. *World Development Report 2012: Gender Equality and Development.* Washington, DC: The World Bank.

World YWCA and World Alliance of YMCAs. 2010. *Women Creating a Safe World. Bible Reading Plan 2010-2011.* Geneva: World YWCA and World Alliance of YMCAs.

Young, Kate. 1988. *Women and Economic Development: local, regional and national planning strategies.* Oxford: Berg/Unesco.

Notes

1 www.unifem.org/gender_issues/violence_against_women/ (website for UN WOMEN, accessed 22.03.12)

2 For an overview of WAD, WID and GAD, see also Payne and Phillips 2010: 125-131.

3 Quoted in the article Transforming participation of youth in Africa through Southern Zone YMCA programmes, http://www.africaymca.org/index.php/template/lorem-ipsum-ii/news-archive/itemlist/date/2009/6?catid=73 (accessed 28.2.12).

4 Gil Harper, in the article Transforming participation of youth in Africa through Southern Zone YMCA programmes, http://www.africaymca.org/index.php/template/lorem-ipsum-ii/news-archive/itemlist/date/2009/6?catid=73 (accessed 28.2.12).

5 Annie Ngwire, national general secretary of Zambia YMCA, in the article Transforming participation of youth in Africa through Southern Zone YMCA programmes, http://www.africaymca.org/index.php/template/lorem-ipsum-ii/news-archive/itemlist/date/2009/6?catid=73 (accessed 28.2.12).

6 Gil Harper, in the article Transforming participation of youth in Africa through Southern Zone YMCA programmes, http://www.africaymca.org/index.php/template/lorem-ipsum-ii/news-archive/itemlist/date/2009/6?catid=73 (accessed 28.2.12).

CHAPTER TEN

Transforming Masculinities Male Care Volunteers in Tanzania

Auli Vähäkangas

Introduction

The recent AIDS research in Africa has noted that an important part of the whole problem on the continent is masculinity (Van Klinken 2013; Wyrod 2008; Colvin, Robins and Leavens 2010). The focus of these previous studies has been transforming the masculinities of HIV-positive people as individuals. Masculinities are constructed in all societies in a community, but community is especially central when constructing masculinities in Africa. There is a need to analyse the transformation of masculinities in the larger communities by not focusing exclusively on a certain group of people. This research responds to this need by focusing on the male care volunteers who are part of their local village communities in Tanzania.

In this chapter, masculinities are understood as social construction(s) of male gender identities and men's place in gender relations following van Klinken's (2010) practical definition. The previous discussion of masculinities in Africa has identified three basic types of masculinities: African theologians driving for gender equality and discussing ideal masculinities (Nadar and Phiri 2012; Chitando 2012; Chitando and Chirongoma 2012), a middle way which van Klinken calls "soft patriarchy" (van Klinken 2012) and at the other end strong, "hegemonic" patriarchy (Morrell et al. 2012). My aim is to evaluate which of these masculinities would come closest to male care volunteers studied in this chapter.

Study context and aim of research

This study analyses the role of male volunteers in serving the dying patients in the Selian Hospice and Palliative Care Programme in Arusha, Tanzania. This program launched the "Tanzanian model" and is renowned for its success and multidisciplinary approach in caring for dying patients. Since its initiation, the number of patients has increased rapidly; in April 2012, the program was serving approximately 5,000 patients, the largest group being those with AIDS although individuals with TB and cancer were also served. This program uses trained volunteers who make regular home visits as well as provide day care service while the multidisciplinary team visits the sick in the villages. I conducted field research on this program in 2009 and found a need to focus more closely on volunteers (Vähäkangas 2010; 2012).

Previous research on volunteers who provide care and support for people living with HIV/AIDS has indicated that most volunteers in Africa are women (Kasimbazi and Sliep 2011: 95–110). Only very few studies have researched the care role of men in Africa (Chindomu and Matinzamhuka 2012). However, one interesting aspect among the studied Selian volunteers is that almost half of them are men. Furthermore, previous research on volunteering has emphasized that the pattern of volunteering might be rather different between men and women (Edgardh 2011; Taniguchi 2006). Thus, the aim of this chapter is to find out:

- Why do many men volunteer in the Selian Hospice and Palliative Care Programme?
- What motivates these men to continue their unpaid service?
- How does the role of male care volunteers contribute to the discussion of masculinities?

Data collection and analysis

In April 2012, I spent two weeks with the Selian Hospice and Palliative Care team, during which time I attended day care in two rural villages (one mining community and one plantation community) and in a semi-urban village outside of Arusha town. I also visited the sick in the Arusha Lutheran Medical Centre, a hospital in Arusha town, and attended team meetings and a monthly meeting organized for the volunteers of one of the districts.

I interviewed forty volunteers: twenty-two females and eighteen males. Eight of the males were church workers, all of them evangelists of the Evangelical Lutheran Church in Tanzania (ELCT). The participants were between twenty-three and sixty-five years old and were from various ethnic and religious backgrounds. Five were Muslims, while the others were members of various Christian churches, the majority belonging to the Lutheran Church. This is natural as the Selian team has an ELCT background and serves in a predominantly Lutheran area. The original objective was to conduct individual interviews; however, on two occasions, a small group of volunteers were in same place at the same time, making it more natural to conduct the interview as a small focus group than to send the additional members away. All three participants in the first focus group were ELCT evangelists, middle-age men and part of the same volunteer training course. Thus, their backgrounds, experiences and views were similar, which they stated during the interview. The second focus group consisted of two female volunteers who similarly shared many views; each had served as volunteers for approximately the same number of years.

Whereas the original intention was to record all the interviews, this was not possible due to the recorder malfunctioning. Thus, the seven interviews that were conducted on the day of the malfunction are recorded in my field research diary only. As an interviewer, conducting interviews by only recording notes was a new experience for me. The interviewees were extremely relaxed during these interviews. For example, they explained one idea and then waited for me to write that down and after my writing, they continued directly from where they had left off. The interviews during this study were generally rather brief, lasting approximately fifteen minutes, with the shortest being less than ten minutes. The interviewee with the shortest interview was very shy and brief in explaining her views. The three-person focus group interview lasted approximately an hour.

The interviews were conducted either during the provision of day care or during volunteers' monthly meeting—in other words, when volunteers were at work. This is one reason why the participants could not devote a long period of time to the interviews. No member of the team was present during the interviews of the volunteers. Prior to each interview, one of the team members introduced me to the volunteers and encouraged them to participate in the interview. These interviews were conducted in Kiswahili, and the interview tapes were subsequently transliterated into English by me.

I also interviewed five team members on the role of volunteers. These team members included the leader of the program, a nurse, a social worker, an evangelist and a pastor. The interviews were supplemented by participant observations as well as by countless informal conversations with team members, volunteers and patients on the role of volunteers in the Selian Hospice and Palliative Care Programme. Furthermore, I was given some statistics on the volunteers and some teaching materials that were either used by the team or prepared for the patients.

The thematic interview was selected to enable a greater number of interviews to be conducted in a short time. The first theme consisted of the volunteer's background information, the second theme inquired about her/his experiences in the service, the third discussed the rewarding aspects of their work, and the fourth theme concerned the challenges that the volunteers encountered during their service. The closing theme discussed their reasons for their wanting to continue volunteering and also evaluated if they had ever served as volunteers elsewhere.

Selected by their communities

Previous research on volunteering has not focused on volunteers selected by their local communities or do not volunteer themselves; in this respect, the Selian volunteers are clearly unique (Grönlund 2011; Kasimbazi and Sliep 2011). In short, the Selian volunteers accept the call of their community to volunteer. This was explained during various interviews, such as when a relatively young man described how three other people had responded negatively to the request by the community and he was only the fourth choice on the list. However, he interpreted this as a plan of God—that it was his place and one that was not meant for others.

During the early years of the project, volunteers were selected through the local parishes of the ELCT. Later, when the program expanded and received some support from the Tanzanian government, most of the volunteers were selected through their local village governments. Tanzania has a unique organization of ten house cells which combine to form village-level governments. This system was organized during the years of *ujamaa* socialism, and it continues contain some of the communality values of the idealistic *ujamaa* of President Julius Nyerere which means living together or living as one family (Green 2010). The local communities recognize that the selected volunteers are capable of serving the sick in their community. The communities suggest the names of suitable candidates to the Selian Palliative Care team, and this team further interviews the candidates to determine whether they qualify for the task in terms of their personal abilities and the availability of sufficient time to serve the sick in their community.

The first volunteer training course was organized in 2004; by April 2012, two hundred fifty volunteers had been trained, of which two hundred four were active in their service. The number of volunteers who no longer continued with their work was very small. My objective was to determine the reasons for their strong motivation to continue unpaid work even though they themselves were in difficult financial situations. I asked the team members why some of the volunteers had not continued with their service. The interviewees provided a number of reasons, including that the volunteers had moved, received full-time work, or died. Others had not been motivated to continue longer with unpaid volunteer work, but it seems that this reason accounted for only a few of the approximately fifty volunteers who had resigned.

All volunteers attend a four-week volunteer training course which uses material produced by the Tanzanian government for caring for HIV-positive patients at home. This training involves basic teaching on the care of sick people and also offers, for example, information on hygiene and a nutritious diet. Furthermore, volunteers are taught how sicknesses affect their patients' psychological conditions. Most of the volunteers only had basic elementary school education (the standard seven years); during the interviews, they indicated that the volunteer training course had taught them important information and had also increased their interest in their a need for further education. Evangelists receive further training from the church after their elementary school education. In addition, one of the evangelists' stated that he was attending pastoral training at a local Bible school. Four of the interviewed volunteers had received some secondary school education, two volunteers had attended vocational school, and one interviewee had started his studies at the university, although he had not finished them.

Volunteering as a privilege

All of the interviewees reported that they had received strong support from their own communities, and this feeling of social support from the community seems to give strength to the volunteers to continue their demanding service of caring for their sick and dying neighbours. Previous research has emphasized that volunteering can be a privilege as well as a responsibility. For example, Taniguchi (2006: 84) observed that volunteering becomes a privilege when participants benefit from it in terms of human interaction, personal growth and life enrichment. This privilege aspect of volunteering was evident during my observations in one day care in a village church. The evangelist of that church wanted to become a volunteer in the program. He clearly had an interest in being involved, but at least this time, his request had been rejected and he was informed that in the area no longer has a need for new volunteers.

The Selian volunteers are clearly proud of their service, which they repeated many times during their interviews, stating how blessed they are when they can serve others in their community. When I contemplated this during one of my many informal conversations with the team, the evangelist responded, "One reason is that we also serve patients other than those with AIDS, and this decreases the stigma." A great number of the patients are HIV-positive, but some have cancer and other sicknesses that require hospice and palliative care. Previous research has revealed that, in some African contexts, the volunteers who serve HIV-positive patients are also faced with stigma. Nonetheless, when the stigma of AIDS is not that strongly imposed on the whole program, volunteering is seen more as a privilege.

The interviewed volunteers also explained the benefits that they received even though they had directly indicated that these were not substantial and not the main reason for their volunteering. In April 2012, all volunteers received pocket money of 40,000 Tanzanian Shillings (slightly less than 20 euros at that time) to reimburse them for bus tickets and other expenses incurred while volunteering. In addition, the volunteers received some small gifts, such as a bicycle, boots or a raincoat. These gifts were not received regularly, as it always depended on visitors or organizations to donate these special gifts. The interviewed volunteers did not recall being offered any gifts recently.

Two of the volunteers had later been offered employment based on their volunteer efforts; this employment can also be categorized under material benefits. The first to receive employment, a male volunteer, was currently employed with an NGO working with youth in the mining community. He continues to serve as a volunteer in the Selian Hospice and Palliative Care Programme as well. The other employed volunteer, a female volunteer, was selected to serve as a secretary in the office of a program in the Arusha Lutheran Medical Centre. She began as a volunteer but became a paid worker; she no longer worked as a volunteer.

The interviewed volunteers regarded the volunteer training as being the most important knowledge-related benefit they had received, and the whole four-week training was important for them. Moreover, many of the volunteers stated that it is important for them to know both how to prevent their own HIV infection and how to take better care of their own families. In other words, knowledge-related benefits were considered to be more far-reaching than material benefits, as the latter seemed to have all been lost by the time of the interviews.

A major motivation to continue volunteering seemed to be the community-related benefits. This was especially the case for the male volunteers, as they emphasized many times how important volunteering was for their status in the community. One of the female volunteers expressed this as follows: "I like to serve the community." One male volunteer explained a similar idea: "Many come to ask my advice. They see that I can guide and counsel them." Whereas the female focus was on the service and the community members, the men seemed to be contented with their own role and additional status in the community. Another male volunteer explained: "They like me and give good feedback on my service.". Two additional women focused again on the community in their comments about how they enjoy seeing the neighbourhood responding to help the patients and how this interaction reduces the stigma in the community.

Many of the volunteers expressed that in their service entailed spiritual benefits. This resembled the prosperity gospel concept of giving. These male and female volunteers stated that they devote their time to the service of others and that, in return, God will reward them. One explained that she visits the sick one week and the next, God blesses her business. Another female volunteer explained how her volunteering meant that her whole family was blessed. Another person expressed that God had protected him from being infected with HIV when he helped a patient to bathe and the gloves broke. He himself had to be tested twice for HIV. The caregiver tested negative for HIV, which he saw as a miracle from God.

Leadership and counselling roles were clearly evident among the evangelists participating in the program, especially during the day care organized in church surroundings and the volunteers' monthly meetings, which for example, opened with a prayer by one of the evangelists. During the interviews, some volunteers emphasized the importance of peer support when faced with difficult psychological or social challenges, but no one explicitly stated that some of the peer support was actually the support from those volunteers who had trained as evangelists and who had experience in counselling.

Male attitudes towards challenges in volunteering

Previous research has reported that volunteering is also considered to be a responsibility or includes various challenges (Jack et al. 2011; Taniguchi 2006: 84). This responsibility aspect was evident throughout the various challenges—practical, psychological and social challenges—encountered in the present study. The volunteers who were interviewed listed various practical challenges that they faced while serving the sick in their community. The men mentioned more often than the women the challenges of transportation and recounted how the bicycles that they had been assigned earlier were either stolen or broken. Many women commented that they could walk or could use their transportation money to travel by bus if a sick person lived further away. Both men and women stated that the major practical problem that they faced was the lack of medicine and other medical supplies.

Only men explained how difficult it was to wake up during the night when they had to travel to visit a sick person and did not even have a torch. I did not notice to ask the women volunteers whether they needed to wake up to visit the sick during the night or whether they merely cope with the darkness of the night. Both men and women mentioned the practical challenges of the rainy season during the interviews, such as obstacles encountered to reach patients' homes through mud and floods.

Both men and women considered their own financial situation as a challenge for volunteering. If they did not have anything to bring when visiting a patient, they could be asked why they came empty handed. In addition, many of the patients seemed to harbour the misunderstanding that the volunteers were compensated for their services or at least were given some food to be distributed to the patients. I also discussed this issue of food distribution with the team, who said that this aspect of the program warrants further patient education. Food is distributed only during day care and given directly to the patient her-/himself. In those few cases when the patient is too ill, someone from the team ensures that the food reaches the patient's home. Financial challenges and unrealistic expectations of the patients were also reported in a study of the palliative care volunteers in Uganda (Jack et al. 2011: 713).

The interviewed volunteers in my study stated that the biggest social challenge they face in their volunteer work is poverty—both to the volunteers themselves and the poor patients of the Selian Palliative Care Programme. One challenge of palliative care is social responsibility. Steve de Gruchy (2007: 63–65) made the important point that, while healing is of great importance to all Christians in Africa, social justice is not considered to have much theological significance. This fundamental relationship between health and social justice requires attention in an era in which AIDS is a grim fact of life for many. The Selian Palliative Care Programme is a good example of a program that focuses both on healing and on social responsibility, but in the context of severe poverty, the ability of one organization to make a substantial change in the life of a client is inevitably very limited.

In the beginning of the program, the sick were extremely sick and there was a strong stigma of AIDS in the community. Now, since ARV medications have become available, many of the patients are stronger and feeling better. This improved physical condition has partly helped the volunteers with the stigma. Among the social challenges, both male and female volunteers mentioned their patients' sexual harassment. In fact, female volunteers expressed that they had been afraid of being raped when visiting some of the patients. When they reported these fears to their supervisors and fellow volunteers, the volunteers were either assigned to other patients or advised to always go with another person on their visits. It is interesting that one male volunteer also indicated having been sexually harassed by a few of his patients. These women intended to have sex with him to receive better benefits from the program. The volunteer also requested that these women be reassigned so that he would not have to visit them alone. All of these narratives on sexual harassment were from the mining community, which has a reputation of having a free sexual atmosphere.

Social challenges focused on the patient and her/his well-being included addictions and promiscuous sexual behaviour (infecting others and contracting more viruses her-/himself). One major social challenge was pregnant women who received HIV test results during their pregnancy check-ups and their spouses later deserted them when they received this information. The deserted wife is left on her own to treat her AIDS and assume the physical and financial responsibility for the child once it is born.

The program is planned so that the role of counselling the local volunteers is the responsibility of the district supervisor. During the interviews, the team emphasized that these supervisors are close to the volunteers and are readily available for counselling. Most of the interviewed volunteers were of the opinion that their supervisors were difficult to contact and that their supervisors do not provide medicine and other supplies to the volunteers. However, the supervisors were not interviewed, so I do not have their perspective on these issues. Most of the volunteers who strongly criticized their supervisors were from the same district, so the situation might be that in that particular district there was a problem with one supervisor.

The volunteers also mentioned the psychological challenge created by facing death and suffering. Many of them were unable to elaborate on these during the interviews. They could only explain how tired they were when their patients were approaching death. The leader of the program used the term "burnout" when referring to the psychological challenges that the volunteers face, yet not a single volunteer used this expression during the interviews. The evangelist of the team also thought that men became tired more easily. However, the leader of the program stated her point of view: Female volunteers face burnout more easily. As I did not adopt psychological scales in my research, it was not possible to determine the levels of interviewee burnout from these findings. In addition, I do not know if the educational background of the leader (a trained nurse) and the evangelist (no medical training) influenced their different points of view or if the difference in their opinion stemmed from their gender, as the leader was female and the evangelist male.

Gender differences in volunteering

In many ways, the traditional situation no longer exists in Tanzania because urbanization has changed Tanzanian society. It is no longer a question of a small community where everyone knows one another and in which it is possible to offer or receive social support (Dilger 2006: 111–112). Indeed this social change has affected the generational and gender hierarchies in Tanzania, but these hierarchies seem to influence gender roles in volunteering in modern society as well. Some aspects of the traditional village setting communality nonetheless have survived in the newly established community organizations, as was evident in the previous examples of the role of volunteers.

The communality aspect of volunteers can be explained by analysing more closely governance as a cultural practice. According to Green (2010: 15), "Governance as a cultural practice in Tanzania enacts the hierarchical relations between the lower and higher tiers in models premised on the conceptualization of the village as both object and lowest level of government." Volunteers in Tanzania seem to act both as part of the civil society and as part of the local governance. The unique selection process of these volunteers strengthens the bond between the volunteer and the local governance. The task assigned to volunteers falls between an official work role and a traditional volunteer role. What makes their role clearly to be that of a volunteer is that they are not paid for their services.

In traditional Tanzanian societies, male identity was constructed not only at home, but in terms of the larger community as well. The attributes that have long been central to this male identity have been fighting skills and leadership within the age group together with the clan system (von Bülow 1995: 7). In a collective culture, identity is not a question of a single individual, as the community is also involved in the process of identity construction. In an African context, identity is continuously constructed and transformed within a discursive process that involves discourses that are ethnic and religious (von Bülow 1995: 3). Although female behaviour is seen as being home-centred, male behaviour is oriented out toward the larger community. Today, contemporary society does not value fighting skills as highly, but the qualities these skills represent—namely, bravery and success—continue to command respect. Another important contributor to the high status of males in an African community is wealth (Howard and Millard 1997). Additional contributors to high status are proper occupation, in the traditional sense, and good moral behaviour. Philip Setel, who has studied the male population in the Kilimanjaro area in northern Tanzania, reported that some occupations are more valued than others. For example, farming is viewed as being honest and tiring work, but other occupations are not as highly valued, such as a businessman or a petty trader (Setel 1995: 41). It is vital to understand that these traditional worldviews and constructions of male behaviour remain highly relevant to the contemporary context (see also Chitando 2012).

The Swahili term *heshima* explains gender roles in Tanzania, including gender roles in volunteering. *Heshima* is a broader concept than the English word "honour"; *heshima* can also mean respect and dignity. Thus, a woman's *heshima* is connected to correct moral behaviour and is mainly related to female sexual behaviour. In contrast, honour is much more than an individual's estimation of self-worth. Instead, a woman is judged by the society in terms of her honour (Silberschmidt 1999: 166). Whereas *heshima* is interpreted as an important aspect of female sexual behaviour, it is not frequently connected to male sexual behaviour. In fact, male sexual behaviour does not necessarily have to adhere to the Christian sexual moral code because social status is more important for male *heshima*. Thus, with regard to female behaviour, *heshima* seems to refer more to personal dignity, whereas for male behaviour, *heshima* is a mark of community respect.

Transforming masculinities through care role in community

The gender differences in volunteering discussed thus far reveal that the Selian program has succeeded in inviting both male and female volunteers to assume the palliative care role in their communities. This further raises the question of how the male volunteers transform their masculine identities during the process of their service.

Another complicating factor in the analysis of masculinities in the context of Arusha municipality is that there is no single contributing community to study. In this transitional society, different cultural categories work side by side. For instance, researchers have identified three different cultural categories that are interconnected in contemporary Tanzania (Hasu 1999; see also Comaroff and Comaroff 1991): *kienyeji* (traditional), *kikristo* (Christian), and *kisasa* (modern). In relation to the present study, a "traditional community" refers to kinship ties and the area of the village community from which the volunteers originally came. The "Christian community" refers to historical church communities in Tanzania; in the case of the Muslim volunteers, it refers similarly to their traditional Muslim religious community. Modern influences include various urban situations, such as the formal organizational level of the Selian Palliative Care Programme. These cultural categories are therefore used by Tanzanian men to construct their personal and social identities. Usually, an individual creates his personal identity from at least two of these categories. The same individual can change his approach during the course of his life; older people tend to rely more on *kienyeji* while younger urban people rely more on *kisasa*. However, the situation is much more complicated than merely age or rural–urban differences.

The male volunteers seem to construct their masculine identities primarily from the previously discussed traditional male identity, where the central feature is their leadership and the role of counselling in the community. However, at the same time, men adopt a modern masculine identity when accepting their roles as caregivers in their community. To accept a caregiving role in an African setting is extraordinary, yet only very limited research exists that analyses the care role of men in Africa. One of these is from Zimbabwean context in which African men are challenged to be "man enough to care" (Chindomu and Matinzamhuka 2012: 423–426; 434–437). Moreover, previous research also in European contexts has discovered that, for example, men in Greece would not consider joining care programs as volunteers (Edgardh 2011: 86). The fact that so many men volunteer in the Selian Programme is a considerable contribution towards transforming masculinities in their local villages. Through their volunteering, men find an important role to play in the fight against HIV (Chitando 2012: 144).

Selian masculinities could be interpreted as what is called "soft patriarchy," a concept coined by van Klinken (2010) in his analyses of the approaches of masculinities in Africa. Van Klinken's case study of a Pentecostal church in Zimbabwe illustrates a similar approach of the transformation of masculinity within the patriarchal framework. This "soft patriarchy" model does not seem to be officially planned, but rather a result of being open to respecting traditions as well as wanting to face new challenges in volunteer work in Tanzania.

The transformation of masculinity in Selian's case occurs within a patriarchal framework that does not support the feminist theological vision of masculinity transforming beyond patriarchy (Nadar and Phiri 2012: 126–127). Two African theologians, Ezra Chitando and Sophie Chirongoma, introduced the term *redemptive masculinities*, which they asserted characterizes and identifies masculinities that are life-giving (2012: 1). According to Chitando and Chirongoma, redemptive masculinities evoke the spiritual dimension of masculinities that they wish to stress. Another reason for not only talking about transforming or liberating masculinities as feminist theologians have previously done might that the book, also titled *Redemptive Masculinities*, is a common venture of male and female theologians in Africa.

Previous research in the South African context has revealed that the new masculinity in Africa often looks to history as a model and is traditionalist (Morell et al. 2012: 25). In contrast, the Selian masculinities are not based on history or tradition, although they respect the local African traditions and offer men the opportunity to build strong social capital through volunteer work in their community. Social capital is defined as community cohesion that results from positive aspects of community life (Putnam 1993; 1995). A lack of traditional communal support creates a strong need for organized support from the faith communities and offers a possibility of strengthening men's social capital through involvement in volunteering.

This soft patriarchy could be further evaluated by adopting Ninna Edgardh's (2011: 83–88) analysis of the ideal and existing gender roles in church-related social work. The ideal in the Selian case is openly explained, the goal of selecting volunteers from villages is gender balance. Through the selection process the programme clearly promotes gender equality in volunteer work. This equality does not require men to lose their masculinity. The departure point of the Selian case seems to be the idea that there is a need to transform slightly the existing gender roles, but not to transform them into unrealistic ideals that would deter men from joining as care volunteers.

Conclusion: Selian "soft patriarchy" promotes reform

The role of male volunteers in the Selian Hospice and Palliative Care Programme indicates that they are rather reforming gender roles than requiring a full revolution of gender equality. A closer examination of the concepts of transformation, reformation and revolution reveal how these are all interconnected and that there are different ways to describe the changing of attitudes and the shifting gender roles (Nielsen 1971).

The liberation theology approach, including the African female and male theologians discussed herein, promotes an all-out revolution of gender equality. Yet revolution does not appear to be very effective way of transforming gender roles in Africa. It seems that the Selian approach—which promotes reform, not revolution—works better. Selian masculinities are realistic and can be effective way of transformation. Male volunteers are a natural part of the program. Selian masculinities combine the good side of existing gender roles and propose the addition of some of the ideal masculinities into the construction of individual male identities.

References

Chindomu, Charles and Matizamhuka, Eunica E. 2012. "Challenging African men to be "Man Enough to Care" in the HIV Era: Special Focus on the Anglican Diocese of Manicaland, Zimbabwe." In *Redemptive Masculinities: Men, HIV, and Religion,* ed. Erza Chitando and Sophie Chirongoma, 423–446. Geneva: World Council of Churches.

Chitando, Ezra. 2012. "Even When There is No Rooster, The Morning Will Start: Men, HIV and African Theologies." *Journal of Feminist Studies in Religion* 28, no. 2: 141–145.

Chitando, Ezra and Chirongoma, Sophie. 2012. "Introduction: On the Title." In *Redemptive Masculinities: Men, HIV, and Religion,* ed. Erza Chitando and Sophie Chirongoma, 1–30. Geneva: World Council of Churches.

Colvin, Christopher J., Robins, Steven and Leavens, Joan. 2010. "Grounding 'Responsibilisation Talk': Masculinities, Citizenship and HIV in Cape Town, South Africa." *Journal of Development Studies* 46, no. 7: 1179–1195.

Comaroff, Jean and Comaroff, John. 1991. *Of Revelation and Revolution. Christianity, Colonialism, and Consciousness in South Africa.* Vol. 1. Chicago: University of Chicago Press.

de Gruchy, Steve. 2007. "Re-Learning our Mother Tongue? Theology in Dialogue with Public Health." *Religion & Theology* 14: 47–67.

Dilger, Hansjörg. 2006. "The power of AIDS: kinship, mobility and the valuing of social and ritual relationships in Tanzania." *African Journal of AIDS Research* 5, no. 2: 109–121.

Edgardh, Ninna. 2011. "A Gendered Perspective on Welfare and Religion in Europe." In *Welfare and Religion in 21st Century Europe: volume 2. Gendered, Religious and Social Change*, ed. Anders Bäckström et al., 61–106. Surrey: Ashgate.

Fynn, Sharl. 2011. "Experiences of social support among volunteer caregivers of people living with HIV/AIDS." In *Response-ability in the era of AIDS: Building social capital in community care and support*, ed. Wenche Dageid, Yvonne Sliep, Olagoke Akintola and Fanny Duckert, 111–128. Bloemfontain: Sun Media.

Green, Maia. 2010. "After Ujamaa? Cultures of Governance and the Representation of Power in Tanzania." *Social Analysis* 54, no. 1: 15–34.

Grönlund, Henrietta. 2012. *Volunteerism as a mirror of individual and society: Reflections from young adults in Finland*. Dissertation, University of Helsinki.

Hasu, Päivi. 1999. *Desire and Death. History through Ritual Practice in Kilimanjaro*. Transactions of the Finnish Anthropological Society No. 42. Helsinki.

Howard, Mary Theresa and Millard, Ann V. 1997. *Hunger and Shame: Child Malnutration and Poverty on Mount Kilimanjaro*. New York: Routledge.

Jack, Barbara A. et al. 2011. "A bridge to the hospice: The Impact of Community Volunteer Programme in Uganda." *Palliative Medicine* 25, no. 7: 706–715.

Kasimbazi, Anette Kezaabu and Sliep, Yvonne 2011. "Unpaid volunteers and perceived obstacles in ensuring care and support of people living with HIV/AIDS." In *Response-ability in the era of AIDS: Building social capital in community care and support*, ed. Wenche Dageid, Yvonne Sliep, Olagoke Akintola and Fanny Duckert, 95–110. Bloemfontain: Sun Media.

Morrell, Robert, Jewkes, Rachel and Lindegger, Graham. 2012. "Hegemonic Masculinity/Masculinities in South Africa: Culture, Power, and Gender Politics." *Men and Masculinities* 15, no. 1: 11–30.

Nadar, Sarojini and Phiri, Isabel. 2012. "Charting the Paradigm Shifts in HIV Research: The Contribution of Gender and Religious Studies." *Journal of Feminist Studies in Religion* 28, no. 2: 121–129.

Nielsen, Kai. 1971. "On the choice between reform and revolution". *Inquiry: An Interdisciplnary Journal Journal of Philosophy* 14: 1–4, 271–295.

Putnam, R. 1993. *Making democracy work*. New Jersey: Princeton University Press.

Putnam, R. 1995. "Bowling alone: America's declining social capital." *Journal of Democracy* 6: 65–79.

Setel, Philip. 1995. "The Social Context of AIDS Education among Young Men in Norther Kilimanjaro." In *Young People at Risk. Fighting AIDS in Northern Tanzania*, ed. Knut-Inge Kepp, Paul M. Biswalo and Aud Talle, 49–68. Oslo: Scandinavian University Press.

Silberschmidt, Margrethe. 1999. *"Women Forget that Men are the Masters". Gender Antagonism and Socio-Economic Change in Kisii District, Kenya*. Uppsala: Nordiska Afrikainstitutet.

Taniguchi, Hiromi. 2006. "Men's and Women's Volunteering: Gender Differences in the Effects of Employment and Family Characteristics." *Nonprofit and Voluntary Sector Quarterly* 35: 83–-101.

van Klinken, Adriaan S. 2010. "Theology, Gender ideology and Masculinity Politics: A Discussion on the Transformation of Masculinities as Envisioned by African Theologians and a Local Pentecostal Church." *Journal of Theology for Southern Africa* 138: 2–18.

van Klinken, Adriaan S. 2011. "Male Headship as Male Agency: An Alternative Understanding of a Patriarchal African Pentecostal Discourse on Masculinity." *Religion and Gender* 1, no. 1: 104–124.

van Klinken, Adriaan S. 2013. *Transforming Masculinities in African Christianity. Gender Controversies in Times of AIDS.* Ashgate: Farnham.

von Bülow, Dorthe 1995. "Power, Prestige and Respectability. Women's Groups in Kilimanjaro, Tanzania." CDR Working Paper 95.11. Copenhagen: Centre for Development Research.

Vähäkangas, Auli. 2010 "The social construction of hope in the lives of PLWHA in Tanzania and Finland" *Africa Theological Journal* 33, no. 1: 1–21.

Vähäkangas, Auli. 2012 "Contextual pastoral counselling among the terminally ill AIDS patients in Tanzania." *Journal of Pastoral Theology* 22, no. 1: 1–14.

Wyrod, Robert. 2008. "Between Women's Rights and Men's Authority: Masculinity and Shifting Discourses of Gender Difference in Urban Uganda." *Gender & Society* 22: 799–823.

CHAPTER ELEVEN

Religion and Development
A Gender Perspective on the Ambiguous Role of the Churches

Marianne Skjortnes

Introduction

Christian churches across the world have long engaged in what we would today term development. Faith-based organizations have been deeply involved in humanitarian assistance and diaconal work. At the same time, the evolution of thinking about gender and development expressed in modern concepts, as we find in secular organizations since the 1970s, has long been far more difficult to trace in faith-based institutions (Marshall and Van Saanen 2007).

However, increasing awareness among faith-based communities, especially within the Christian tradition, indicates that all work which aims to create positive processes of change needs to include a gender perspective. This applies to churches as well as mission and humanitarian organizations. The reason for this is that a community will always be marked by the fact that conditions are different for women and men and that there are different perceptions of what women's and men's roles in society are based on social and cultural constructions and understandings of what is "natural."

Diaconal work of the churches, in the sense of development work related to improving people's living conditions, might lead to changes in social and cultural conditions in society. As such, changes that are the result of diaconal work might also threaten the stability of important social institutions and of the fellowships that are central in meeting the population's basic needs. This might include changes in how one's daily bread is produced, technological innovations for farming and livestock keep, changes in the fellowships tied to production and economic networks and changes in the gendered division of labour and in the relationship between the sexes.

Churches are agents of change, but they can also represent hindrance to change. Therefore, there will always be a need to incorporate critical self-reflection around the role of the church. Important areas of reflection for churches might, amongst other things, be tied to living conditions for women and men. Thus, this chapter will focus on three questions:

1. What does "gender equality" mean across cultures? I especially want to highlight the point that "being equal" does not necessarily mean "being the same."
2. Which gender role patterns are communicated by churches? Here I especially wish to emphasize that these gender roles can be ambiguous.
3. How can the church and religious organizations become more aware of their own role in this situation?

Churches are powerful arenas for transforming gender role patterns. Based on this knowledge, my aim in this chapter is to challenge churches and church actors, and on this occasion, particularly Sub-Saharan African churches, to become more aware of the key role that religious faith and practice serve as both a resource and a limitation in relation to creating equal opportunities for women and men in society.[1]

Equality and complementarity

Gender is a complex and dynamic set of ideas, actions and feelings about what it means to be a woman or a man in a specific place, culture and time (Kabeer 2003). My theoretical perspective is based on the assumption that femininities and masculinities are historical, social and cultural constructions (West and Zimmermann 1987; Butler 1997). As Simone de Beauvoir put it: "One is not born a woman, one becomes one" (de Beauvoir 1952: 249). When gender involves cultural constructions, we cannot assume what gender means in different cultures and contexts; rather, we have to empirically study what it means. This is also the case when it comes to gender in the context of churches.

How differently women and men are perceived can vary. One might place different perceptions about women and men along a continuum between complementarity and equality. In those societies where the ideals include few defined differences between women and men and where these differences are not given much weight, the understanding of gender might be said to be marked by equality. Many of today's Western societies—such as Scandinavia, where ideologies of gender equality are central—stand as an example of this. At the opposite end of the continuum one could place societies in which gender is marked by complementarity. This means that according to local values and understandings, men and women are defined as different—and different in a complementary way to the other. For example, if men are defined as strong, women are defined as weak; if men are rational, women are emotional. They are understood as two different parts of the same whole and, therefore, mutually dependent on each other. These complementary characteristics form the starting point for complementary tasks. Women give birth to children and take care of the household, while men provide. Women need protection, and men protect them. Men cannot take care of themselves when they are at home; women can take care of them. This type of role pattern is common in today's non-industrialized societies (Eriksen 2010: 137).

Complementarity should not necessarily be understood as hierarchical in the sense that some tasks, such as men providing for the family, are more important and worth more than others, such as women's tasks in the household. Complementarity does not mean that some tasks should be thought of as better and more important than others. In a Norwegian context, many seem to perceive such complementary role patterns to be expressions of male dominance and female oppression. This is based on a line of thought in which "being equal" means "being the same," which then becomes something positive. Being different is seen as "being not equal" and is therefore perceived negatively. Instead one might think that equality needs to be related to reality as it is understood and lived by people themselves in various societies and cultures. These perspectives can shed light on processes of changes to which churches also need to relate.

Complementarity represents a way of thinking and organizing differences, but in itself does not tell us anything about whether the different parts are perceived as equal or not and whether one or the other has the most power. These issues need to be seen as empirical questions and need to be examined in each specific case in question. Many immigrants and refugees who live in Norway organize their lives around more or less complementary roles. In many Pakistani families, for instance, family members seek to keep the husband as the provider and the woman as the mother and housewife who stays at home for as long as possible. This same type of family organization was found in Norway in the 1950s, when complementarity was the usual form in which to organize a gendered division of labour. The ideal of gender equality came as a result of the battle for gender equality in the 1970s. This happened as the private sphere (the homes) were emptied of important functions and power; as a result, women—contrary to previous experience—started to feel isolated, marginalized and oppressed. From a Norwegian cultural perspective, the development of Norwegian gender roles—from complementarity to what we today call gender equality, or at least an ideal of gender equality—is defined as liberating for women and therefore per definition as something positive.

A complementary gendered division of labour can be challenged by new ideologies and new interpretations, such as through the presence of Christian churches, where women's and men's equal worth are an important perspective. How should one relate to the fact that women and men in different parts of the world have different experiences of which tasks and roles are natural for the two sexes? Here I wish to present two experiences and my reflections on them, which point toward how important it is to understand one's own position (e.g., as a Western woman) when one responds to these questions (Narayan 1997).

Experience and reflection 1

In 1995 I became engaged in reading coverage and reports from the UN World Women Conference in Beijing. This was an arena where women from the whole world met and exchanged points of view and experiences. Women who participated had different backgrounds, different languages and experiences and different religions and values. They also expressed different perceptions about the division of labour between women and men in society and about what is important in order to achieve a better existence and a better life. The women wished to further different themes and put these on the agenda of the conference.

The conference can be said to be an expression of a societal debate about what is the good life for women and how can better living conditions be created for women in different societies. At the conference, disagreement emerged about the answer to these questions. Norway was officially represented by then-Family Minister Grete Berget and Prime Minister Gro Harlem Brundtland, who presented themselves as representatives from a country in Scandinavia which had been successful in creating good living conditions for women and had come far in achieving gender equality. They gave the following examples to illustrate their claim: Women have great influence over their own situation in Norway, women are active in the workplace and in political life, women are financially independent, women make decisions about their own bodies (cf. the legal right to self-chosen abortion), and most women in Norway have had their basic needs met, such as food, clothing, health, housing and education. At a general level, this is probably a conclusion that many of the women at the conference could agree upon: Most women in Norway have, materially speaking, achieved a good life and good living conditions.

But on a few points there was much disagreement. For example, there was a discussion about how one should relate to the question about inheriting land, and from

Western women, amongst others, a demand was put forward that in all countries women and men should have the right to inherit land in the same way. For women in Scandinavia and a few other Western countries it has become taken for granted that sons and daughters should have the same opportunity to inherit land, in line with the ideology of gender equality that often underlies a Western thought process. But female representatives from Muslim countries protested this demand and thought it would be unfair. In line with their tradition, it was claimed, men ought to provide for women. If the sole right to inherit land were taken away from men, then providing would become an unreasonable responsibility.

The discussion from the women's conference shows what is often observed at global conferences—namely, that it is Western women's values and aims which are put on the agenda and turned into general demands and standards for women, regardless of their cultural and geographical background. This raises key questions that are important to consider when including a gender perspective on churches' role in a global context: Who should decide what the good life for women is?

Experience and reflection [2]

At a theological seminary in Madagascar, both female and male students attended. It was tradition at the school that the female spouses of the theology students also be taught. In addition to bible classes, they were taught cooking, sewing and embroidery, including the Norwegian stitch *Hardangersøm*. This was a tradition that Norwegian missionaries had introduced several decades previously. Their thought was that these women were going to be pastors' wives and the Norwegian model of what it meant to be a pastor's wife was the natural association. The ideal and frame of reference were pastors' wives who stayed at home during the first half of the twentieth century in Norway and for whom sewing and embroidery were important tasks at the vicarage. These structures and ways of thinking, based on a gendered division of labour in Norway more than fifty years ago, have persisted at these theological seminaries until recently. For most of the future pastors' wives in Madagascar, however, farming, vegetable growing, and poultry and livestock keep would be important and necessary activities in order to contribute to the household finances in a financial situation with few resources. After a while the education offered to the future pastors' wives was changed—for example, courses in vegetable growing were started—based on students' demands who perceived such experience to be relevant.

Church organizations are ambiguous as seen from a gender perspective

The second question to consider is: Which gender role patterns are communicated by churches? For example, what has the church meant for gender role patterns in Madagascar? Seen from a different perspective than the experience at the theological seminary, one might say that the church in Madagascar has simultaneously considered the different roles of women and men in society seriously and based its work on this. The church has appealed to women to take financial responsibility for activities in the congregations, such as through women's groups. This is in line with women's independent financial role in society.

Women also have an important and influential position in the congregation, as evident in the Revival Movement, *Fifohazana.* This is a charismatic and diaconal revival movement that is part of the church structure. Such work tasks are also in line with women's strong position and actual influence in local communities.

The presence of churches in Malagasy society can also be said to have a liberating function, especially for women who, according to their tradition and culture, have not had tasks in the public sphere, but who have primarily been tied to family and the household.2 For some women, the act of participating in a church context has opened doors to new work areas and new living conditions.

But if we look at little more closely at this, we will see that the work of the church has resulted in both changing and cementing existing gender role patterns. The effects of the church's work are ambiguous. Churches have often been important arenas for women's participation and activity and have also been places that have given women education and duties. Women have been central in church organizing; they often hold their own meetings and discuss issues that concern them and, in this way, have their own arena. Through this kind of training and experience, women have also become able to participate in the public sphere in church and society. Through this, they are given opportunities for development and tools to be agents of change.

Many Sub-Saharan African churches today have their own women's work, partly organized within a separate structure, such as "Femmes pour Christ" in Cameroon. In this way the church has created a space that makes it possible for the women to create networks at different levels and to organize themselves in relation to social and economic challenges. In Cameroon, the church's women's organization is today a dynamic element in the church and society, and women have achieved positions in the church administration, including in relation to financial oversight.

Churches such as the Malagasy Lutheran Church, the Evangelical Lutheran Church in Cameroon and the Ethiopian Evangelical Church Mekane Yesus have been concerned that girls should go to school, and some have constructed their own boarding schools for girls. The education of girls and women has led to considerable change in those countries where the church is present. (At the same time, there are still areas where few girls receive an education, even though there are more girls who go to school among church members than among others.)

In some Sub-Saharan African countries, a separate office for women's work has been established in the central church administration, such as in Madagascar, Ethiopia, Cameroon and Tanzania. In addition, in some of these Lutheran synods they have their own women's coordinators. One might ask what this means for women in the church. On the one hand, women are active in the congregations; they are often the ones who collect money and who do most of the practical work. On the other hand, we see that churches can result in a cementing of various existing gender role patterns.

Christian churches wish to offer people a Christian value system and, through diaconal work, they wish to contribute to better living conditions for people. Several churches have integrated this double activity with a claim that women's subordinate position is divinely ordained, as a theological truth that lies as a fixed premise for the work that is carried out. Many leaders in these churches perceive the question of equal access to opportunities and resources for women and men, often expressed in terms of gender equality, as a Western phenomenon, and the topic is often avoided (Walker 1999).

For similar reasons, the existing division of labour between women and men in society is not questioned either. Most non-industrialized societies have traditionally had a patriarchal structure, in which women have had responsibility for the home while the men's arena has often been tied to the public sphere and participation in public decision-making processes. This patriarchal tradition is also found in churches. Churches' work in relation to women and women's situation and position is therefore ambiguous.

To my knowledge, the churches' women's work seldom raises questions about women's subordinate position in society. Much of the training for women emphasizes the roles that are perceived to be accorded to women in general, in relation to raising children, caring for others, cooking and sewing. Women's tasks in the congregation often follow along the same lines: They visit the sick, prepare food for meetings and gatherings, tidy up and keep things in order, but usually are not allowed to participate in making decisions. In some churches, in Tanzania and South Africa, for example, historical processes have contributed to the emergence of female church leaders and pastors, but there is still a lot of resistance to this in parts of the churches (*Hope in Africa* 2003). The recent focus on organizational capacity strengthening within various churches is an example of diaconal work that contributes to strengthening men's roles in the church as women are usually marginal in the church's central administration.

In some countries where women are very active in church, and where they also have their own women's work, there are often very few women with central management positions or responsibilities. In relation to the rest of the local community women have a clear position, but it is often subordinate, as men still do not allow them to participate when decisions are made.

My communication with churches in *inter alia* Ethiopia and Madagascar reveals a tendency to underline and confirm cultural perceptions about the relationship between the sexes and to put forward or accept the view that making decisions is a task for men whereas women ought to be subordinate, in both the family and society. Church members have therefore claimed that churches oppress women and contribute to cementing a culture that can lead to the social and physical abuse of women. In these conditions, it has proved to be difficult for women to become free of a man who abuses his superior position.

Seen in this light, churches can stand out as protectors of the status quo. An alternative approach is to question the status quo—the complementary distribution of tasks and responsibilities between women and men—which will challenge power relations between the genders and in society. In this way, church organizations will stand out as agents of change who pave the way for positive processes of change.

Balancing between the local and the global

We shall now move from an analysis of the ambiguous effects that churches can have, to more applied reflection around what churches can do in this situation. Question 3 asks: How can churches and religious organizations become more aware of their own role in relation to gender roles and gender equality? When thinking about this issue, we need to keep two thoughts in mind at the same time—namely, gender equality and difference.

On the one hand, as a Christian-proclaiming and diaconal church, we advocate that all human beings—women and men—should have the same rights and opportunities in relation to joining a church and gaining access to basic rights, opportunities and resources. At the same time we need to acknowledge that women and men in different societies and cultures have such different experiences that they are actually living in different worlds. Understanding local churches and cultures from their own point of view means trying to understand the choices and priorities that churches make in the cultural context in which they work. This also means that one can try to understand women's and men's ways of organizing and structuring their lives without turning this into a question of right and wrong. In other words, societies, churches or ways of organizing one's life can be qualitatively different, and their value cannot be judged based on what is natural from one's own cultural point of view.

This cultural relativist approach marks a break with a position with a specific cultural perspective of gender. Our own perceptions about gender and gender roles commonly do seem not only right for me, but also natural, and therefore right for everybody. The female spouses of the theology students at the seminary were seen as part of a Norwegian tradition from the 1950s and 1960s, based on a past ideal of Norwegian pastors' wives; therefore they were seen in relation to what was perceived to be the natural role of future pastors' wives. Taking a cultural perspective on gender as our starting point, the question is to what degree the "natural" is actually a question of culture. Femininity and masculinity might be something that is constructed in different cultures and among women and men.

In the encounters that a church faces as well as the establishment of churches in new cultural contexts, one aim would be to be adopting a cultural relativist perspective in one's approach to understanding and empathizing with other people's and groups' experiences of their own reality while still holding on to and maintaining one's Christian, ideological viewpoint as one's position. Churches can use methods of cultural relativism to a certain degree and still present and offer the proclamation of the gospel and diaconal activities as a right and an opportunity for all people, as something that is a common resource for all societies and individuals. This does not mean, that one necessarily "loses oneself" or one's Christian position. Making an effort to understand the logic behind a society's gendered division of labour, female circumcision, arranged marriages or rules for inheriting land is not the same as agreeing with these cultural practices. Here it is important to see the difference between cultural relativism as a method (used in order to understand), and cultural relativism as a worldview or an ideological position (used in order to act morally).

For example, international church fellowships such as the World Council of Churches (WCC) and the Lutheran World Federation (LWF) have in several instances challenged the practice of local churches concerning their gender perspective. The LWF contributed to making it possible to ordain female pastors in Hong Kong and Tanzania. The WCC has established inter-faith dialogue programs, thereby furthering dialogue within the church and highlighting projects that further women's position and groups' rights to define themselves. In addition, organizing regional women's conferences in Asia has put a gender perspective on the agenda and has created greater awareness of the significance of gender roles in a local context. In this way, churches have been active contributors to establishing new practices.

The relationship between local and global values is not a new issue, but it is especially relevant in a time where participants in the global church need to relate to each other and where church organizations need to relate to other cultures, other value systems and other perspectives on gender. In today's world, it is expected that the encounter and collaboration between north and south ought to be marked by mutual understanding and the exchange of impulses. This might be played out in contacts made between churches, congregations, organizations and local communities. The experience of having come closer to each other in a global world is clear. We might say that everyone is in the same boat, ecologically, economically, militarily, and politically speaking. The world has become one place—"a global village," as McLuhan (1962: 291) said. This kind of description of the cultural situation in the world glosses over the fact that globalization needs to be spoken of in relation to two different levels: a micro and a macro level, or a local and a global level. When speaking of the activity of churches, it is necessary to clarify the relationship between the global church on the one hand and the local church on the other, so that one can find the balance between local uniqueness and global fellowship. Relationship to the global church gives churches the possibility to look at themselves and keep on to what they have while also being inspired and challenged by the global universal church.

Churches are actors in a global arena, and in today's world churches are challenged to develop a reflexive attitude towards themselves and their lives as well as to what it means to be a church.

Conclusion: Gender roles and equality

Churches' active efforts to improve women's and men's living conditions incorporate a dual perspective. One perspective concerns change, while the other concerns equality. However, as a starting point, the work for better living conditions must be based on the gendered needs and pre-conditions that women and men experience in their own culture as well as on how resources can be used to strengthen women on their terms and men on their terms. The situation the churches in Sub-Saharan African societies find themselves in is characterized by the fact that, in each local community, a complementary gendered division of labour exists in some form or another. The gendered division of labour in a society is usually related to differences and power. The aim can therefore be equal access to resources and opportunities for women and men within a perspective of equality. This does not mean that women's and men's work tasks necessarily ought to be the same, in the sense of having few differences between women's and men's gender roles, but rather that both genders ought to have the opportunity to improve their living conditions based on their situation. These objectives can be put on the churches' agenda.

A Christian faith and perspective on life are experienced by many as a good starting point for mobilizing and stimulating a broader perspective on a worthy life (Goldewijk and Fortman 1999; Walker 1999). The Christian church can, through its activity, stimulate more people to create better living conditions and life situations for themselves and their families as well as contribute to giving greater capacity and ability to reach this goal. A Christian ideology that emphasizes the worth of human beings can also bolster perceptions of a more humane and meaningful life, where women and men gain access to opportunities and rights that are given as religious faith and practice are manifested. In the work for dignified lives, people's worldview, their culture and religion are important resources (Goldewijk and Fortman 1999).

If churches and religious organizations are to take the fight for poor, hard-pressed women and men seriously, it will have consequences for a church's understanding of its own vocation. This requires one to be clear that being human means that nobody can take your dignity away from you, whether you are poor, female or male, belong to an ethnic minority or are mentally or physically handicapped. Therefore, dignity means respect for all human beings, regardless of what their life situation is like. This fight can also be seen as a fight over power tied to decision making, authority and resources (Tyndale 2000).

In this context, churches can, first, contribute by being a source for a deeper understanding of the human worth of women and men (Lutheran World Federation 2009). Second, religion can also be a platform for mobilization as well as have the potential to contribute to conflict resolution. Last but not least, churches and faith groups can act as role models that show how women and men live with dignity, mutual respect and self-respect.

Historically speaking, Western churches' proclamation of faith and diaconia has been carried out in a context in which one has often not been very humble about one's own culture and gender role pattern. In addition, churches' expression of religious faith and practice has from time to time taken the form of a Western modernization project. A relevant response would be to develop a contextualized Christian church based on cultural values and identity in the local context. At the same time, one must be able to state that there are universal values regarding what it means to be human and that Christianity is a bearer of these values. It is at the intersection among these universal, global values and local cultural experiences and practice that churches have something to communicate and offer women and men in a society. The challenge for churches will be to create awareness of others' right to hold a different point of view and other perceptions of what counts as relevant interpretations in a local universe of meanings as well as when one shares a common biblical basis.

For churches this means acknowledging the roots of religious faith and practice in different social, cultural and religious contexts while simultaneously tying local expressions of religious faith and practice to global, interdenominational standards and mechanisms for implementing Christian faith and diaconal deeds. Expressions of religious faith and practice can only be developed in a space of freedom, where both one's own freedom and the freedom of others are acknowledged. In order to realize this project, we need visions. It is not enough for churches to preserve the status quo and relate to established gender roles as they exist in each culture. We need churches that wish to be agents of change and speak about what could have been and what can still be.

References

Beauvoir, Simone de. 1952. *The Second Sex*. New York: Bantham.

Butler, Judith. 1997. "Performative acts and gender constitution." In *Writing on the body: female embodiment and feminist theory*, ed. Katie Conboy, Nadia Medina and Sarah Stanbury. New York: Columbia University Press.

Eriksen, Thomas Hylland. 2010. *Small Places, Large Issues: An introduction to social and cultural anthropology*. Revised ed. London: Pluto Press.

Fattigdom och utveckling. Religionen som värdegrund. 2001. Stockholm: Svenska Missionsrådet.

Klein Goldewijk, Berma and de Gaay Fortman, Bastian. 1999. *Where needs meet rights: economic, social and cultural rights in a new perspective*. Vol. 88. Geneva: World Council of Churches.

Lutheran World Federation. 2009. *Diakonia in context : transformation, reconciliation, empowerment.* Geneva: The Lutheran World Federation.

Hope in Africa. The role of the churches in the development of civil society. 2003. Oslo: Bistandsnemnda.

Kabeer, Naila. 2003. *Reversed realities: Gender hierarchies in development thought.* London: Verso.

Marshall, Katherine and Van Saanen, Marisa. 2007. *Development and faith: Where mind, heart, and soul work together*. Washington, DC: World Bank.

McLuhan, Marshall. 1962. *The Gutenberg Galaxy: The Making of Typographic Man.* Toronto: Toronto University Press.

Narayan, Uma. 1997. *Dislocating cultures: Identities, traditions, and Third-World feminism.* New York: Routledge.

Thorbjørnsrud, Berit and Engebrigtsen, Ada. 1995. *Norge som flerkulturelt samfunn.* Oslo: Kommunaldepartementet.

Tyndale, Wendy. 2000. *Poverty and Development: Has Religion a contribution to make?* Millennium World Peace Summit of Religious and Spiritual Leaders.

Walker, Bridget. 1999. "Christianity, development, and women's liberation." *Gender and Development* 7, no. 1: 15–22.

Weber, Max. 1919/1978. *Economy and Society: An outline of interpretive sociology.* Ed. Günther Roth and Claus Wittich. Berkeley: University of California. Press.
West, C. and Zimmermann, Don H. 1987. "Doing Gender." *Gender & Society* 2: 125–151.

Notes

1. In 1978–82, I worked for the Norwegian Mission Society, working with the Lutheran Church in Madagascar *inter alia* as a teacher. With my professional background as a social anthropologist, I also worked on the Women and Development program in Madagascar in 1985–88 on a research assignment from the Norwegian Council of Applied Social Research. Since then, I have worked as a researcher and associate professor and have regularly visited the Lutheran Church of Madagascar and other faith-based organizations and churches in Sub-Saharan Africa. It is based on this background and these empirical studies that I have written this chapter.
2. The concept of *tradition* and its dichotomy *modernity* are oversimplified and are of a different order than the social reality that they presume to describe. My use of the concept *tradition* is stylized as an abstracted model of aspects of the world (Weber 1919/1978). The act of differentiating between *traditional* and *modern* values is meant to bring out contrasts and models to consider.

CHAPTER TWELVE

Religion and Development
Lessons from Three Donor Countries

Nikolai Hegertun

Introduction

During the last fifteen years, large bodies of work have been produced by well-respected institutions and scholars on the subject of religion and development. The ever-growing scholarship has assumed many different approaches to the complex relationship between the world of religion and the discourse of development. Much of the existing literature has focused on, among other topics, how religion can be included in mainstream thinking about development, what the contributions of religious non-governmental organizations (NGOs) are and how one can implement religious aspects in development policy. In addition, a great deal of research is case-study based in order to capture the interplay of religion and development policies in different development contexts (Tyndale 2003; Holenstein 2005; Clarke 2006; Deneulin and Bano 2009; Ter Haar 2011).

This chapter, however, is an attempt to discuss and evaluate how this growing discussion on religion has been received by European donors. More specifically, what are the donors' experiences in trying to engage with both the discourse of religion and development and faith-based development-actors? The paper assesses the experiences of two specific countries with a history of engagement in the field of religion and development: the Netherlands and the United Kingdom (UK). The work has been guided by three research questions: i) What has been done? ii) Why has this been done? iii) What are the lessons learned?[1]

These questions consequently led into an analysis of the relations among the state, the academia and the faith-based actors, whose dynamic is important to understand as it influences the domestic discourse in donor countries. As a result of the increasing cooperation and interdependency between state donors and civil society, the need for assessment of the nexus among the state, the academia and NGOs has increased. Finally, the article accounts for the recent project that has taken place in Norway initiated by the Norwegian Ministry of Foreign Affairs (MFA), suitably entitled Religion and Development.[2]

As such, the chapter brings the focus back to Europe and sheds some light on how this discussion is framed and understood by important donor countries.[3]

Two countries: Crossing paths and unfinished business

As donor countries, the Netherlands and the UK are considered pioneers in the field of religion and development. However, although the two countries were engaged at an early stage and chose somewhat different approaches, their respective processes have not led to adequate policies or institutionalized ownership. In short, the processes can be described as unfinished business and mixed experiences. Two common features mark the processes in both countries: the emphasis on building research and an equal focus on, and increased dialogue with, faith-based organizations (FBOs).[4]

In terms of research, the British initiative has been exceptional. The Department for International Development (DFID) sponsored a £3.5-million research program from 2006 to 2011. For a variety of reasons this comprehensive research project did not live up to the expectations of DFID and other stakeholders. In short, the field's complexity, uncorrelated expectations, ambiguous mandate and limited existing knowledge all contributed in making the research process difficult.

The push to engage FBOs and their networks occurred for several reasons. Donors have collaborated with FBOs for decades; they are extensive service deliverers, and religious communities are often the only functional institutions and reliable representatives for civil society in weak states. However, there are other less obvious reasons for this focus as well. First, donors have not necessarily had a reflected attitude toward religion as a non-confessional field of knowledge. Many still believe that *religiosity* per se automatically yields competence on religion and its complex relation to the rest of society. As such, the recruitment of religious actors becomes self-evident. Second, there has been a widespread rhetoric on the added value of FBOs in development. Both their network and structures are emphasized as unique; their religious worldview is perceived as more in tune with the "religious South." Finally, and in line with the latter point, there exists an on-going critique from religious actors of the West's materialistic and secular agenda in development. This reductionist understanding of development is not sustainable in deeply religious contexts in the South. What is needed, the critics claim, is a more culturally sensitive development approach, often labelled as "holistic" or "integrative", that implements individuals' well-being in a much broader sense, including spiritual needs. These tendencies will be further elaborated on, but first a short discussion of the processes in the two countries will be presented.

The Netherlands

The period around 2000 was marked by an increased recognition of the role that religion and religious actors play in contexts where the Netherlands had interests. For the Dutch Ministry of Foreign Affairs (MFA), it was the combination of the obligations of the Millennium Development Goals (MDGs) on the one hand and the state of fragile states on the other hand that first made the politicians aware of the contributions of FBOs. In addition, there was a general recognition of religion as a potent force in global politics. These developments led to a renewed reflection on religion and development as well as how the Netherlands as a secular state could relate to religious actors in development. The Dutch MFA identified two main areas of interest where the knowledge gap was imminent: the development context and the political landscape therein—both areas that more or less directly dealt with religion and religious actors.

Yet several dynamics contributed to putting religion on the map. In 1999, the International Institute of Social Studies in the Hague (ISS) established a Chair devoted to the thinking around religion, human rights and development. Professor Gerrie ter Haar was appointed to the Chair and became a dynamo for this focus the following decade. In 2000 the Catholic organization *Justitia et Pax* arranged a conference on the freedom of religion which resulted in the establishment of a network for religious freedom which also included the Dutch MFA. The 9/11 attacks the following year warranted heightened sensitivity on religion, although it drew the focus towards the security discourse.

In 2002 representatives of the MFA took part in a conference with several FBOs which offered a critique of the materialistic and 'secular' fundamentalism in development theory. The conference led to increased mobilization within the ministry concerning the knowledge of, and engagement with, religious actors. In 2003 the Dutch MFA and several FBOs agreed to establish a joint forum for religion and development. The Dutch Advisory Council on International Affairs supported the initiative, but emphasized the focus on human rights and international law. The same year elections led Agnes van Ardenne to the post of Minister for Development Cooperation. As a Christian Democrat with close ties to some of the Dutch faith-based development organizations, she became a key actor in including the focus on religion within the MFA. In 2005, the forum was formalized as The Knowledge Forum for Religion and Development Policy. The forum's main partner was the FBO initiative The Knowledge Center for Religion and Development.[5] From 2006 until the time Ardenne left office, the centre collaborated closely with the ministry on building up knowledge and competence. In addition, the ministry financed research, conferences and publications on the issue of religion and development. When Bert Koenders succeeded Ardenne in 2007, the forum was restructured and its focus became more academic, trumping the more practical focus of the FBOs' centre. On the other hand the members of the forum were now invited to have an annual meeting with the minister. However, the initiative and agenda were usurped by the ministry, and the FBOs lost momentum and influence.

Despite good intentions and sincere expectations, the forum did not quite develop as hoped and was dismantled three years later. Neither the MFA nor the FBOs were significantly disappointed by this. The activity level had peaked in 2008 and had subsequently grown to be an anomaly compared to its creators' hope. The meetings with the minister had resulted in very few practical consequences, partly because it became clear that Koenders and the FBOs had quite different plans and agendas for the forum. The change of government in October 2010 gave the forum its final blow. The chair at ISS was dismantled in 2012 due to a lack of financing. In contrast to previous years, the focus on religion and development at the MFA is currently at a low level.[6]

However, the focus on religion is not the only neglected idea in contemporary Dutch politics. From being one of the world's leading nations on development, the last VVD-led and PVV-supported government in the Netherlands cut one billion euro in its development budget and halved the number of partner countries in 2011. Further cuts are planned that will leave the Netherlands below the threshold of 0.7 per cent of the GDP to development, if the new government of 2012 does not change course.

In short, ten years after the first initiative began the work on increasing the knowledge on religion and development, few concrete results remain. According to informants, a positive shift in the attitude has occurred within the Dutch MFA; however, the current conditions do not allow any further engagement.

United Kingdom

The year 1997 marked a watershed in the history of religion and development in the UK. The change of government led Claire Short to the position as Minister of International Development. Short's leadership signalled a radical change regarding *how* DFID approached partners and *who* they approached. Short was sceptical of the comfortable relationship DFID had with the culturally homogeneous mainstream NGOs and demanded an increased collaboration with the wider civil society, including religious organizations.

A few years into her first term as Minister of International Development, Short ordered an internal mapping of how DFID worked with religious actors. The mapping revealed a systematic lack of competence in DFID's own ranks concerning religious actors in development. Professor Gerard Clarke from the University of Swansea was asked to expand the mapping and produce recommendations on how DFID could follow up. In the wake of Clarke's work, DFID started consulting with several faith-based institutions and organizations, with participation from the highest levels in DFID. However, there were still few consequences in terms of policy, and according to informants from DFID the new line on religion was quite contested within the department. However, as in the Netherlands, reasons outside DFID contributed to legitimizing the focus on religion.

Domestically, the Catholic and Anglican schools grew steadily in popularity, and FBOs were very useful partners in keeping the focus on development in the general public. In addition, faith communities' initiatives to tackle inner-city problems related to poverty, low educational levels and drugs were a welcomed help for the Labour government. Internationally, the UK's closest ally, the USA, doubled their support for FBOs from 2001 to 2005. Indisputably, the 9/11 attacks in New York and the 7/7 bombings in London consolidated the focus on religion in several ministries. In addition, religiously motivated violence in Nigeria, India and other partner countries gave DFID further incentives to understand the role of religion in development.[7]

In 2005 a £3.5-million research project on religion and development was put out on tender and won by Birmingham University. While this project was on-going, DFID promised to double the support for FBOs in their 2009 White Paper (this was also the first timed FBOs were mentioned in a White Paper). The Birmingham project was finalized in 2011, yet despite several comprehensive papers and policy briefs, DFID's response was somehow lukewarm. A recurrent critique from DFID has been that the research was too theoretical and did not produce enough concrete recommendations and results.

The last initiative from the government taking office in 2010 is the work called Faith Partnership Principles: Working effectively with faith groups to fight global poverty. The initiative is intended to increase the transparency, document FBOs' influence and increase understanding on contested issues. Today, DFID has three advisors who spend half their time working on religion and is consequently still engaged with the issues of religion and development to a greater extent than the Netherlands.

Lessons learned

The tension between policy and research

The Birmingham project is an appropriate point of departure in the discussion on research on religion and development. In order to provide the employer with the most practical and concrete findings as possible, the researchers approached the field with an emphasis on *lived* religion—in short, what religion does and how it influences human interaction. Still, at the end of the day, the criticism from DFID centred precisely on the lack of practical and relevant findings and recommendations. According to informants at DFID, this is the main reason why the research has not received any response from DFID yet. FBOs also criticized the research along the same lines. One informant from a British FBO even labelled it "a major opportunity lost." In addition, some informants underscored the fact that, although comparing findings from four countries (Nigeria, Tanzania, Pakistan and India) is a good idea, the researchers' poor ability to carry it out resulted in eschewed and poor comparative studies. Accordingly, the researchers did not deliver adequately or on time. A final complicating factor was the shift of government in 2010 which robbed the project of its anchor-points and left it somewhat orphaned.

From Birmingham's side the disappointment was mutual. First, expectations from DFID were both unclear and alternating. DFID usually provides clear operational guidelines as to their areas of research which generally tend to focus on more established fields, such as medicine, demographics and nutrition. According to the research leader, Carole Rakodi, the only order from DFID was that the research had to be relevant, whilst being aware of the gradual nature of "explorative" research. However, during the research period, these terms changed, and Birmingham was asked to deliver more concrete results more frequently. The increased emphasis on monitoring and documentation was a far more crude and mechanic approach to reporting than first agreed upon and changed both the conditions and Birmingham's possibilities of meeting DFID's expectations.

Second, the project had an inherent challenge in that Birmingham was to build up local research institutions in the focus countries in addition to performing their own research. The idea of local partners was not disputed from Birmingham; however, in practice it would prove very difficult to carry out. Providing first-rate research and building up capacities in other countries are two entirely different activities, and the latter delayed the actual research by more than a year.

Third, there was no institutional "home" for this research within DFID. Nor was there any plan for follow-up. The project became an island with no connections to the institutional landscape in DFID. It consequently led to poor "institutional memory" as the people working with it were frequently moved around. New people with limited interest and experience concerning the project were sent to briefings at Birmingham, leading the researchers to constantly have to re-start from square one. In sum, there was little institutional buy-in, and DFID lost interest.

Finally, and related to the previous points, there was a systematic lack of dialogue between the employer and employee. Relevant recommendations for the policymakers require continuous and mutual briefs on challenges and needs. However, dialogue presupposes will and, according to a number of informants, no such dialogue was forthcoming on the part of DFID.

> I tried to keep DFID in the process, but we could not find anyone to interact with. We asked them and said: "We would like to have more interaction with and directions from DFID." We spoke to the people directly responsible for the program [in the Central Research Department]. When we occasionally succeeded it was more from our efforts than theirs. [. . .] We weren't really given the opportunity to enter into such a dialogue because on the whole DFID lost interest. (Rakodi 18.01.12)

The experiences from Birmingham demonstrate the challenges confirmed by informants in both countries within the field of religion and development. Professor Ter Haar warns that explorative research on religion, which by nature is more anthropological and sensitive, is rarely compatible with the inconstant nature of politics and the development industry. In addition, there is the sensitivity of religion. According to Rakodi, religion is not necessarily more complex than other social phenomena. However, because of religion's unique position in peoples' lives, it is very hard to disregard ones prejudices and subjective biases and treat it as neutrally and scientifically as it deserves. Katherine Marshall equates religion to gender research:

> It took a lot of time, knowledge and evidence for gender to be mainstreamed. For a long time it was person depended. People also have their emotions invested in gender. It is not easy to have a sober, cold discussion about gender relations because it affects people personally—and the same is true for religion. (Marshall 25.05.12)

In general, three recurrent challenges faced the research in both countries. First, the establishment of scientific research on religion is a tardy process. It involves "naturalizing" and mainstreaming a new and detached way of thinking about religion that people (both religious and secular actors) and institutions are not accustomed to. Because of the unique experience and history Europe has in handling religion, it is perceived as something personal and often problematic. Thus, it is not only ignorance, but also a certain opposition among social scientists towards mainstreaming studies on religion. Second, the task of operationalizing both analysis and applying existing research has proven to be difficult. Although there has been a certain success in illuminating the knowledge gap among donors, there is still a way to go in converting this into tangible policies for development, notwithstanding the current regime on monitoring and documentation. Finally, there are serious challenges in terms of disparity among the mindset, practices and daily life of politicians, bureaucrats and researchers. Research thus needs to unfold in close dialogue with the employer. As Ter Haar remarks:

> Development has become very much a matter of measuring, figures and counting. We do not know how to measure the immaterial dimension. We need to make the connections between the "what" and the "how" [. . .] however, the nexus between "the what" and "the how" is difficult to make. (Ter Haar 10.02.12)

FBOs and their added value

In much of the literature on religion and development, there has been an eminent focus on FBOs and their potential contribution to development. Ever since James Wolfensohn "discovered" these faith groups at the end of the 1990s and linked them to the MDGs, there has been a clear instrumental focus on these groups.

However, given the highly diverse nature of FBOs, most attempts to categorize them have been inadequate. FBOs vary in terms of their belief systems, how faith influences their *modus operandi*, what partners they have, goals, methods, results and documentation. The discussion regarding their added value has been centred on qualities like unique outreach, network, grassroots presence, trust among the poor, legitimacy, advocacy, motivation and 'religious literacy'. This debate has received a lot of attention in both the UK and the Netherlands; however, there are few unambiguous answers to be found.

Many informants expressed frustration regarding the problems of generalizing the issue. Wherever there seemed to be a unique merit, one could always find drawbacks that made general conclusions hard to draw. For example, although some FBOs were excellent service deliverers, donors could still have serious trouble with their conservative attitude towards issues like birth control or gay rights.

Informants from FBOs were naturally more inclined to approve of their added value, although they often found it hard to prove. Some underscored the fact that professional standards and objective categories precisely tended to miss the intricacies of their added value. Others asserted that the systemic secular opposition of donors and big multilateral agencies implied that FBOs would need more than evidence; what was needed was an attitudinal shift for FBOs' uniqueness to be accepted.

The Birmingham project's findings from Nigeria demonstrate the differences between NGOs and FBOs in terms of the design of programs and organizational characteristics. However, the advantages of FBOs were often perceived and not necessarily factual.[8] In fact, context was considered equally important, if not more so, as inherent characteristics of the FBOs.

In light of donors' current emphasis on transparency and documentation, there is a dire need for more information about the myriad FBOs. Due to the increasing requests for proof of FBOs' purported efficiency, critiques of their conservative values and the recognition of the vast complexity of the field, several informants from FBOs are today far more hesitant and cautious in flagging their own added value. From their side, the debate seemed somewhat fatigued and exhausted.

Principles regarding non-conditionality, non-exclusivity and reproductive health are some of the most difficult questions donors face in the ever-growing landscape of faith-based partners. DFID experiences this every day in fragile states, such as in Somalia. In a country where there is no *de facto* state and a negligible amount of public schools, one simply has to engage with a range of FBOs that do not necessarily share DFID's principles on equal rights of gender, reproductive health and the freedom of religion. Considering the increased domestic pressure and scrutiny of DFID's grants in tough financial times, the link to religious partners is very much a contested one. Former DFID advisor Ian Linden explains:

> They [DFID] are constantly being scrutinized for what they do, so they have to be extremely cautious about where they go and what they do. Anything that would smack of religious partisanship would be very bad obviously. (Linden 18.01.12)

The struggle of individuals

Individual efforts, not institutional continuity, is characteristic of the processes in both countries. Experiences from the UK, the Netherlands, the World Bank and the United Nations (UN) clearly show that religion is treated on an *ad hoc* basis and as a result of the initiative of individuals.

James Wolfensohn was instrumental in putting religion on the global agenda. Both the World Faiths Development Dialogue (WFDD) and the World Bank's Development Dialogue on Values and Ethics are products of his commitment. However, since his retirement in 2005, the World Bank's engagement with faith groups has been basically nil. Within the UN system, Thoraya Obaid kept the focus on religion while she was director of UNFPA, but few leaders have followed her fearless promotion of this important field of knowledge.[9]

In the Netherlands, van Ardenne and Ter Haar played essential parts in establishing the field of religion at the governmental level and in academia. Today Ter Haar is retired and the Chair at ISS dissolved. Van Ardenne left office in 2006, and much of the means that financed the Dutch MFA's initiatives on religion have dried up. Religion is currently not a prioritized area for the Netherlands, and the few people still involved with it within the ministry consider it a "luxury" from when the budgets allowed such engagement. One informant explained:

> It is very vulnerable. [. . .] We really have to ask ourselves, who is keeping and protecting the knowledge that we have built up on religion, politics and development? The Ministry of Foreign Affairs is squeezed; it is quite likely that the whole religion agenda will disappear. (10.02.12)

In the UK, Short lifted and carried the focus on religion and religious actors for many years. Former DFID advisors Linden and Paul Spray were both important promoters of the initiatives that later came from within DFID (e.g., the Birmingham project). Both Linden and Spray had earlier worked with these issues for the Catholic Institute for International Relations. Hence, it is timely to ask whether the focus on religion would have been as vibrant without these individuals. The initiatives taken by these individuals benefitted from a stable government for thirteen years. When the new government took office in 2010, the initiatives from its predecessor hung by a thread. Fortunately, the new Minister for International Development, Andrew Mitchell, started his own initiative, Faith Partnership Principles, aimed at increasing knowledge on the interplay between DFID and religious actors in development. Hopefully, the latter initiative will outlive the current government.

However, beyond the Faith Partnership Initiative, there are few signs that the focus on religion will be institutionalized and mainstreamed in the UK. One informant even compared DFID's engagement with religion—in particular, the vulnerability of being dependent on individuals—as playing the game 'snakes and ladders', where you constantly fall back to where you started.

Religious interests

Despite a few honourable exceptions, a striking observation from both countries is that the debate and research on religion and development for the most part interested religious actors themselves. The risk one runs if the field is usurped by faith-based actors is that is remains a "special" field of research outside mainstreamed development agenda. Another caveat is the question concerning scientific independence and disinterest. Considering the potential financial support affirmative findings would yield, how critically can religious actors themselves assess their own contributions?

Yet representatives from Dutch FBOs expressed frustration over the constant suspicion from secular partners over what they considered a genuine attempt to increase important knowledge on religion. One cannot with ease promote a field of knowledge of which oneself is a part without being rendered suspect. However, at the same time many of the FBOs did not find the reports or conclusions from the Birmingham project to be very fruitful. They believed that the research was too theoretical and not practice oriented. Moreover, in their opinion, the criteria to measure the added value of FBOs were too rigid. Birmingham, on the other hand, contends that their approach was precisely on practical "lived religion"; however, this entails much more than FBOs. Some FBOs also felt ignored and underestimated by the research. FBOs' interest in the research is seemingly restricted to their own contributions and not the broader field of religion and development per se. Consequently, the critique from religious actors of donors' limited and instrumentalized approach might turn back on them, considering their own restricted scope of interest.

It seems the knowledge field on the whole suffers from the sheer self-interest of the different actors who raise and present the theme in the public discourse. DFID initiated the research on religion and development to enhance existing projects and develop better policy. When the research unveiled a complex field where clear recommendations were hard to produce, DFID lost interest. In the Netherlands, Christian Democrat van Ardenne had clear incentives for involving religious actors as they made up parts of her constituency. The FBOs had a mutual desire of being acknowledged and included in development policy. When Koenders chose a fundamental knowledge approach, many of the FBOs lost interest in the forum.

There are those who genuinely want to lift the knowledge of religion and development into the mainstream thinking in development and foreign policy analysis. However, the processes in both the UK and the Netherlands are marked by restricted agendas and vested interests of specific actors, not an adequate commitment to the knowledge field in and of itself.

Conservative agenda and acute rhetoric

On the whole, informants from both countries underscored the continued challenges related to the lobbying of religious conservatives in multilateral human rights forums. In step with the increasing recognition of religion, conservative religious actors have increased their commitment, arranged global conferences, interfered in human rights debates and built alliances with like-minded states in order to challenge more progressive forces on certain human rights issues (Butler 2006). The axis from conservative to moderate is in many ways overriding the traditional boundaries of religious faiths. Carole Rakodi considers this one of the most important concerns of the current debate:

> Today you have a spectrum in the debate, which is not a divide between faiths, but you get a spectrum from socially conservative to socially liberal and this cut through each of the faiths and you can place actors along that spectrum. In Christianity you have very socially conservative views among evangelicals and Catholics, but you find the same views in Islam and Hinduism. You also have the liberal end of the spectrum in all those faiths as well. But we have a tendency of lumping all those of a single faith together, but in fact it's more useful to say: where on this conservative-liberal divide do they sit? This has important implications for development. (Rakodi 18.01.12)

Informants from FBOs also recognized the pattern, but highlighted that the phenomenon should only increase our incentives for engaging in dialogue with the conservative actors. Others took a more apologetic approach and attributed these conservative and fundamentalist expressions of religion to external causes like politics, culture and egocentrism, labelling it "manipulated religion" while the positive effects of religion were "true religion."

Informants from the Dutch MFA warned of what they considered to be traditional politics enrobed in religious symbols and rhetoric. The intertwining of religion and politics is a method for the leaders of each realm to mutually boost their positions and gain influence. They understood religion as a powerful tool in which actors could shape global politics; thus, they sought a sober analysis of power. For example, the collaboration between the Vatican and countries like Malta and Poland is slowing progressive development within the EU by hindering consensus on issues like reproductive health.

Two trends can be seen in the wake of this. On the one hand, faith-based development actors are reluctant to admit the double nature of religion; on the other hand, secular development actors categorically write off all religious actors (including religious progressives) because of the actions of some strong conservatives. This feeds into a dawning polarization in the debate.

Moreover, religious actors are not just on the receiving end of criticism. Much of the FBOs' rhetoric carries with it an inherent critique of what they see as Western states' and the MDGs' materialistic and secular understanding of development. FBOs consequently want more than recognition of their useful structures and services; they want recognition of their religious worldview. In a sense, the processes and debates in both the UK and the Netherlands can be traced to a deeper ontological and epistemological debate: What is development? What are human needs? What is man? What sort of knowledge do we need in order to understand man? What is the ideal society?

The faith-based critics contend that development cannot be sustainable if we continue to impose our Western secular ideas and do not integrate the existing structures and spiritual resources in the local society. Most development contexts are deeply religious, and religious institutions play a large role here. Religion forms an essential part of peoples' identity, values and well-being and cannot be separated from the state. Consequently, agents of change should arguably apply religion, not attempt to ignore it or change the ways of beneficiaries. As one informant from a British FBO said, "It is about not imposing our own worldview, a secular Western point of view, but actually understanding the local worldview in that context" (19.01.12). On the other hand, although the researchers at Birmingham warned about the neglect of religion in development, they were quite sceptical about applying religion in development (Rakodi 2011). Katherine Marshall also warns against development policy based on alternative models to development that emphasize local religious worldviews. Such policies risk promoting a relativism that romanticizes traditional societies where many children die before they are five and few live to see their forties. Needless to say, just as religion can be the agent for change, it can also be the keeper of the status quo.

Informants from the Dutch MFA also claimed that adherents of more "holistic" approaches to development tended to overlook the influence of politics on religious leaders. The religious actors in a development context are very often limited by both ethnicity and political positioning. Thus, the analysis should not overemphasize the role of religion. One informant attributed FBOs' emphasis on religion to their desire to be recognized and have a "seat at the table."

Hence, for the donor countries it seems that the timing for the inclusion of religion is not right for at least three reasons. First, although the ministries appreciate the awareness raised regarding religion and development, the secular state of the Netherlands or the UK simply cannot fundamentally change their idea of development and start implementing spiritual dimensions. Second, the development agenda in Europe is currently threatened by the debt crisis. Accordingly, any fundamental revision of the development discourse should arguably take place in the recipient countries where religion is an integrated part of society. Third, the debate has stagnated due to the lack of documentation, proving that alternative models actually lead to more efficient development.

Faced with these arguments, some of the FBOs responded by questioning the very principles of the secular state and the problems this causes in the "religious South." Thus, they maintained a polarized rhetoric that envisages a fundamental division between people of faith and people with a secular worldview. Consequently, the debate has stirred up ideological controversy and risks constructing insurmountable divides and conflict. As Katherine Marshall comments:

> A vision that suggests a world divided between "people of faith" and "people without faith" suggests that there are clear and neat distinctions in values and approaches between two groups. That applies, for example, to a subtle implication—sometimes, as in Vatican documents not so subtle—that suggests that people are only moral if they believe in God and practice their faith. A much more nuanced view is needed that recognizes both overlap and also accepts that very religious people can be immoral and that irreligious people are guided by a deep sense of ethics. (Marshall 27.06.12)

Mindful of the fact that words matter, it seems imperative to counter such rhetoric, albeit without veiling genuine disagreement. After all, in practice informants from state agencies, FBOs and academia seemed more in agreement than not.[10] Yet on the rhetorical level, the essentialist versions of different cultures and the clashing of lofty principles seemed irreconcilable. In short, one can say that most informants agreed that religion matters. However, they differed on the consequences this should have for development policy.

The Norwegian experience

Former Minister of International Development Erik Solheim initiated a project on religion and development as a response to the challenge from Norwegian missionaries to take religion more seriously in Norwegian foreign policy. In an article in a Norwegian newspaper, the minister called for increased knowledge among Norwegian diplomats of the religious dimension in development contexts in which Norway is involved. Moreover, he elucidated the relationship between solid contextual knowledge and a more effective development policy. From January 2011 to September 2012, the Oslo Center for Peace and Human Rights led the project. The aim of the project was twofold: to increase knowledge on the nexus between religion and development and to have engaging public debates on these issues. Thus, there were two target groups: the Norwegian diplomatic corps and the general Norwegian public.

The project emphasized knowledge as its central perspective. It was a first step towards gaining more knowledge on how religion influences contexts in which Norway is engaged and how Norwegian development policy could include this knowledge. It differed considerably from initiatives in the UK and the Netherlands in terms of both scope and focus. The Norwegian process was quite limited (18 months) and myopic (the state administration and domestic opinion); consequently, the output of the process did not contribute much to the international debate. Considering Norway's broad agenda when it comes to development, we chose to focus on four main areas:

- Religion and conflict, peace and reconciliation
- Religion and democracy and human rights
- Religion and economic development
- Religion and aid assistance

From the thematic areas, it is clear that the project had a focus on the politicization of religion and how to meet the challenges of symbolic politics, particularly in human rights issues—issues Norwegian diplomats face as a result of their development policy. The problem of such an approach is that it limits the transfer value. However, we soon found patterns that pointed to general challenges that was recognizable and common in other donor countries as well. The findings from UK and the Netherlands were immediately recognized as familiar challenges by researchers and development actors in Norway, and proved to be an important part of the foundation upon which we built our recommendations.

The Oslo Center arranged three public meetings and one full-day seminar on each of the thematic areas. The public meetings were arranged as debates, with representatives from different faiths, researchers and even Cabinet ministers attending. The meetings attracted a vast number of people and gave the Oslo Center an indicator of the general public's level of interest in the topic. Mindful of the technical research required to discuss the relationship between religion and economic development, a full day was spent on this issue at the Norwegian School of Economics (NHH).

The Oslo Center established an experienced reference group at the start of the project. The group consisted of researchers, development workers and representatives from different faiths. Their mandate was to strengthen the Oslo Center's work by drawing on a range of perspectives and concrete experiences from the field.

Main challenges

In Norway there is a broad consensus about religion's important role in international relations and development. In spite of this, the thinking and handling of religion is still very much dependent on individuals' knowledge, interest and initiative. Both among the development actors and within the state administration, there is a need for more systemized knowledge. In particular, there is a need to understand and assess religion's societal and organizational role in development contexts.

The secular nature of the Norwegian state and the traditional perception of a state's dual nature differs from those of many developing countries. Whereas Norway constantly builds bulkheads between religion and state institutions, the societal development in many countries is going in the opposite direction, such as the Russian Orthodox Church steadily growing together with the state since the fall of the Soviet Union.

This has led to a knowledge gap in terms of how religion influences Norway's development policy and diplomacy (e.g., our own understanding of "Norway"). Norwegian diplomats have not been adequately aware of how other people, especially in religious contexts, perceive Norway and its representatives. The fact that many partners perceive Norwegians as Christians has important implications for the country's diplomacy and approach to other countries' political context.

However, the current consensus of religion's important role in development has implied that our discussions have now moved from the stage of diagnoses to that of treatment. According to the Norwegian Agency for Development Cooperation (NORAD), the religious or secular nature of partner organizations is irrelevant; the point is how well they are functioning. The goal of reaching target groups outside the ambit of the state oblige NORAD to engage actors like religious groups. However, religious actors are indisputably a heterogeneous group, with various consequences for development.[11] As such, Norway—as an important donor—is required to undertake serious assessments of the context and its actors. Yet this does not entail focusing exclusively on FBOs or the somewhat constructed dichotomy between religious and secular development organizations.

As in the UK and the Netherlands, the debate on religion and development policy in Norway tends to be somewhat tense and polarized. The close collaboration between NORAD and FBOs has contributed to professionalization and a critical self-evaluation on the part of the Norwegian FBOs, which has resulted in a debate on holism, added value and who knows religion "better". However, although the debate seems polarized, the divides are not very deep. NORAD has a pragmatic relationship to the FBOs and respects many missionaries' deep knowledge of context and language. NORAD is first and foremost interested in professional development partners.

Furthermore, the tension between progressive religious actors and conservative religious actors has increased, especially on issues related to reproductive health, which is of particular concern for Norway. The intersection between modernity and tradition within religions has given rise to more fundamentalist reactions that materialize in the issue of women's rights. The control of women's sexual conduct has become a heated issue in multilateral arenas. Conservative religious forces have attempted to de-legitimize these rights by rendering them as Western concepts which have little relevance in more traditional societies. Norwegian ambassadors are seeking a language to address this and warn against a cultural relativism that might weaken time-honoured values such as equal rights between men and women. The refutation of these tendencies requires a certain level of insight into these actors' way of thinking and perspectives.

In addition, the challenges of ethnic and religious minorities in connection to religious freedom and the freedom of speech is also a prioritized area for the MFA. Norway has just appointed its first Special Envoy on Minorities, Harald Neple, whose main focus will be on religious minorities. The MFA is currently building up its competence on this. The following are the main recommendations from the project:

- Knowledge of religion has to have both practical and theoretical approaches.
- There is a potential for improvement within the state administration regarding the coordination of efforts and sharing of information. There are also challenges connected to systemizing and institutionalizing existing knowledge within the administration. When religious actors pose serious challenges to development goals and human rights, systematic efforts and strategic thinking is required.
- Religion should not be treated as a special case, but rather as an interdisciplinary field of knowledge that requires cooperation and dialogue across different sections and departments.
- There is a need for a joint plan for competence development. This has to happen at two levels: First a general basic understanding of the relation between religion and society must be developed; second, the specific context-based knowledge in areas where religion plays a particular role needs to be strengthened.
- Courses on religion should be a basic part of the education of diplomats. This includes introduction to the study of religion and analysis of religious dynamics in specific contexts.
- Diplomats and ambassadors who work in countries where religion and politics are especially interwoven should receive extra guidance and material for competence development.

- Embassies should engage with local centres for religious studies and include these concerns in their reporting and assessment of projects whenever it is pertinent.
- The Norwegian MFA and NORAD should invite external experts and researchers on religious studies in the strategic planning and policy discussions of projects where religion is an important factor.
- The MFA and NORAD should seek more research on the concrete challenges they face. To ensure relevance, close and continuous dialogue between employers and researchers must be guaranteed.
- The MFA and NORAD should develop checklists with instructive questions to ensure competent analysis and assessment, especially in contexts where religion or religious structures play a part in conflict and development.

Whether or not the MFA and NORAD will follow-up on these recommendations remains to be seen. The project has gained praise from both agencies, including the current Minister of International Development Heikki Holmås. A working group consisting of representatives from both the MFA and NORAD is currently looking into possible courses of action. However, mindful of the absence of concrete plans for follow-up, actual institutionalization of the project and the contingency experienced in other countries regarding the field of religion, most Norwegian development actors remain sober in their expectations.

References

Balchin, Cassandra. 2011. *Avoiding Some Deadly Sins: Oxfam learnings and analysis about religion, culture, diversity and development*. Oxfam GB: Oxfam Discussion Papers.

Butler, Jennifer. 2006. *Born Again: The Christian Right Globalized.* London: Pluto Press.

Clarke, Gerard. 2006. "Faith Matters: Faith-based Organisations, Civil Society and International Development." *Journal of International Development* 18, no, 6: 835–848.

Deneulin, Séverine and Rakodi, Carole. 2010. "Revisiting Religion: Development Studies Thirty Years On." *World Development* 39, no. 1: 45–54.

Gifford, Paul. 2009. *Christianity, Politics and Public Life in Kenya.* London: Hurst & Company.

Holenstein, Anne-Marie. 2006. *The Role and Significance of Religion and Spirituality in Endogenous Development: a learning process between SDC and NGO's*. Paper for Endogenous Development and Bio-Cultural Diversity, 3–5 October, Geneva, Switzerland.

Rakodi, Carole. 2011. *Inspirational, Inhibiting, Institutionalized: Exploring the Links between Religion and Development.* International Development Department, University of Birmingham.

Ter Haar, Gerrie (ed.). 2011. *Religion and Development. Ways of Transforming the World.* London: Hurst & Company.

Tyndale, Wendy. 2003. "Idealism and Practicality: The role of religion in development." *Development* 46, no. 4: 22–28.

Notes

1 The analyses of the processes in the Netherlands and UK are based on a more comprehensive report in Norwegian. The chapter is therefore a limited selection of the main findings.

2 The reason for the paper's focus is twofold. First, as the initiator of the Norwegian project, the MFA naturally wanted to see how other donors had handled the complex field of religion and development. Second, the interplay between the state and civil society is of increasing relevance as the borders between them are diminishing and mandates converging. As some of the biggest donors, many European states are influential in this process.

3 Methodically, the report was based on qualitative interviews with key actors within development ministries, academia and organizations in the Netherlands and the UK. Informants include people from institutions such as the Birmingham University, the Department for International Development (DFID), the Tony Blair Faith Foundation, the University of Swansea, Lambeth Palace, Islamic Relief, the International NGO Training and Research Centre, the International Institute for Social Studies in the Hague, The Knowledge Center for Religion and Development, the Dutch Ministry of Foreign Affairs, the Knowledge Forum for Religion and Development Policy, People With a Mission, the Catholic Organization for Relief and Development Aid (Cordaid), Georgetown University and United Nation Population Fund (UNFPA).

4 Although "faith-inspired" might be a more suiting term, the term faith-based organizations (FBOs) is an established term and thus applied in this chapter. Gerard Clarke divides the group into five: faith-based representative organizations or apex bodies; faith-based charitable or development organizations; faith-based socio-political organizations; faith-based missionary organizations; and finally faith-based illegal or terrorist organizations (Clarke 2006: 840). Other researchers emphasize the difference between "Western" and "local" FBOs as a requirement in order to adequately assess the contributions from the complex group.

5 Consisting today of Cordaid, Edukans, ICCO Action by churches together, Islamic Relief, Dutch Consortium of Migrant Organizations, OIKOS Foundation, People with a Mission and Seva Network Foundation.

6 In the wake of the closure of the forum, the ministry initiated an internal forum called Network on Religion and Diplomacy. However, as of this autumn, it has come to a standstill.

7 However, these incidents did not lead to a distorted security bias in DFID's approach. All informants underscored what they experienced as a genuine interest in religion in and of itself.

8 See Policy Brief 13: http://www.religionsanddevelopment.org/files/resourcesmodule/@random454f80f60b3f4/1315400250_policy_brief_13_for_web.pdf

9 However, today the UN has two initiatives that aim to institutionalize the knowledge on religion: the Inter-Agency Task Force on FBO Engagement and the annual course on Faith and Development as part of the UN System Staff College.

10 Cassandra Balchin found similar contradictions in her study of 18 common challenges facing development actors in work related to religion (Balchin, 2011).

11 Although FBOs are essential contributors to the welfare of millions of people, we are for instance acutely aware of the subversive effect Christian NGOs with international support have on the Kenyan government's commitment to welfare services (Gifford, 2009).

List of Contributors

Tomas Sundnes Drønen is professor in global studies and religion at School of Mission and Theology, Stavanger, Norway. He has authored many publications on globalization, intercultural communication, and religious change in Africa; including *Communication and Conversion in Northern Cameroon* (Brill, 2009) and *Pentecostalism, Globalisation and Islam in Northern Cameroon* (Brill, 2013).

Kjetil Fretheim is professor in ethics and Christian social practice (diaconia) at MF Norwegian School of theology, Oslo, Norway. He is author of *Rights and Riches. Exploring the Moral Discourse of Norwegian Development Aid* (Peter Lang 2008). He has published articles on intercultural communication, Christian ethics, and religion and development, and is currently working on the public and political role of Christian theology.

Gerrie ter Haar is the emeritus professor of Religion and Development at the International Institute of Social Studies of Erasmus University Rotterdam, The Netherlands. She is the author of numerous books and articles on religion, with special reference to Africa.

Päivi Hasu is Adjunct Professor at the University of Jyväskylä and Academy Research Fellow at the University of Helsinki. She has researched on traditional life cycle rituals and the Lutheran form of Christianity in Northern Tanzania as well as the charismatic revival within the Lutheran church. Her later research involved urban Pentecostalism. She currently holds a research position of the Academy of Finland with research on Evangelical and Pentecostal faith-based organizations and their development projects in Tanzania.

Nikolai Hegertun is the project coordinator for the democracy assistance program at the Oslo Center for Peace and Human Rights. He worked extensively with research on the project "Religion and Development". He holds masters degree in Peace and Conflict Studies from the University of Oslo.

Anne Kubai is associate professor of World Christianity and Interreligious Studies, and a researcher at the Hugo Valentin-centre and Faculty of Theology, Uppsala University, Sweden. She has edited books and published articles on Christian-Muslim relations in Africa, religion and international migration, religion and the Rwandan genocide and challenges of post-genocide reconstruction. Currently she is working on perpetrators' perspectives of the genocide and the processes of re-integration and social cohesion in Rwanda.

Karen Lauterbach is Assistant Professor at the Centre of African Studies, University of Copenhagen, Denmark. She did her Ph.D. (*The Craft of Pastorship in Ghana and Beyond*, 2009) on the making of pastoral career trajectories in Ghanaian Pentecostal churches. She is currently working on Congolese refugee churches in Uganda, spiritual economies and the politics of access to assistance.

Ville Päivänsalo is assistant professor in global theology, worldviews and ideologies at the Faculty of Theology, the University of Helsinki, Finland. He is the author of *Balancing Reasonable Justice: John Rawls and Crucial Steps Beyond* (2007) and a number of other publications on theories of justice as related to social contract thought, Christian life-views, global ethics and human capabilities, and is currently working on religion and health justice.

Marianne Skjortnes is Associate Professor in Social Anthropology at School of Mission and Theology in Stavanger, Norway. She has extensive experience from work with development issues in several African countries, particularly in Madagascar, where she has lived and worked with research and consultancy on development issues for several years, as well as employee of Norwegian Mission Society working with the Malagasy Lutheran Church as a teacher. Her focus has been on culture, social change, and gender and development. She is currently involved in research on religion and development.

Magne Supphellen is a Professor of Marketing at the Department of Strategy and Management, Norwegian School of Economics (NHH), Bergen. He teaches and does research in the areas of consumer psychology, marketing, and entrepreneurial psychology. In his research on entrepreneurship he has focused on small businesses in developing countries and the relationships between faith, values, and entrepreneurial psychology and behaviour. Supphellen has published in journals such as the Journal of Marketing, Journal of Consumer Psychology, Journal of Business Research, Psychology and Marketing, Public Opinion Quarterly, and World Development.

Auli Vähäkangas is acting professor of practical theology at the faculty of Theology, University of Helsinki, Finland. She is author of *Christian Couples Coping with Childlessness; Narratives from Machame, Kilimanjaro*. Vähäkangas's research has focused on those at the margins: HIV-positive and childless people in African communities. She has additionally done research on African feminist theology, and is currently working with a large international project which studies contribution of faith-based organizations to social cohesion of marginalized youth in South Africa and in the Nordic countries.

Mika Vähäkangas is professor in mission studies and ecumenics at Lund University, Sweden. He is also the president of the International Association for Mission Studies. He has published books and articles on African Christianity as well as inter-religious and intercultural encounters. He directs currently research project "Looking for Wholeness in an Enchanted World: Healing, Prosperity, and Ritual Action in African Charismatic/Pentecostal Churches".

Index

A

B

C

D

E

F

G

H

I

J

K

L

O

P

S

T

U

V

W

Y

Z

Bible & Theology in Africa

The twentieth century made sub-Saharan Africa a Christian continent. This formidable church growth is reflected in a wide range of attempts at contextualizing Christian theology and biblical interpretation in Africa. At a grassroots level ordinary Christians express their faith and read the bible in ways reflecting their daily situation; at an academic level, theologians and biblical scholars relate the historical traditions and sources of Christianity to the socio- and religio-cultural context of Africa. In response to this, the Bible and Theology in Africa series aims at making African theology and biblical interpretation its subject as well as object, as the concerns of African theologians and biblical interpreters will be voiced and critically analyzed. Both Africans and Western authors are encouraged to consider this series.

Inquiries and manuscripts should be directed to:

Professor Knut Holter
MHS School of Mission and Theology
Misjonsmarka 12
N-4024 Stavanger, Norway
knut.holter@mhs.no

To order other books in this series, please contact our Customer Service Department:

(800) 770-LANG (within the U.S.)
(212) 647-7706 (outside the U.S.)
(212) 647-7707 FAX

Or browse online by series:

www.peterlang.com